UNIVERSITY OF
GLOUCESTERSHIRE

Environment, Society and Natural Resource Management

Environment, Society and Natural Resource Management

Theoretical Perspectives from Australasia and the Americas

Edited by

Geoffrey Lawrence

Professor of Sociology and Executive Director of the Institute for Sustainable Regional Development, Central Queensland University, Australia

Vaughan Higgins

Associate Lecturer in Sociology, Monash University, Australia

Stewart Lockie

Senior Lecturer in Sociology and Associate Director, Centre for Social Science Research, Central Queensland University, Australia

Edward Elgar
Cheltenham, UK • Northampton, MA, USA

Published by
Edward Elgar Publishing Limited
Glensanda House
Montpellier Parade
Cheltenham
Glos GL50 1UA
UK

Edward Elgar Publishing, Inc.
136 West Street
Suite 202
Northampton
Massachusetts 01060
USA

A catalogue record for this book
is available from the British Library

Library of Congress Cataloguing in Publication Data
Environment, society and natural resource management: theoretical perspectives from Australasia and the Americas/edited by Geoffrey Lawrence, Vaughan Higgins, Stewart Lockie.
    p. cm.
  Includes bibliographical references and index.
  1. Natural Resources—Management—Case studies. 2. Natural resources—Social aspects—Case studies. 3. Environmental policy—Case studies. I. Lawrence, Geoffrey. II. Higgins, Vaughan, 1974– III. Lockie, Stewart.

  HC59.15 .E58 2001
  333.7–dc21   00–065406

ISBN 1 84064 449 4

Printed and bound in Great Britain by MPG Books Ltd, Bodmin, Cornwall

Contents

Figures

Tables

Contributors

Ian Barns is a Lecturer at the Institute for Science and Technology Policy, Murdoch University, Western Australia. He has published in *Environmental Politics* and *Science, Technology and Human Values*, and is co-editor of *Poststructuralism, Citizenship and Social Policy* (Routledge, 1999).

David M. Bates is a Professor of Botany in the L.H. Bailey Hortorium, Cornell University, New York. His recent work has been concerned with the interrelationships among humans, the plant environment, and development. A recent chapter in this field was published in Buck et al., (eds) *Agroforestry in Sustainable Agricultural Systems* (Lewis Publishers, 1998).

Ruth Beilin is Senior Lecturer in the Department of Resource Management and Horticulture, Institute of Land and Food Resources, University of Melbourne. A landscape sociologist, Ruth is interested in socio-environmental assessment in landscape policy. Recent research includes a longitudinal study of Landcare; gender in the landscape; and the place of the commons in landscape management.

Joan M. Bentrupperbäumer is a Research Fellow at James Cook University, Cairns, Australia. Her research interests include human–natural environment transactions using social, psychological and biophysical perspectives; endangered species management and recovery; and impact assessment. Of particular theoretical and applied interest is the issue of interdisciplinarity across the natural and social sciences.

Kate Brinkley is a Graduate Administrative Assistant with the Bureau of Rural Sciences in Canberra. She has a background in geology, geography, archaeology and anthropology. She has an interest in social science issues as they relate to natural resource management, and has conducted research in areas relating to environment management systems, ecologically sustainable development, and complexity.

David J. Brunckhorst is Chair of Rural Futures at the University of New England, Armidale, Australia. His research interests include landscape ecology and bioregional planning and management. He is involved in the

UNESCO Biosphere Reserve Program. His latest book is *Bioregional Planning: Resource Management Beyond the New Millennium* (Harwood Academic, 2000).

Frederick H. Buttel is Professor and Chair, Department of Rural Sociology and Professor of Environmental Studies, University of Wisconsin, Madison. His interests are in critical rural/environmental sociology and he has co-edited *The Rural Sociology of the Advanced Societies* (Allanheld, 1980), and *Towards a New Political Economy of Agriculture* (Westview Press, 1991). He is co-editor of *Society and Natural Resources*.

Phil Coop is a doctoral student at the University of New England, Armidale, Australia. Phil has a background in business management and economics. His research interests include regional approaches to social and ecological sustainability in agro-ecological systems. His current research includes mapping of social and ecological functions of landscapes to elucidate innovative socio-ecological institutions.

Sarah Ewing is a Research Fellow in the Department of Civil and Environmental Engineering, University of Melbourne. She is a member of Victoria's Catchment Management Council and has had extensive involvement in natural resource management. Her current research interests include the policy and practice of Landcare, and adaptive policies and institutions for catchment management.

Melanie Fisher is the Director of the Social Sciences Centre of the Bureau of Rural Sciences in Canberra, Australia. She has a Bachelor of Arts degree majoring in psychology and anthropology, a Graduate Diploma of Science (Psychology) and a Master of Public Policy. Her research interests range from risk cognition, social data and indicator development, to social impact assessment.

Gerard Fitzgerald works for Fitzgerald Applied Sociology in Christchurch, New Zealand. He has also worked for government social research, and social assessment, agencies in New Zealand and Western Australia. Recent research includes resource communities, community participation in conservation management, domestic energy, and social forestry and development issues in Asia and the Pacific.

Barbara J. Geno is currently lecturing at the Sunshine Coast University in Queensland, Australia. During the 1970s she was a policy adviser at the Science Council of Canada. Her doctoral thesis embraced the idea of 'accounting' for sustainability in the Australian rural sector. Present research seeks to integrate the principles of 'best practice' with the new sustainable forestry paradigm.

Sonya Gray is a Graduate Administrative Assistant with the Bureau of Rural Sciences in Canberra, Australia. She majored, in her first degree, in micro- and macroeconomics and international development. She has undertaken preliminary research into natural resource management through environmental management systems. Sonya is currently promoting Quality Assurance Systems throughout Australia's agri-food industries.

Lynda Herbert-Cheshire is a doctoral student in Sociology at Central Queensland University, Australia. Her research takes a governmentality perspective of the community 'self-help' approach to rural development in Australia. Her recent publications include 'Contemporary Strategies for Rural Community Development in Australia: A Governmentality Perspective' in the *Journal of Rural Studies*.

Vaughan Higgins is a Lecturer in Sociology at Monash University, Gippsland. His doctoral studies focus upon the emergence and governance of farm adjustment as an 'economic' problem in Australian agricultural policy. Vaughan has published a number of articles on rural adjustment and has an ongoing interest in issues of governmentality and power, economic restructuring, agricultural policy and environmental governance.

Christopher D. Irons is a Research Associate with the Water Research Foundation of Australia, based in Canberra. Originally trained as an agricultural engineer, Christopher is developing techniques for managing interactions between people and natural resources. A forthcoming publication is *PADI: a Performance Assessment and Diagnostic Instrument for Resource and Environmental Management* (ANU, in press).

Emma Jakku is a PhD student at Griffith University in Brisbane, Australia. She works across three schools: the Australian School of Environmental Studies, the School of Science, and the School of Humanities. Emma is focusing her attention on the boundary-work between science and advocacy – a relatively under-researched area of research in the area of society and natural resource management.

Geoffrey Lawrence is Foundation Professor of Sociology and Executive Director of the Institute for Sustainable Regional Development at Central Queensland University. Recent books include *Restructuring Global and*

Regional Agricultures (1999), *Altered Genes II: The Future* (2001) and *A Future for Regional Australia: Escaping Global Misfortune* (2001). He is Australasian representative on the International Sociological Association's Research Committee on Sociology of Agriculture and Food.

Luis Llambí is Associate Professor at the Venezuelan Institute for Scientific Research and Chair of the Rural and Agricultural Studies Laboratory. He has worked extensively on rural development and agri-food issues in Latin America. His most recent book is *La Reforma del Estado en Venezuela* (Fundacion Polar, 1998). He is currently the Latin American representative of the International Rural Sociological Association.

Luis Daniel Llambí was trained in biology and recently completed an MSc in environmental economics at the University of York (UK). He is currently engaged on a PhD in ecology at the same university. His research interests span the agroecosystems of the Andes to those of the Amazonian region. He has published several papers on environmental issues and on the epistemological foundations of ecology.

Stewart Lockie is Senior Lecturer in Sociology and an Associate Director of the Centre for Social Science Research at Central Queensland University, Australia. He is undertaking research into the 'greening' of food production; sustainable farming practices; and the social impacts of water infrastructure development. Recent co-edited publications include *Critical Landcare* (1997) and *Consuming Foods, Sustaining Environments* (2000).

Wayne McClintock is a social scientist with the firm Taylor-Baines and Associates in Christchurch, New Zealand. His current specialities are social impact assessment, community development, rural sociology and the socio-economic aspects of natural resource policy and planning. He has also worked as a development practitioner and cross-cultural researcher in Tanzania and Pakistan.

Bruce Moon is a researcher dealing primarily with land-use planning, environmental and political economy issues in the School of Planning, Landscape Architecture and Surveying at Queensland University of Technology, Australia. He has written extensively on matters associated with how governments – and public sector administration – manage natural resource issues (especially environmental issues).

Sharon Pepperdine is a doctoral student at the University of Melbourne, where she is designing a methodological tool to monitor social sustainability for catchment management – funded by the Land and Water Resources Research and Development Corporation. Her project is part of 'Integration and Adoption of R&D Results at the Catchment Scale Program', within the Centre for Environmental Applied Hydrology.

Joseph P. Reser is a Reader in Applied Psychology at the University of Durham and an Adjunct Associate Professor of Psychology at James Cook University, Australia. He teaches in the areas of social psychology, environmental psychology and cross-cultural psychology. Research interests include applied social psychology, environmental perception and valuation, and theories of human-setting transactions and encounters.

Nick Taylor works for Taylor-Baines and Associates, Christchurch, New Zealand, specialising in social research and assessment relating to natural resource management. Previously he was a researcher at the Centre for Resource Management, Lincoln University. He has been involved in the development of approaches and techniques for social assessment and has conducted training courses in social assessment internationally.

Terry W. Tucker is Assistant Director of Cornell University's International Institute for Food, Agriculture and Development, and the University's International Agriculture Program. He was formerly on the faculty of the State University of New York at Alfred, where he taught agricultural economics. His current interests include farmer experimentation and learning in resource-poor environments (such as the Philippines).

Tabatha Jean Wallington is a doctoral student at the Institute for Science and Technology Policy, Murdoch University, Western Australia. She has a BSc in environmental science and a Masters degree in ecologically sustainable development. Tabatha has worked as an environmental consultant in Perth, and her current research investigates the application of theories of deliberative democracy to environmental decision making.

Acknowledgments

In July 1999 over 1500 delegates from throughout the world gathered in Brisbane, Australia, for the International Symposium on Society and Resource Management (ISSRM). This was the eighth such meeting held by the organisers of ISSRM. The broad theme of the conference was *The Application of Social Science to Resource Management in the Asia Pacific Region*. There was a great diversity in content with symposium themes including Indigenous Land and Resource Management, Community Participation in Resource Management, Human–Wildlife Interactions, Gender and Resource Management, Watershed Management and Soil Conservation, and Integrated Conservation in Developing Countries.

We thank the Symposium Co-chairs, Professors Geoff McDonald, Terry de Lacy, Roy Rickson and Donald Field for their kind offer to us to organise Session 1 of the conference – Theoretical Issues in Environment and Natural Resource Management. We also thank the more than 40 participants who provided papers in our session, and especially to those whose papers form the basis of this book. Sally Brown and Madeleine Boyd provided excellent 'behind the scenes' support in the organisation of Session 1. Associate Professor David Burch assisted us in making initial contact with the Edward Elgar publishing group, while Dymphna Evans and staff of Edward Elgar provided editorial guidance and assistance, and were enthusiastic supporters of the book. Dania Lawrence assisted us with referencing, Dimity Lawrence produced camera-ready copies of the entire manuscript and Janet Norton provided editorial support and compiled the index.

One of the 'findings' of the conference was that there is a paucity of material theorising the environment/society/natural resources nexus. We believe this book will not only help to foster conceptual clarity in this area, but will also suggest some new choices in the theoretical frameworks adopted by researchers in future field studies. We sincerely thank all those who have assisted us in our task of compiling what we hope will be a valuable collection of papers dealing explicitly with the 'social' in natural resource management.

Geoffrey Lawrence
Vaughan Higgins
Stewart Lockie

1. What's Social about Natural Resources and Why do we Need to Theorise it?

Stewart Lockie, Vaughan Higgins and Geoffrey Lawrence

INTRODUCTION

For decades, social scientists have struggled for recognition as valid contributors to natural resource management (NRM). Overshadowed by the seemingly obvious importance of soils, hydrology, agronomy, biology, ecology and a host of other apparently 'natural' dimensions of NRM, the social dimensions of NRM have all too often been ignored. So, how much have things changed? Since the report of the World Commission on Environment and Development in 1987 (WCED, 1987) there has been growing international recognition of the relationships between what we understand as natural and social resources (or between environments and people). The WCED argued that sustainable use of natural resources was impossible in the absence of equity, justice and social and economic development. Environmental issues were thus also social, trade and economic issues. While it would be misleading to trace widespread change to a single report or event, it is nevertheless evident that, as we begin the new century, NRM policy statements from governments, non-government organisations and multilateral organisations alike embrace components of a new 'language' of partnerships, capacity building, institutional support, public participation, community initiatives, environmental health, community health, social capital, international cooperation, education, and a host of concepts and ideas once foreign to the natural sciences.

The social dimensions of NRM are clearly on the international agenda. However, many natural resource managers are confronted by confusion as to what incorporating the 'social' might actually mean. They also face an array of social science disciplines with which they may have had no prior experience. It is not enough simply to get social issues on the agenda and then to commence research in the traditional mould. This ignores the potential and desirability of having a new set of theoretical and methodological 'tools' available to understand the social factors and processes underpinning resource use management. The role that we envisage for the social sciences in NRM is an ambitious one, but if growing demand for social scientific input is to be satisfied it is incumbent upon social scientists to develop robust and adaptable theoretical and methodological approaches that are appropriate to the understanding and governance of human–environment relationships. Theory-building is not simply an academic exercise with little connection to the practical task of managing resources. It is an exercise fundamental to the conduct of this management in a systematic, reflexive and informed manner. With this in mind, this introductory chapter outlines the theoretical issues raised through the rest of this book. It offers a critical assessment of the implications of these issues for NRM, and suggests areas in which the social sciences may make their most important contributions. One thing that will become clear is that there are potentially many ways in which natural resources might be considered social, and so particular attention is given to highlighting the basic assumptions raised in the various theoretical approaches.

THE ROLE OF THE SOCIAL SCIENCES IN NATURAL RESOURCE MANAGEMENT

There can be no doubt that natural resource management is an inherently social pursuit. But just as the general activity of NRM is pushed and pulled by changing political priorities, policy settings, social values and scientific knowledge, so too is the more specific contribution of the social sciences. In other words, the roles that social scientists have taken in NRM have been very much subject to changing understandings of the relationships between people and their environments and to the power dynamics and projects involved in those relationships. Further, the 'applied' orientation of NRM has placed pressure on social scientists to address the apparently practical issues concerning programme or policy implementation and often to ignore the full complexity of social issues implicated in human–environment relationships.

Nowhere has this been clearer than in 'technology transfer' (TT) and 'barriers to adoption' research. The TT paradigm assumes that problems related to NRM are to be best understood through objective scientific research, the results of which should then be transferred to resource managers for adoption and implementation. Yet, with regard to the difficult issues confronting multiple resource managers, TT has been shown time and time again to fail. It is now accepted that one of the earliest roles that social scientists took in NRM – research into the 'barriers to adoption' of scientifically-designed solutions to scientifically-defined problems – was a flawed part of, rather than a challenge to, the 'top down' approach by science.

Adoption research took what might best be described as a social-psychological approach that focused on measuring correlations between the adoption behaviour of resource managers and a range of individual characteristics such as education, socioeconomic status, social participation and so on (Buttel et al., 1990). *TT and adoption research thus dealt with natural resources as social by acknowledging that natural resources are necessarily managed by people.*

While early studies were found to be quite useful in the development of education and extension programmes, they were also criticised for a range of reasons including: (1) an overemphasis on the discovery of associations between variables and frequent failure to identify or theorise causal relationships; (2) a naive acceptance of the desirability of new technologies and a lack of attention to processes of resistance to that technology; (3) a tendency to blame resource managers for the failure to adopt rather than questioning the effectiveness or desirability of the innovation; (4) a lack of attention to the interrelationships between processes involved in technology generation and utilisation; and (5) an inability to deal with complex packages of technological innovation (Buttel et al., 1990; Ruttan, 1996; Vanclay and Lawrence, 1995). Further, the ability of adoption studies to predict adoption behaviour in agriculture, for example, using socioeconomic and social-psychological variables decreased markedly following the 1950s as technological innovation became normalised and the adoption of successful technologies comparatively rapid (Buttel et al., 1990).

The point here is not to develop an extensive critique of the TT paradigm, despite its continued prevalence among scientifically-oriented NRM agencies. It is, rather, to emphasise the potential problems that develop when social aspects are inadequately conceptualised and the social sciences are incorporated into NRM in tokenistic ways in order to help shore up ineffective technocratic programmes. The imperative will always be placed on resource managers to develop practical, implementable strategies – an imperative that will be reflected in the demands resource managers place on the social sciences. The challenge is to construct tools for doing social science that meet this imperative while not becoming a handmaiden to the 'needs' of the natural sciences. Only in this way will social science escape incorporation and avoid becoming utilitarian and 'functional' for the disciplines with which it interacts. It must, if it is to develop its own critical edge, be in a position to remain conceptually and theoretically sophisticated in the face of attempts by those in the natural sciences to appropriate – sometimes unwisely – its language and insights.

Fred Buttel takes up this argument in Chapter 2 by arguing that more attention needs to be given in the subdiscipline of the sociology of natural resources to issues prominent in the less practically-oriented environmental sociology. In particular, he is concerned that what may appear to be macro-level theoretical issues such as globalisation and the changing role and shape of the state are used to strengthen and inform the sociology of natural resources. Buttel notes that a sociology of natural resources is well equipped to examine both environmental degradation and protection – provided it engages in a more intimate way with trends in political sociology, and better theorises the role of the nation state. *Natural resources are thus considered social in the sense that their management is governed by social forces and institutions extending beyond the locale of the individual resource manager.*

There is more that can be explored within environmental sociology. A more overtly Marxist political economy, for example, would argue that environmental degradation is virtually inevitable due to the pressures placed on resource managers to increase efficiency in order to maintain profitability in capitalist marketplaces. Dealing with the environmental costs of resource use may be rational in the long term, but in the short term there is more incentive to ignore them or to pass them on (O'Connor, 1993). From this perspective, *natural resources are social in the sense that their management, or mismanagement, is shaped by the contradictory imperatives of capital accumulation.* While many would argue that the externalisation of environmental costs by resource managers should not be regarded as inevitable, it is still surprising how little policy actually attempts to come to terms with the effects of constant drives towards greater efficiency and productivity (see discussions in Redclift and Woodgate, 1997). Indeed, as noted by a number of chapters in this book there is a noticeable trend in policy towards voluntarism, an approach that asks resource managers to improve their practice while offering few additional resources and doing little to change the economic environment. At the very least this suggests an important role for the social sciences in analysing the limitations of NRM policy and programmes that fail to take account of the wider networks of social relationships in which resource managers are enmeshed.

At what is perhaps the other end of the theoretical spectrum is social constructivism, an approach that emphasises the importance of theorising the ways in which environments and resources are understood as cultural or ideological artefacts (Hannigan, 1995). *Natural resources are understood as both symbolic and material entities constructed through processes of social interaction.* Environments are not mere figments of the social imagination, but our understanding of them is necessarily shaped by our values, priorities and self-identities, as well as by what it is that we think we already know. Despite the aura of objectivity surrounding science and scientists, this perspective argues the importance of coming to terms with the social processes through which knowledge of environments and natural resources has been constructed. Social constructivism does not suggest that scientific knowledge is either naive or fraudulent (see Jakku, Chapter 8), but it does offer tools to understand both: (1) why resource managers so frequently disagree with scientific problem definitions and solutions; and (2) why social movements (such as the environmental justice movement) have arisen over the last decade to contest the knowledge claims of scientific agencies they believe are subservient to powerful vested interests. This analysis is supported by sociological work on risk. Beck (1992), for example, argues that the risks generated by industrial society (pollution, food contamination, nuclear fallout and so on) have replaced natural hazards (such as droughts, floods and earthquakes) as the major threats facing human life. The authority of science has become problematised in sociologically interesting ways for, at the same time that oppositional social movements see institutionalised science as part of the problem, the tools of science have been taken up to criticise the project of modernisation and industrialisation.

As the need to apply the social sciences to the conceptualisation and understanding of resource management issues and conflicts becomes clearer, so too does the need to find ways of integrating social scientific knowledges with other knowledges, a theme taken up in the remaining chapters in Part II of this book. Yet, as Joseph Reser and Joan Bentrupperbäumer argue in Chapter 3, with the exception of economics the social sciences have historically been all but absent from scientific and policy discussions concerning NRM. Further, the particular ways in which multi-disciplinarity has been operationalised within research projects, they argue, has been as much to blame as the skewed priorities of funding agencies. Similarly, in Chapter 4, Luis Llambi and Luis Daniel Llambi draw upon work in the Amazonian region of Latin America to argue that the changes in natural ecosystems brought about by the marketisation of previously subsistence economies demands a transdisciplinary approach by scholars that they believe has so far been lacking. There is much work to be done, therefore, in the development of strategies through which environmental, economic and social sustainability considerations might be incorporated into an analysis of tropical agoecosystem transformations.

Sharon Pepperdine and Sarah Ewing (Chapter 5) take up the Llambis' challenge of transdisciplinarity by evaluating the merit of a number of different approaches to dealing with *social* sustainability. By defining social sustainability as a set of measurable indicators, the authors suggest that 'the social' is more likely to be considered by decision makers in the resource management arena. We would argue that the current level of interest in social indicators of sustainability – reflected by Pepperdine and Ewing in their analysis of indicator systems including State of the Environment (SoE) reporting, Sustainable Regional Development (SRD), Quality of Life (QoL), capacity for change and community sustainability research – suggests that indicators are useful devices in the new politics of NRM.

One of the remaining questions – one that is taken up by David Brunckhorst and Phil Coop in Chapter 6 – is how these sorts of data might be combined with others in the process of NRM decision making. Brunckhorst and Coop argue that it is necessary to recognise and combine three building blocks of resource governance, namely: the influence of institutional structures; the distribution of social, environmental and political values; and the functional–ecological connectivity between landscape components. Reflecting the perspective of most of the chapters in Part II of this book, for Brunckhorst and Coop *natural resources are social in the sense that biophysical relationships and social and institutional processes are interdependent*. Sustainability is viewed as being dependent on the matching of culturally appropriate local and regional systems of resource governance, and resource exploitation with the bioregional capacity to provide resources and ecosystem services. We do need to be careful here. There is a tendency whenever quantifiable social attributes are identified for the purposes of indicator development or mapping to neglect the more subtle, and yet important, processes through which power and agency are enacted in decision making. This is a theme to which we will return in a number of the following chapters.

PLANNING AND IMPACT ASSESSMENT

Environmental impact assessment in its various guises has become one of the principal ways in which environmental and social concerns are integrated into planning and decision making regarding large-scale infrastructure developments. Some of the more common criticisms of the practice of impact assessment have included the lack of attention generally given to the cumulative impacts of successive developments and the limited attention given to full public participation and the application of local knowledge in decision making. *Natural resources may easily be reduced, in other words, into predictable cogs in a mechanised environment manipulable by expert technocrats*. This results in the marginalisation of less influential social groups and a widespread failure to translate the substantial amounts of work conducted on individual assessments into holistic, long-term, planning processes. Interestingly though, in a number of worldwide legislative frameworks for impact assessment, social and cultural impacts are explicitly defined as types of environmental impact. In the letter, if not the application, of the law *there is often no rigid distinction between society and nature or between social and natural resources.*

The application of impact assessment is taken up by Wallington and Barns in Chapter 7. The authors question whether a distinctly 'social' agenda can be incorporated into NRM policy practice given the underlying economic rationality of the bureaucratic process. Wallington and Barns focus on Western Australia's system of environmental assessment and argue that, despite the rhetoric of public involvement in environmental decision making, the structures and practices of public participation have been highly vulnerable to co-option by broader economic agendas of government. *An underlying instrumental rationality is evident, they argue, that at one and the same time reduces natural resources to their economic exchange value and public involvement in decision making to a 'thin' procedural politics.* One of the key points to be drawn from this analysis is that much of the 'force' of technocratic approaches to impact assessment and planning lies in the extent to which they appear to 'make sense' from the perspective of instrumental and economic rationality. Developing alternatives requires not simply paying more attention to social impacts, therefore, but changing the rationality that underpins the impact assessment and planning system. Wallington and Barns draw on Habermas (1984) to propose a deliberative discursive rationality of public enquiry that might help to overcome the technocratic and elitist tendencies characteristic of current environmental assessment procedures (see also Dryzek, 1987, 1992). This rationality would shift the focus in impact assessment from the application of science in order to discover the truth about natural resources, to a new *focus on the negotiation of common understandings about natural resources involving multiple stakeholder groups, knowledges and perspectives.*

The potentially tenuous nature of technocratic approaches to impact assessment and planning is further explained in Chapter 8, where Emma Jakku examines the roles of scientists in environmental disputes. Rather than discovering clear boundaries separating the knowledge of expert scientists from that of the public and politicians, Jakku's work demonstrates the contested nature and content of these characterisations. Using the Magnetic Keys resort development in North Queensland as her case study, Jakku employs the concept of 'boundary-work' to examine how scientists construct their roles in environmental disputes variously as providers of independent advice or as advocates of a particular position. She notes that the expectation that scientists will provide objective advice is fraught with difficulties. Where some scientists believed that any involvement in advocacy compromised their position as independent and impartial sources of information, others believed their understanding of the scientific dimensions of the issue behoved them to become politically involved. In neither case was the unique perspective of science challenged, but its relationship to value judgements and to political processes was clearly contested. If the perspective of Wallington and Barns becomes more widely adopted, scientists will have no choice but to become more directly involved in advocacy and decision making as it will be through these processes that their knowledge is integrated with those of others to generate new understandings and mutually acceptable strategies. As utopian as this might seem, a number of impact assessors have noted the reduction in conflict associated with developments where technocratic approaches have been put aside in favour of more genuine involvement and negotiation (Dale et al., 1997).

Chapter 9 also focuses on planning in resource management. However, instead of examining how assessment procedures might be democratised, the authors seek to develop a broad conceptual framework for understanding formation and change in communities dependent on primary industries or processing of natural resources – what the authors call 'resource communities' – for the purposes of providing a stronger basis for social assessment and planning. *Natural resources here are social in the sense that their exploitation is closely linked to the creation and maintenance of nearby communities of workers and their families.* Using a comparative case-study approach, Nick Taylor, Gerard Fitzgerald and Wayne McClintock argue that few rural communities in New Zealand remain dependent on a single resource sector. Changes in technology and the organisation of work, industry restructuring, centralisation of social services and loss of population have all had an impact on the structure of resource communities. These are now less clearly defined spatially by locality, and need to be understood more in terms of networks of localities that interact with extra-local processes. For the authors, this suggests the need for a more dynamic concept of community that accounts for the mosaic of production activities and social relationships within a network of physical settlements. The authors argue that their research provides a useful conceptual and empirical basis for social assessment and resource planning in New Zealand.

A practical means for attempting to integrate multiple perspectives on resource planning, that take into account a diversity of social relationships and productive uses, is proposed by Christopher Irons in Chapter 10. Irons outlines the design and application of PADI, a Performance and Diagnostic Instrument used to formalise and compare social values in relation to sustainability. For the author, this diagnostic instrument allows environmental managers and practitioners to better assess what it means, from the perspectives of different stakeholders, for a catchment to be 'healthy' – at the same time as identifying both the bases for conflict and the impediments to be overcome.

SUSTAINING RESOURCES

While impact assessment tends to focus primarily on large-scale infrastructure developments, NRM activities related to enterprises such as agriculture and forestry are, of course, more diffuse. Chapter 11 provides a provocative introduction to issues associated with agriculture by focusing on biodiversity as the key to sustainability of rural communities. This may not seem like a novel suggestion in itself, but it is an important one due to its positioning of *natural resources as social through the complex networks of relationships that characterise ecological processes.* In contrast to the mechanised and manipulable environments of technocratic and instrumental rationality, this approach emphasises the complexity and indeterminacy of socio-ecosystems. However, rather than suggesting that biodiversity needs to be preserved at all cost, David Bates and Terry Tucker note that human occupation inevitably leads to some alteration of landscapes. Using an example of the Philippines-based development programme known as Conservation Farming in the Tropical Uplands (CFTU), the authors argue for a much more modest approach to sustainability that, while recognising biodiversity as a worthy goal in developing rural communities, takes into account the constraints posed by the immediate needs of rural people, and the non-government organisations and government agencies that serve them. The task of academics here is to refine the parameters within which the conservation of biodiversity may realistically proceed, rather than to produce idealistic models of sustainability. How, though, we might ask, are we to determine what is 'realistic'? Perhaps here the answer might lie in ideas of deliberative rationality and their operationalisation through tools for participation such as Irons' Performance and Diagnostic Instrument.

Chapter 12 also takes up the issue of landscape as a site of conflict over values. Ruth Beilin argues that there exists in Australia a diversity of landscapes that are constituted through trade and agricultural policy decisions, as well as by local people. The author draws attention to how changes in landscape reflect power relations and, in turn, how this affects production regimes and land management. Taking catchment management in Australia as an example (known as watershed management in the US and elsewhere) Beilin argues that a participatory rhetoric of 'local knowledge', 'partnerships' and 'ownership of issues' has been used by government to distract attention from the penetration of these landscapes by transnational capital. The mechanism through which this has occurred, she argues, has been a network of unelected Catchment Management Authorities that prioritise state expenditure on NRM initiatives. Barbara Geno, in Chapter 13, also develops the idea that the profit-making imperatives of transnational capital have influenced resource management policies and programmes but, in this case, in the context of the emergence of 'managerialism' as a strategy to regulate Australian forest industries. Managerialism is based on the idea that public sector agencies should adopt similar practices, organisational structures and accountability procedures to the private sector, and that economic efficiency should be considered an achievable endpoint in itself. Geno notes, however, that there is a potential conflict between bureaucratic discourses of 'managerialism' and attempts to institute and regulate sustainable development. For example, the focus on process rather than outcome in ISO 14001 Environmental Management Systems means that the objective of environmental sustainability becomes reframed within a language of efficiency, measuring, and monitoring. Similar to Wallington and Barns in Chapter 7, Geno argues that this creates a situation in which the process of cost-effectiveness, driven by a calculative rationality, is privileged over goals of ecologically sustainable development.

The theoretical approach developed by Vaughan Higgins, Stewart Lockie and Geoffrey Lawrence in Chapter 14 suggests that in terms of the processes through which the pursuit of profit seeking becomes institutionalised in NRM, Geno's identification of managerialism as a way of 'thinking' NRM is ultimately more convincing than Beilin's identification of top-down control by government. This is not to suggest that different actors have equal access to resources of power, but rather to suggest that power does not reside in a central repository from which NRM may be controlled. Reflecting the resources available to both groups, relationships between governments and agricultural land users in Australia (and elsewhere) have been characterised by a diversity of frequently unsuccessful strategies to influence NRM practice. Rather than equating sustainability with 'local' knowledge, and efficiency with 'scientific' knowledge and macro-social forces, Higgins, Lockie and Lawrence argue that both have been used simultaneously in attempts to govern Australian agricultural environments. Using the case study of a local 'action-learning' initiative in the cotton industry, the authors show how state agencies attempt to shape farmer behaviour by influencing the environment in which they make decisions and the ways in which they understand – and, therefore, respond to – that environment. But knowledge creation and dissemination is far from a linear 'top-down' or 'bottom-up' process and concessions may need to be made by all parties in order to operationalise a particular initiative. Similar to the constructivist perspective outlined above, *natural resources are thereby considered social in the sense that their management is shaped by the heterogeneous strategies through which 'sustainable knowledge' is created.*

INSTITUTIONS AND REGULATION

Debate over appropriate institutional structures for sustainable NRM is frequently concentrated on Hardin's (1968) thesis of the tragedy of the commons, the essence of which is the argument that when a resource is owned in common, the rational course of action for each individual with access to that resource is to increase her or his exploitation of it. Even when widespread over-exploitation and degradation of the resource becomes evident, individuals continue to increase their exploitation because the costs of their actions are shared by the whole community while the benefits are appropriated individually. In this manner, the common property resource is eventually destroyed. But as a number of authors have pointed out, Hardin confused common property resources, to which access is regulated by common property institutions, with unregulated open-access resources. In Chapter 15, Phil Coop and David Brunckhorst show that common property institutions have a proven track record of sustainable management and are still widely found today. Applying these insights to rural communities, Coop and Brunckhorst argue that common property institutions can provide a realistic basis for maintaining the ecological and social fabric of such spaces, and may also minimise the effects of rural decline. Obviously, the establishment of common property institutions has a number of limitations and the authors take these to include issues relating to enterprise consolidation and operation, establishment of managing bodies, and identification of key infrastructure and equipment. Despite these limitations, Coop and Brunckhorst point to the many benefits of common property resources. These include the efficient management of resources without affecting land tenure, the efficient utilisation of labour, the buffering of long-term risk associated with primary production ventures and collective decision making, and the greater sustainability and efficiency offered by the larger land area.

In contrast, Kate Brinkley, Melanie Fisher and Sonia Gray argue in Chapter 16 that an evaluation of common property resource management suggests that the key issue is the development of models by which decision makers can better understand and predict natural resource interactions. These authors are thereby more pessimistic than Coop and Brunckhorst about the potential of common property institutions. Using a complex adaptive systems approach, the authors argue that effective resource management policy requires an understanding of the links between the social, biophysical and economic drivers of behaviour. These are conceptualised as interdependent factors that form a complex adaptive system. The adaptive nature of such systems means that policy makers have to become used to formulating policy in an uncertain environment. However, we would argue that, while on the surface the importance attributed here to relationships between social, biophysical and economic factors seems reasonable enough, there is a danger that the behaviourist assumptions underlying this argument may favour technocratic attempts to intervene in resource management in ways that actually ignore the wider social context within which resource managers find themselves. It is for this reason that some systems theorists have sought to abandon the cybernetic models guiding that approach in favour of hermeneutic models based on similar notions of discursive rationality to those developed by Wallington and Barns in Chapter 7 (see Jackson, 1990; Martin, 1991; Ulrich, 1988). The emphasis from this point of view would be less on the ability of policy makers to predict resource manager behaviour and more on processes of negotiated 'meaning making' with those resource managers.

Bruce Moon takes up this concern with the role of policy makers in Chapter 17 by assessing the implications of post-structuralist theory for public sector management of natural resources. Moon argues that a paradigm shift has occurred in the way government administration is theorised. Rather than 'rational choice' underpinning decision making, administration is characterised by a choice between prescriptive models or a 'best fit' approach in which the relative 'goodness' of a policy reflects culturally-defined influences. This means that natural resource managers must rely less on the most logical or 'rational' outcome and more on the ideologies and expectations of other actors involved in the network. Moon's central point is that more attention needs to be given by policy makers to the action and culture of other actors within policy networks rather than relying on prescriptive models for policy formulation and implementation. However, while Moon presents this as a case of what policy makers *ought* to do, Lynda Herbert-Cheshire demonstrates in Chapter 18 both that it is already the case that policy makers avoid prescriptive models, and that the models they do use raise a number of further issues concerning power and knowledge (see also Higgins, Lockie and Lawrence, Chapter 14). Specifically, Herbert-Cheshire examines the discourse of community self-help, which has become increasingly prevalent in recent years. She argues that programmes of 'self-help' are more complex than a simple 'empowering' of community groups. In a similar vein to Chapter 14, Herbert-Cheshire argues that many community-focused programmes entail various forms of 'action at a distance' through which state agencies attempt to shape the ways in which individuals make their decisions. Herbert-Cheshire sees community development 'experts' as key agents in the formation of entrepreneurial attitudes. These 'experts' attempt to train individuals in the 'art' of self-government. Self-help, therefore, focuses on the building of 'active' subjects who can achieve the aims of government without direct regulatory or fiscal intervention. This is viewed, in critical fashion, as encouraging local people to work within the existing economic and political environment – rather than to provide a challenge. It also structures the field of possible action by denying the rationality of alternative resource management practices. This is not to suggest that there is something sinister or underhand here, but that processes of control are more complicated than the linear processes implied by top-down or bottom-up models.

CONCLUSION

Returning to the question that heads this chapter it is now possible to identify a number of ways in which natural resources are conceptualised as social. In summary, it can be seen that these conceptualisations revolve around three key questions: the relationship between people and nature; the management of those relationships; and the processes through which knowledge is generated about those relationships. Perspectives on the relationship between people and nature range from those that argue that there is no essential difference between society and nature, through those that consider biophysical, social and institutional processes to be interdependent, to those that reduce nature and natural resources to their economic exchange value from an exclusively human perspective. Clearly, one of the common threads running through the chapters of this book is a critique of the latter perspective and an assumption that society and nature are closely interrelated. To those involved in natural resource management this may seem self-evident. But what if we were to take the more radical perspective that there is no essential difference between society and nature? What tools would we have as social scientists to deal with such a perspective? Although such a perspective has not been taken up in this book we believe it is one that deserves greater attention. The recent popularity of Actor–Network Theory (see Lockie and Kitto, 2000; Murdoch, 1997) in some academic circles shows that it is possible to develop sociological accounts of change that neither privilege the agency of humans over non-humans, nor fall back onto crude behaviourist versions of environmental determinism. The task remains to apply such insights to the more preemptive research required to inform NRM.

A further – apparently self-evident – statement is the proposition that natural resources are managed *by people*. Certainly, none of the chapters in this book directly challenges this proposition. But again, we need to treat it critically. Individual natural resource managers do not exercise absolute control over mechanistic systems. Rather, they are faced with indeterminacy, uncertainty, and a range of social and political imperatives. NRM strategies focused solely on resolving discrete technical or scientific problems or on changing the behaviour of individual resource managers ignore the full complexity of the decision making environment faced by those managers. Clearly, there is a role for social scientists in improving our understanding of this environment. However, there is an even greater role, we would argue, for the social sciences in problematising what it is that we 'know' about NRM and how it is that this knowledge has been constructed. The role that we envisage here is not one based on deconstruction for its own sake – positioning social scientists as a bunch of killjoys ready to dismantle scientific knowledge claims and point out the unintended consequences of policy interventions (although all these activities may be legitimate and necessary). The social sciences offer powerful tools with which to construct more holistic understandings of NRM issues, to pursue discursive rationality and to encourage widespread participation in NRM decision making. By acknowledging the jointly material and symbolic dimensions of natural resources the social sciences are uniquely placed to understand and to translate the competing knowledge claims and value judgements that often characterise environmental conflicts. This does not deny unequal access to resources of power, but it does potentially provide a basis for negotiation by giving voice and legitimacy to alternative knowledges and, thus, a genuine alternative to technocratic agendas.

REFERENCES

Beck, U. (1992), *Risk Society: Towards a New Modernity*, Sage: London.

Buttel, F., O. Larson and G. Gillespie (1990), *The Sociology of Agriculture*, New York: Greenwood.

Dale, A., P. Chapman and M. McDonald (1997), 'Social Impact Assessment in Queensland: Why Practice Lags Behind Legislative Opportunity', *Impact Assessment*, **15** (2), 159–179.

Dryzek, J. (1987), *Rational Ecology: Environment and Political Economy*, Oxford: Basil Blackwell.

Dryzek, J. (1992), 'Ecology and Discursive Democracy: Beyond Liberal Capitalism and the Administrative State', *Capitalism, Nature, Socialism*, **3** (2), 18–42.

Habermas, J. (1984), *The Theory of Communicative Action, Volume One: Reason and the Rationalisation of Society*, Cambridge: Polity Press.

Hannigan, J. (1995), *Environmental Sociology: A Social Constructionist Perspective*, London: Routledge.

Hardin, G. (1968), 'The Tragedy of the Commons', *Science*, **162**, 1243–1248.

Jackson, M. (1990), 'The Critical Kernel in Modern Systems Thinking', *Systems Practice*, **3** (4), 357–364.

Lockie, S. and S. Kitto (2000), 'Beyond the Farm Gate: Production–Consumption Networks and Agri-Food Research', *Sociologia Ruralis*, **40** (1), 3–19.

Martin, P. (1991), 'Environmental Care in Agricultural Catchments: Toward the Communicative Catchment', *Environmental Management*, **15** (6), 773–783.

Murdoch, J. (1997), 'Inhuman/Nonhuman/Human: Actor-Network Theory and the Prospects for a Nondualistic and Symmetrical Perspective on Nature and Society', *Environment and Planning D: Society and Space*, **15**, 731–756.

O'Connor, J. (1993), 'Is Sustainable Capitalism Possible?', in P. Allen, (ed.), *Food for the Future: Conditions and Contradictions of Sustainability*, New York: Wiley, pp. 125–137.

Redclift, M. and G. Woodgate (eds) (1997), *The International Handbook of Environmental Sociology*, Cheltenham, UK: Edward Elgar.

Ruttan, V. (1996), 'What Happened to Technology Adoption-Diffusion Research?, *Sociologia Ruralis*, **36** (1), 51–73.

Ulrich, W. (1988), 'Systems Thinking, Systems Practice, and Practical Philosophy: A Program of Research, *Systems Practice*, **1** (2), 137–163.

Vanclay, F. and G. Lawrence (1995), *The Environmental Imperative: Eco-social Concerns for Australian Agriculture*, Rockhampton: Central Queensland University Press.

World Commission on Environment and Development (WCED) (1987), *Our Common Future*. Oxford: Oxford University Press.

PART I

The Role of the Social Sciences in Natural
Resource Management

2. Environmental Sociology and the Sociology of Natural Resources: Strategies for Synthesis and Cross-Fertilisation

Frederick H. Buttel

INTRODUCTION

It remains relatively uncommon within contemporary sociological circles to devote serious consideration to the natural world and the social relations that shape and are shaped by it. It is thus surprising that the minority of sociologists interested in societal–environmental relationships would be divided into two separate – and largely harmoniously coexisting – subdisciplines: environmental sociology (ES) and the sociology of natural resources (SNR).

While environmental sociology and the sociology of natural resources nominally focus on the same subject matters, in practice the literatures in the two subdisciplines have tended to be quite separate intellectual enterprises. Environmental sociology and the sociology of natural resources have different origins, their practitioners tend to have distinctive institutional locations, their problematics are different, and their theoretical tendencies differ considerably.

This chapter provides an overview of the divergent courses that have been taken within these two areas of inquiry, focusing on some possible avenues for cross-fertilisation and synthesis. The first avenue of opportunity is that of the roles of states in environmental degradation and protection. Mainstream environmental sociology has tended to overtheorise or overgeneralise the role of the state, while the sociology of natural resources has tended to undertheorise or ignore it. Here, I will argue that some provocative trends in political sociology (in particular, embedded autonomy, state–society synergy and state-in-society theories) can help to bridge this gulf. Second, while mainstream environmental sociology has tended to pay little attention to place or region, the sociology of natural resources has usually emphasised –

if not overemphasised – the specificities of place and downplayed generalisation across space. I will suggest that there are several promising perspectives such as commodity chain analysis, staples-related theories, and theories of the distinction between extraction and production, that have considerable promise in bridging this gulf.

ENVIRONMENTAL SOCIOLOGY AND THE SOCIOLOGY OF NATURAL RESOURCES

The divide between environmental sociology and the sociology of natural resources has been a longstanding one, reflecting the relatively distinct origins of the two subfields. The major contours of this divide are summarised in Table 2.1.

While practitioners of both the sociology of natural resources and environmental sociology have made a good many claims that their fields have long and distinguished histories – dating back even to the nineteenth and early twentieth century classical sociologists – it is most accurate to say that the sociology of natural resources is the older, at least as a recognised subdiscipline and as an organisational entity in the US. The sociology of natural resources was a relatively well established area of work by the mid-1960s. The sociology of natural resources field at this time consisted of three very closely related groups of scholars. First, there was the growing cadre of social scientists (among whom sociologists were well represented) who were increasingly being employed by natural resource management agencies such as the US Park Service, US Forest Service, Bureau of Reclamation, Corps of Engineers, and so on. Second, there was a sizable community of scholars interested in outdoor recreation, many of whom would become active in editing and publishing in the *Journal of Leisure Research* and *Leisure Sciences*. Third, there was a significant group of rural sociologists interested in the sociology of resource-oriented rural communities and in rural natural resource issues. These rural sociologists, along with many resource agency social scientists and social scientists interested in outdoor recreation, joined groups such as the Natural Resources Research Group (NRRG) of the Rural Sociological Society. The NRRG was quite active by 1965. Both intellectually, and in practical or personal terms, these sociologists of natural resources were interested in matters pertaining to effective resource management, in more rational and socially responsive policy making by resource agencies, in enhancing the cause of resource conservation, and, in the mid-1970s and thereafter, in social impact assessment of natural resource development projects. In addition, professional societies of resource biologists (such as the Society of American Foresters) would establish

Table 2.1 *Tendencies Within Environmental Sociology and the Sociology of Natural Resources*

Dimension	Environmental Sociology	Sociology of Natural Resources
Origins	Grew out of the environmental movement	Longstanding emphasis among rural sociologists, leisure/outdoor recreation researchers and social scientists in resource agencies
Definition of Environment	'Singular', encompassing, cumulative disruption	Local ecosystem or landscape
Main Features of the Environment Stressed	Pollution, resource scarcity, global environment, ecological footprints	Conservation, (local) carrying capacity
Definition of Sustainability	Reduction of aggregate levels of pollution and raw materials usage	Long-term sustained yields of natural resources, social equity in allocation and use of resources, reduction of social conflict over natural resources
Predominant Cadre of Practitioners	Liberal arts sociologists	Natural resource agency staff; college of agriculture/natural resources staff; rural sociologists
Scale/Unit of Analysis	Nation state Metropolitan focus	Community or region Nonmetropolitan focus
Overarching Problematic	Explaining environmental degradation	Improving public policy, minimising environmental impacts and conflicts, improving resource management
Theoretical Commitments	Highly theoretical, often metatheoretical	De-emphasis on social theory

networks in which sociologists of natural resources would play very significant roles. The journal *Society and Natural Resources* would shortly become the flagship journal of the sociology of natural resources, though many sociologists of natural resources would publish the bulk of their work as agency bulletins or in biophysically-oriented natural resource journals.

Most sociologists of natural resources today are either employed in a public or private resource management agency or, if they are employed as academics, are most likely to be found in resource departments (forestry, wildlife, range management, fisheries, environmental studies) or related departments or programmes (development studies or international agriculture programmes), in colleges of natural resources, or in colleges of agriculture.

Environmental sociology had quite different origins and institutional characteristics. Vocationally, most environmental sociologists have tended to be in conventional liberal arts sociology departments and to be scholars who were personally and professionally challenged by the rise of the environmental movement in the late 1960s and early 1970s. Most environmental sociologists were relatively new converts to the field, either as young or middle-career professionals (for example, Denton Morrison and Allan Schnaiberg), and especially as graduate students (such as Riley Dunlap). This cohort of environmental sociologists was especially likely to have strong commitments to environmentalism, and to have elected to orient their scholarship to be relevant to environmentalism. In the very early days of environmental sociology the core issue was the nature and dynamics of environmentalism and the structure of the environmental movement. It is significant and striking that in the 1970s virtually all of the sociological attention paid to the environmental movement was by environmental sociologists, rather than by sociologists of collective behavior and social movements, since the former saw this movement as being fundamental while the latter did not accord it this level of significance. Nonetheless, by the end of the 1970s the field of environmental sociology would change very rapidly, and matters of theory – if not metatheory – would become particularly critical.

As can be seen from Table 2.1, the historical and institutional divergences between environmental sociology and the sociology of natural resources have led to some longstanding differences between the scholarship in the two fields. The sociology of natural resources tends to stress rural/nonmetropolitan topics, in large part as a reflection of the work its practitioners do for natural resource agencies, and of the strong representation of rural sociologists and related rural social scientists. Accordingly, the predominant conception of the environment from the vantage point of the sociology of natural resources is that of consumptive, preservationist, recreational and related uses of primary resources (forests, fisheries, mining, coastal zones, riparian zones, and so on). The sociology of natural resources retains a strong emphasis on management and policy, and thus tends to be relatively applied and empirical in orientation. The characteristic unit of analysis in the sociology of natural resources is that of the individual resource manager/user or the resource group or locality (particularly the nonmetropolitan community).

Environmental sociology, by contrast, tends to be more metropolitan in focus and tends to be preoccupied with manufacturing industry and with metropolitan-centred consumption and metropolitan social groups. The treatment of primary resources is a highly aggregate one, with very little local detail, reflecting the industrial- and metropolitan-oriented focus. Environmental sociology's conception of the environment is basically about pollution and resource scarcity induced by metropolitan- and industrially-driven tendencies in production and consumption. Environmental sociology has largely tended to have a national societal unit of analysis, but increasingly environmental sociology has taken on a global or international level of analysis (Gould et al., 1996; Redclift, 1996; Redclift and Benton, 1994; Roberts and Grimes, 1997).

While the summary of the argument thus far as presented in Table 2.1 shows that the sociology of natural resources and environmental sociology exhibit a great many differences, perhaps the three most significant differences lie in the definition of environment, the scale of research or unit of analysis, and the overarching problematic. In the remainder of the chapter I will stresses strategies for synthesis and cross-fertilisation that revolve around these three key dimensions of difference.

Before proceeding, it is important to mention that the differences between environmental sociology and the sociology of natural resources ought not to be exaggerated. It should be noted that this divide is probably most evident in the US, and is arguably not so pronounced elsewhere (for example, in the UK). While US exceptionalism in this regard should be reassuring in the sense that there is nothing intrinsic to the ES/SNR divide, it also suggests that there ought to be some readily available bases for synthesis and cross-fertilisation. Furthermore, there is a significant cadre of sociologists whose work has creatively straddled the divide. The fact still remains, however, that ES and SNR reflect significant enduring divergences in styles of scholarship that have led the two subdisciplines to have less synthetic potential than could possibly be the case.

STRATEGIES FOR SYNTHESIS AND CROSS-FERTILISATION

The Definition of the Environment

Perhaps the most obvious place to begin regarding synthesis and cross-fertilisation between environmental sociology and the sociology of natural resources is the matter of the definition of 'the environment'. As much as mainstream environmental sociology and sociology of natural resources practitioners see themselves as adhering to an objectivist view of the natural world,[1] neither of these two groups' definitions of the environment would be a comfortable fit for most professional ecologists. The environmental–sociological view of the environment is essentially one that views the natural world in a singular, undifferentiated, sense as an overarching 'thing' or 'whole' which is tending to be progressively degraded and polluted (Buttel, 1996).[2] This view of the environment is typified by Schnaiberg's (see Schnaiberg, 1980; Schnaiberg and Gould, 1993) categories of 'additions' and 'withdrawals', by O'Connor's (1994) concept of the 'second contradiction of capital', and by sociological use of notions of global environmental change (with national, and especially global, totals of carbon dioxide emissions being viewed as a overarching indicator of the state of the natural environment). This view of the environment is thus overly comprehensive if for no other reason than it does not take into account that the social implications of environmental change are not uniform across space.

The sociology of natural resources, by contrast, has tended to be built on a foundation of community and regional sociology that privileges local or regional landscape dynamics. Sociology of natural resources practitioners often tend to have a fairly sophisticated understanding of local or regional ecological dynamics and trade-offs, due not only to the commitment to community and regional sociology but also to the fact that many work within, or have close relationships with, public resource agencies. Very often, though, the work that is done by sociologists of natural resources makes little mention of cross-border or global environmental phenomena and dynamics. Thus, to a considerable degree the strengths and weaknesses of environmental sociology's conception of the environment are the mirror image of those that tend to prevail within the sociology of natural resources.

Both groups of resource sociologists can benefit from focusing more specifically on the relations between diverse local environments and the macro (if not global) environment. Of possible use here are strategies that revolve around more active consideration of concepts from the ecological community such as 'discordant harmonies' (Botkin, 1990), 'nestedness', and 'patches'. These concepts provide ways of understanding both the wholeness of the global biosphere as well as the diversity and highly variegated relations among natural systems and their levels (from the genetic to the landscape and global biospheric levels). The larger imperative is, however, for both environmental sociologists and sociologists of natural resources to become more self-reflective about their conceptualisations of nature, landscape, and environment, and to recognise that these definitions can play a key role in shaping the conceptualisation and results of research.

The Role of the State in Environment and Natural Resources

Environmental sociology practitioners, along with those from the sociology of natural resources, are by no means strangers to public policy analysis. This said, there are very different scholarly traditions of examining the roles of governments/states in the two literatures. Mainstream environmental sociology, in large part as a result of its tendency to privilege national or extra-national units of analysis, tends to work from macrostructural – typically political–sociological or political–economic – frameworks. Some of the most influential literature in environmental sociology is, in fact, quite closely anchored to specific theories of the nation state. Allan Schnaiberg's highly influential environmental sociology, for example, is anchored in a synthesis of neo-Marxist and neo-Weberian political sociology in which many of the major concepts (accumulation, legitimation, fiscal crisis) are derived from O'Connor's *Fiscal Crisis of the State* (1973). Even the non-Marxist branches of environmental sociology (such as Catton, 1980 and Dunlap, 1997) have tended to have in mind a conception of the role of the state which is macro or national in scope, and in which it is implicitly, if not explicitly, posited that there is some powerful dynamic within the contemporary state and policy making which leads to decisions that have the effect of exacerbating environmental destruction.

The bulk of the sociology of natural resources, by contrast, tends to approach states and state policy making and policy analysis as a reflection of locality or regional units of analysis. By employing the locality or regions as the basic spatial units of analysis, the sociology of natural resources tends to de-emphasise recognition that there are overarching imperatives and patterns of state rule and nation-state-level policy formation. In other words, in nonmetropolitan localities it is primarily the regional or field offices of federal and state government resource management agencies who are seen to comprise the most visible state actors. It is typically the case that sociology of natural resources practitioners work formally or informally from pluralist-type theories of the role of the state and politics. The group or groups that tend to prevail in policy and resource management struggles in a particular locale or site are viewed as those that are able to overwhelm opponents or that are strategically agile enough to form effective coalitions or formulate effective discourses. Accordingly, the outcomes of policy struggles are, in principle, indeterminate, and are shaped by the differential intensity of group strategies and mobilisation that are brought to bear at the local level or within the resource management agency.

Again, the strengths and weaknesses of the characteristic approach to politics and state policy making within the sociology of natural resources are in an important sense the mirror image of those from the environmental sociology tradition. Just as environmental sociology practitioners are prone to overgeneralisation about states, toward exaggerating broad structural imperatives about roles of states (accumulation, legitimation, and the growth-augmenting functions of the state for example) and toward ignoring the specificities of state action in decentralised contexts or peripheral areas, the sociology of natural resources is prone to undergeneralisation and to a lack of attention to the macropolitical parameters of resource policy making.

Two possible analytical cornerstones for synthesis and cross-fertilisation with regard to the policy-analytic styles of the sociology of natural resources and environmental sociology will be explored below. The first is to recognise conceptually that contemporary nation-states intrinsically have very contradictory imperatives relating to environmental quality and resource consumption. One way of discussing these imperatives of state governance is to use the language of state functions developed by O'Connor (1973) – that the most basic or fundamental imperatives or functions are to undergird private capital accumulation, and to do so while maintaining legitimisation. The notions of the accumulation and legitimation roles of states have been incorporated into the environmental sociologies of Schnaiberg (1980; Schnaiberg and Gould, 1993), O'Connor (1994), and a number of others (Benton, 1996; Dickens, 1996; Foster, 2000). Equally fundamental, though, is the growing imperative on the part of states in regard to societal rationalisation – that is, the minimisation of social disruption and the achievement of social efficiencies, one critical dimension of which is environmental protection. Put somewhat differently, to the degree that environmental protection is achieved, it will be largely due to the role of states in rationalising the human relationship to the environment and resources (see Andrews, 1999; Buttel, 1998; Murphy, 1994).[3] Thus, instead of assuming that the state plays a relatively unitary role regarding the environment, it is more useful to anticipate that state policy will be contradictory and that conflicts over environmental protection and resource conservation will be played out within the state itself.

A second analytical opportunity is for practitioners in the two subdisciplines to draw on new lines of thought in the political sociology and political science literatures on state effectiveness and state–society synergy. Over the past half decade or so there has been a decisive shift in the perspectives of political sociologists and political scientists about what makes states effective. It had traditionally been assumed that state autonomy or state power was a property of states (see the critique in Evans, 1995, and in Migdal et al., 1994). In particular, it was stressed that, all things being equal, centralised states would tend to have the greatest level of autonomy *vis-à-vis* the competing interests and demands within civil society, and would be best able to implement a coherent set of policies to accomplish goals such as economic growth, monetary stability, national security, and so on.

This has been called into question in recent years, however, and has begun to give way to a 'state-in-society', embedded-autonomy, or state–society synergy perspective (see Evans, 1996).[4] The essence of these alternative perspectives is that what makes states effective is not the degree to which they are autonomous, or are able to insulate themselves from groups in civil society, but rather the degree to which states are 'embedded' (Evans, 1995) within groups in civil society. Both state actors, and actors in civil society, can obtain influence or autonomy on one hand, and achieve their goals on the other, through establishing synergistic (though often conflictual) mutual relations – hence the expression state–society synergy (Evans, 1996). This embedded-autonomy or state–society synergy perspective has thus moved from a zero-sum conception of state power to a positive-sum notion of power in which state/civil society relationships can lead to synergy and to more power for both groups of actors.

Davidson's (1999) research on the role of federal and state government agents in the implementation of the Endangered Species Act in California is a very useful illustration of how concepts such as state–society synergy allow one to understand the macrostructural features of resource policies while doing so in ways that do not gloss over the details and specificities of local environmental and resource management struggles.

Globalisation

In less than a decade 'globalisation' has become one of the most widely used concepts in the social sciences (as well as in popular discourse). Unfortunately, the notion of globalisation is typically employed in vague and inconsistent ways, essentially as an undifferentiated but powerful trend toward: closer communication linkages across nations; increasingly integrated and competitive global markets; cultural homogenisation (together with heterogenisation); trade liberalisation; and the growing role of international organisations. While the term 'globalisation' may be nebulous and inconsistent, there are many obvious, and some not-so-obvious, reasons why environment and natural resources sociologists must grapple with the forces of globalisation. The very notion of 'environment' conjures up a global scale conception of habitat such as 'global environmental change' or the 'global commons'. At the same time, many grassroots environmental groups have become critical of the excessively global emphasis of the symbols and strategies of mainstream environmental organisations. International organisations and regimes, and international negotiations over the practices of these regimes, play an increasingly important role in environmental protection and resource management (Andrews, 1999). Most natural resources are implicated in global markets, and even those resources that are widely traded internationally are indirectly affected by global markets in substitute or complementary fuels, resources, materials, and so on.

Neither environmental sociology nor the sociology of natural resources (with important exceptions to be noted later) has had a particularly distinguished record of scholarship relating to globalisation. In part, this is no doubt due to the fact that the literature on globalisation has tended to be imprecise, and there has been a lack of clear exemplars for incorporating globalisation forces into the conceptualisation of research problems (although see Buttel, 1998; McMichael, 2000). It has also been largely the case that the sociology of natural resources, given its tendency to stress local and regional units of analysis, has not dealt systematically with late twentieth century world economic and political integration. Also, the principal unit of analysis in environmental sociology has tended to be the nation-state (Buttel, 1997), and, accordingly, while globalisation pressures are often acknowledged (for example, Harper, 1997), these pressures have essentially been viewed as exogenous to societies or as extensions of societal level dynamics.

To provide a basis for future work in ES and NRM, globalisation needs to be understood historically, relationally, and with respect to differential incidence and impacts. Globalisation is not merely a pattern of closer contacts and communication among nations and their peoples, of the cultural homogenisation wrought by the culture of consumerism, or of the increasing pervasiveness of cross-border trade and investment circuits. We must remember that market-based trade and investments among nations and international flows of raw materials have occurred for a very long time (Andrews, 1999).

The core force underlying present global relations is the mobility of money capital across borders in search of both speculative profit as well as profitable investment opportunities. This is not to say that globalisation trends and processes have been uncontested. There are social movements and NGOs across the globe for which resistance to trade and financial liberalisation is among their major goals. Most major global environmental groups are ambivalent about, if not opposed to, World Trade Organisation (WTO)-style trade liberalisation, mainly because of the threat that the WTO regime will result in 'downward harmonisation' of national environmental policies. Environmental organisations, for example, played a key role in the mass protests at the November–December 1999 Seattle WTO Ministerial Conference.

A few examples of the not-so-obvious relevance of globalisation to the environment and resources should also be mentioned at this point. First, the fundamental pattern of contemporary globalisation, in which relatively unregulated cross-border movements of money capital assume the lead role, are likely to create pressures for the natural resources industries to become more globally concentrated as a result of market competition, and of acquisitions and mergers driven by stock speculation and currency disorders. Second, however, given the tendency for long lead times of investment in the natural resources industries, footloose money capital is likely to go disproportionately to the financial/services sector and to industries (such as information technology) with shorter cash flow horizons than are typically the case in agriculture, mining, and forestry. Third, globalisation's differential impacts on social groups, nations and continents will prompt changes in the geography of extraction, production, consumption and waste disposal (in large part because footloose investment capital can be particularly agile in seeking out cheap labour and sites with fewer environmental regulations). To the degree that globalisation processes exacerbate income inequalities and reinforce patterns of social exclusion, globalisation will not only affect directly productive resources and resulting patterns of ecosystem change and pollution, but will also affect the distribution politics of natural reserves. In an increasingly unequal world, in which growing numbers of people are excluded from basic needs such as food and shelter, it is likely to become increasingly difficult to justify the cordoning off of ecosystem reserves.

Recent work of particular relevance is that of Bunker and colleagues, who have demonstrate the critical role that the physical characteristics of resources and materials play in shaping the social organisation of their extraction and industrial conversion (see especially Bunker, 1989, and Ciccantell and Bunker, 1998). These researchers have examined the historical development of the global commodity chain of copper, from the site of bauxite mining in countries such as Brazil, to the manufacture of aluminium, to the incorporation of aluminium into finished products, and to the consumption and recycling of aluminium (see especially Bunker and Ciccantell, 1994). They have explored the socioeconomic processes that accompany the extraction of raw materials and the industrial conversion of these raw materials into finished products in order to demonstrate how extraction is associated with underdevelopment (Bunker, 1989, 1992).

There are three other noteworthy contributions to the global context of resources and environment that can show the way to cross-fertilisation between environmental sociology and the sociology of natural resources. One particularly useful corner of scholarship is that by researchers such as Freudenburg et al. (1995) and Boyd et al. (1999) on the relationships between the biophysical characteristics of materials and resources and human modes of appropriation and extraction. It is striking that in a good share of the scholarship in both environmental sociology and the sociology of natural resources there is relatively little consideration of the role that the biophysical characteristics of materials and resources play. For example, in his otherwise impressive book, *Wasted*, Redclift (1996) documents the parameters of the (highly unequal) expansion of global materials consumption, but he has very little to say about the local, biophysical, conditions of extraction or appropriation of these materials. The challenge for environmental sociology is to recognise the roles that the biophysical parameters of materials and pollutants play across space and time.

Another promising focal point for research that can lead to ES/SNR cross-fertilisation is to consider the methodological device of exploring cross-border commodity chains. It is seldom that practitioners in either environmental sociology or the sociology of natural resources pay attention to the actual flows of resources from sites of extraction/appropriation to consumption. But for most materials appropriated from nature there is a 'chain' of activities of greater or lesser length which affects the form and character of the material, and which affects the environment and social groups.

Pioneered in the sociology of agriculture (especially by Friedland, 1984, as 'commodity systems analysis') and in world-systems theory (by Gereffi and Korzeniewicz, 1994), commodity chain analysis is a set of methods aimed at tracing flows of materials and commodities from their inputs through their extraction/harvesting, production, processing, marketing, and consumption. Commodity chain analyses are often very useful in demonstrating where and how control is exercised over processes of production, particularly when these materials cross national borders. In wheat production, for example, control tends to be exercised at two pivotal points along the commodity chain: the role of grain traders as first-handlers of grain (particularly grain destined for export) and of millers of wheat, who transform it into different types of flour for various baking and manufacturing purposes. The nature of commodity chains is also very closely shaped by the biophysical character of materials. To take a simple example, the value per volume and weight of asparagus produced under contract in Peru enables it to be shipped by airplane to North American markets during the off season, whereas the value per volume and weight of wheat causes it to be transported primarily by rail and on ships and barges, and thus relatively slowly.

Commodity chain analyses are of obvious relevance to studies relating to natural resource commodities (timber, minerals, fish, and so on in addition to food commodities and products). With a little more imagination one can understand how commodity chain analysis could be a useful adjunct to more conventional perspectives for studying industrial pollution.

As a final note about globalisation and the global aspect of resources and environment, it has become apparent that resource flows and environmental protection processes have taken on increasingly global regulatory dimensions during the late twentieth century. As deregulation has taken place within most nation-states, and thus as international market flows have assumed greater importance, there have been persistent struggles over the degree to which 'liberalisation' should be further generalised. International regimes and organisations represent, to some extent, a 're-regulatory' thrust. It is relatively obvious, then, that there is a need for natural resources and environment scholars to understand the global environmental practices and struggles, even if the objects of their research remain local or regional.

Environmentalism and Environmental Movements

There are relatively few environmental sociologists and sociologists of natural resources who do not, in some manner, address environmentalism and environmental movements. The reason for this is quite obvious. It is self-evident that environmentalism and the movements which are environmentalism's bearers (which I will hereafter refer to coterminously) directly or indirectly affect virtually every environmental and resource phenomenon in the world today. Further, environmental movements are the principal catalyst in prompting governments, firms, and other social groups to be cognisant about environmental quality, resource conservation, ecosystem integrity, and so on. In other words, it is environmental movements that substantially account for the tendency of states to face the imperative of environmental rationalisation, as noted earlier.

There are a number of oversimplifications about the nature and role of environmentalism which are extant in both ES and SNR and which warrant being addressed. Perhaps the most common oversimplification is the assumption, even if only implicit, that environmentalism is, in essence, a relatively singular phenomenon. In other words, there is typically a presumption that an 'environmentalist' in one context will have considerable commonalities with an 'environmentalist' in another context, and/or that there is in principle, if not in practice, an organic connection among the issues which are the objects of environmental mobilisation. Among the typical – and yet problematic – assumptions about the commonalities among environmentalists is that these people are more knowledgeable about environmental science, more progressive, less interested in material goods and/or economic growth, more 'public regarding', and so on than are nonenvironmentalists.

The type of perspective on environmentalism that I feel has the most to contribute to environmental sociology and the sociology of natural resources has several interrelated components (see also Buttel, 1996, 1997, 1998). First, there is a need to recognise that, in some sense, there is no such 'thing' as environmentalism, since the range of concerns, interests and claims that has been and can be assembled under the banner of environmentalism is amazingly diverse. Second, there is comparable diversity in the range of social groups which can become bearers of environmentalism – or, in other words, environmentalism, unlike most other types of social movements, does not have a 'natural constituency'. Perhaps the most interesting example of this concerns the choices that many elites of indigenous groups must take in deciding whether to align their societies with international environmentalists who hold out the promise of preserving traditional extraction regimes, or to cast their lot with developers and state officials who promise modernisation and jobs. Whether they 'become environmentalists' (in our western sense of the term) is not structurally given, but rather may be more the result of decisions made about strategy based on means–ends calculation. Third, while environmental mobilisation in particular nations or places may involve a fairly definite structure of recruitment and pattern of discourses,[5] these structures and patterns vary enormously across cultures and over space. This variability is captured effectively, though incompletely, by Martinez-Alier (1995) through his use of the notions of environmentalism of the rich and environmentalism of the poor. Fourth, even within a particular social location (such as an advanced industrial country such as the US or Australia, or within tropical rainforest zones in Latin America), the particular shape that environmentalism takes is often highly situational (compare, for example, the modus operandi of the Brazilian rubber tappers with those of Earth First! and Greenpeace–Netherlands). Fifth, given these highly variable processes, the tendency within organised environmentalism is as often as not internal dissent as it is coalition.

The notion of 'movement' leads social scientists to make somewhat arbitrary distinctions between groups and actors that are 'within the environmental movement' and those that are not. This is why it is important to distinguish between environmentalism and environmental movements, since 'environmentalism' needs to be understood as the diversity of impulses among groups and actors to protect the environment (or to make claims that they want to protect one or another feature of the environment), while 'the movement' pertains to those who do so within the confines of specific social movement organisations. Even so, there is a considerable grey area as to what is an environmental social movement organisation. A good example of this ambiguity is Davidson's (1999) research on ESA implementation in Northern California in which she has observed the emergence of local 'watershed defence' groups whose agendas are formed in contrast to both the interests of logging corporations and those of mainstream environmentalists. Watershed defence groups are strongly oriented to preserving private property rights, putting them at odds with most mainstream environmental groups which want to establish the principle of government regulation of and control over the cut of old-growth forests. At the same time, watershed defence groups are insistent that lumber company abuses of the environment do not result in soil erosion, floods and other environmental harms that would adversely affect their own private property rights. Thus, our conceptual tools for depicting the boundaries of social movement organisations and the nature of movement discourses may be problematic in understanding 'hybrid environmental movements' (my term) such as those of watershed defence groups in California. In general, then, there is a need to take a broader comparative view of environmentalism and environmental mobilisation, and a need to be prepared to evaluate assumptions about the nature of environmental movements and environmentalism.

CONCLUSION

In this chapter I have documented the historical origins and current nature of the gulf between environmental sociology and the sociology of natural resources, and most importantly suggested some possible strategies for synthesis and cross-fertilisation. I have argued that both groups of scholars can improve the comprehensiveness of their work by becoming more self-reflective concerning their conceptualisations of the environment, by being more systematic in understanding the roles of states in natural resource and environmental phenomena, by taking globalisation processes seriously, and by taking a broader view of the role of environmentalism and environmental movements than is often the case.

In closing it is also worth mentioning that there are two literatures that deserve special note in relation to the arguments made in this chapter. First, the sociology of agriculture literature – seldom treated within the sociology of natural resources because SNR has not traditionally regarded agricultural resources as appropriate for study within this framework – deserves notice because of its advances in the areas of globalisation, the biophysical character of resources and materials, commodity chains, and the role of environmental mobilisation (see, for example, Bonanno and Constance, 1997; Bonanno et al., 1994; Goodman et al., 1987; McMichael, 1994, 2000). The sociology of agriculture literature has made particular gains in understanding the role of international organisations and regimes during the era of globalisation at the end of the century (see Goodman and Watts, 1997). Second, as suggested by Wilson (1999), the sociology of fisheries has been the area of the sociology of natural resources that has been most comprehensive in grappling with the biophysical specificities of the resource, the economic sociology of production, and the role of the science, the state, environmental movements, and globalisation processes. The sociology of agriculture and sociology of fisheries show that a number of the suggestions in this chapter are realistic and have practical value.

Finally, it is worth returning to a matter, mentioned briefly at the beginning of the chapter, concerning whether the ES/SNR gulf is itself a problem. A reasonable case can be made that there is a division of labour, and, at least potentially, a complementary relationship, between environmental sociology and the sociology of natural resources. There is little overt rivalry between the two approaches, and the weaknesses of one field of scholarship are often areas of strength on the part of the other. While the complementarity interpretation is no doubt true to a degree, my guess would be that the rate of cross-citation between environmental sociology and the sociology of natural resources is very low, and so what complementarity does potentially exist is not being very fully manifest in practice. My hope is that this chapter might suggest opportunities for a more sustained dialogue between environmental sociology and the sociology of natural resources. This closer dialogue will help scholars from both fields come to grips with their differences and learn through looking at these differences self-reflectively.

NOTES

1. It should be noted that environmental sociology and the sociology of natural resources have strong tendencies to take on both objectivist *and* subjectivist definitions of the environment. In other words, practitioners of both subdisciplines tend to see the natural world as a constellation of objective constraints that concretely affect humans and which are also affected in concretely observable ways by humans.
2. Perhaps the most convenient way to convey the predominant environmental–sociological view of the environment is to view it from the 'ecological footprint' perspective (Wackernagel and Rees, 1996), which involves converting a society's or locality's

consumption and waste disposal into a land and water area estimated to be required to meet these needs on a sustainable basis.

3. It should be noted that one particular line of scholarship in environmental sociology – that of ecological modernisation (Mol, 1997) – has achieved progress in understanding the rationalisation imperative of nation-states and how this imperative relates to environmental protection. There is some debate, however, as to the degree to which ecological modernisation theories have exaggerated the scope and power of the rationalisation imperative (Bluehdorn, 1997). Related to, though not identical with, rationalisation is the notion of environmental 'governmentality' – the historic expansion of the scope, responsibilities, and autonomy of the state (see Sairinen, 1999).

4. Much of the evidence in support of this proposition has come from studies by scholars such as Evans (1995), who has demonstrated that the successful role played by the Korean state during its economic ascent of the past three decades has not been due to the state's being insulated from Korean civil society, but rather because of the close, synergistic relations between the state and civil society groups (especially capital).

5. The typical pattern in the industrial countries, for example, that movement officials and active adherents tend to be drawn from the upper-middle classes, to be employed outside of corporate environments, and to be least attractive to conservative political parties.

REFERENCES

Andrews, R. (1999), *Managing the Environment, Managing Ourselves*, New Haven: Yale University Press.

Benton, T. (1996), *The Greening of Marxism*, New York: Guilford.

Bluehdorn, I. (1997), 'Ecological Modernisation and Post-ecologist Politics', paper presented at the ISA RC 24 conference on Social Theory and the Environment, Woudschoten Conference Center, The Netherlands.

Bonanno, A. and D. Constance (1997), *Caught in the Net*, Lawrence: University Press of Kansas.

Bonanno, A. et al. (1994), *From Columbus to ConAgra*, Lawrence: University Press of Kansas.

Botkin, D. (1990), *Discordant Harmonies*, New York: Oxford University Press.

Boyd, W., W. Prudham and R. Schurman (1999), 'Industrial Dynamics and the Problem of Nature', unpublished manuscript, Department of Sociology, University of Illinois.

Bunker, S. (1989), 'Staples, Links, and Poles in the Construction of Regional Development Theory', *Sociological Forum*, 4, 589–610.

Bunker, S. (1992), 'Natural Resource Extraction and Power Differentials in a Global Economy', in S. Ortis and S. Lees (eds), *Understanding Economic Process*, Washington, DC: University Press of America, pp. 61–84.

Bunker, S. and P. Ciccantell (1994), 'The Evolution of the World Aluminum Industry', chapter 2 in B. Barham et al. (eds), *States, Firms, and Raw Materials*, Madison: University of Wisconsin Press.

Buttel, F. (1996), 'Environmental and Resource Sociology: Theoretical Issues and Opportunities for Synthesis', *Rural Sociology*, 61, 56–76.

Buttel, F. (1997), 'Social Institutions and Environmental Change', in M. Redclift and G. Woodgate (eds), *International Handbook of Environmental Sociology*, Cheltenham: Edward Elgar, pp. 40–54.

Buttel, F. (1998), 'Some Observations on States, World Orders, and the Politics of Sustainability', *Organisation and Environment*, 11, 261–286.

Catton, W. (1980), *Overshoot*, Urbana: University of Illinois Press.

Ciccantell, P. and S. Bunker (eds) (1998), *Space and Transport in the World-System*, Westport, CT: Greenwood Press.

Davidson, D. (1999), 'Federal Policy in Local Context: The Influence of Local State–Societal Relations on Endangered Species Act Implementation', unpublished manuscript, Department of Rural Sociology, University of Wisconsin, Madison.

Dickens, P. (1996), *Reconstructing Nature*, London: Routledge.

Dunlap, R. (1997), 'The Evolution of Environmental Sociology: A Brief History and Assessment of the American Experience', in M. Redclift and G. Woodgate (eds), *International Handbook of Environmental Sociology*, Cheltenham: Edward Elgar, pp. 21–39.

Evans, P. (1995), *Embedded Autonomy*, Princeton: Princeton University Press.

Evans, P. (1996), 'Government Action, Social Capital, and Development: Reviewing the Evidence on Synergy', *World Development*, **24**, 1119–1132.

Foster, J. (2000), *Marx's Ecology*, New York: Monthly Review Press.

Friedland, W. (1984), 'Commodity Systems Analysis: An Approach to the Sociology of Agriculture', *Research in Rural Sociology and Development*, **1**, 221–235.

Freudenburg, W., S. Frickel and R. Gramling (1995), 'Beyond the Nature/Society Divide: Learning to Think About a Mountain', *Sociological Forum*, **10**, 361–392.

Gereffi, G. and M. Korzeniewicz (eds) (1994), *Commodity Chains and Global Capitalism*, Westport, CT: Praeger.

Goodman, D. and M. Watts (eds) (1997), *Globalising Food*, London: Routledge.

Goodman, D., B. Sorj and J. Wilkinson (1987), *From Farming to Biotechnology*, Oxford: Basil Blackwell.

Gould, K., A. Schnaiberg and A. Weinberg (1996), *Local Environmental Struggles*, New York: Cambridge University Press.

Harper, C. (1997), *Environment and Society*, New York: St. Martin's Press.

Martinez-Alier, J. (1995), 'Commentary: The Environment as a Luxury Good, or "Too Poor to be Green"', *Ecological Economics*, **13**, 1–10.

McMichael, P. (ed.) (1994), *Global Restructuring of Agro-Food Systems*, Ithaca: Cornell University Press.

McMichael, P. (2000), *Development and Social Change*, second edition, Thousand Oaks, CA: Pine Forge Press.

Migdal, J., A. Kohli and V. Shue (eds) (1994), *State Power and Social Forces*, New York: Cambridge University Press.

Mol, A. (1997), 'Ecological Modernisation: Industrial Transformations and Environmental Reform', in M. Redclift and G. Woodgate (eds), *International Handbook of Environmental Sociology*, Cheltenham: Edward Elgar, pp. 138–149.

Murphy, R. (1994), *Rationality and Nature*, Boulder, CO: Westview Press.

O'Connor, J. (1973), *The Fiscal Crisis of the State*, New York: St. Martin's Press.

O'Connor, J. (1994), 'Is Sustainable Capitalism Possible?', in M. O'Connor (ed.), *Is Capitalism Sustainable?*, New York: Guilford.

Redclift, M. (1996), *Wasted*, London: Earthscan.

Redclift, M. and T. Benton (eds) (1994), *Social Theory and the Global Environment*, London: Routledge.

Roberts, J. and P. Grimes (1997), 'World-system Theory and the Environment: Toward a New Synthesis', paper presented at the ISA RC 24 Conference on Social Theory and the Environment, Woudschoten Conference Center, The Netherlands.

Sairinen, R. (1999), 'Environmental Governmentality as a Basis for Regulatory Reform – Analysing the New Policy Instruments and Changes in Policy

Strategies', paper presented at the RC 24 Conference on The Environmental State Under Pressure, Chicago: August.

Schnaiberg, A. (1980), *The Environment*, New York: Oxford University Press.

Schnaiberg, A. and K. Gould (1993), *Environment and Society*, New York: St. Martin's Press.

Wackernagel, M. and W. Rees (1996), *Our Ecological Footprint*, Gabriola Island, BC: New Society Publishers.

Wilson, D. (1999), 'Fisheries Sociology in the Late 1990s', *NRRG Newsletter* (Rural Sociological Society), Spring/Summer, 6–8.

3. 'Social Science' in the Environmental Studies and Natural Science Arenas: Misconceptions, Misrepresentations and Missed Opportunities

Joseph P. Reser and Joan M. Bentrupperbäumer

INTRODUCTION

This chapter reflects the authors' joint experience over the past five years of undertaking social science-based research in the context of protected area management, and in particular the Wet Tropics World Heritage Area (WTWHA) of North Queensland. This work builds on our respective individual experiences and disciplinary backgrounds as an environmental and social psychologist and a field biologist and behavioural scientist. What is very clear to us is the yawning gulf between social science assumptions and paradigms, on the one hand, and the assumptions and models of the natural and physical sciences in the environmental arena in Australia, on the other. While it is hardly novel to bring attention to the many 'cultures' which characterise 'environmental' research and management practices, it is surprising that such different understandings and worldviews continue to frustrate genuine collaboration in the environmental arena and in protected area management contexts. This is especially so, given the multidisciplinary and interdisciplinary nature of the problems, the applied management context, management discourse and rhetoric – and indeed the history of protected area management elsewhere in the world. It is clear that this divide between social science and natural science is the product of multiple factors, many of which are poorly recognised and understood in terms of causes, mediating processes and ultimate consequences. These, in our view, include fundamental misperceptions and misunderstandings of the nature of a generic social science perspective on environmental problems and research, fundamental differences in understanding with respect to the nature of the enterprise of environmental protection and management, and multiple and interacting problems of cross-discipline, cross-agency, and management–stakeholder–community communications, interests and concerns.

We have chosen to frame the nested set of problems faced in disciplinary and professional practice in terms of *misconceptions, misrepresentations,* and *missed opportunities* as this provides a strategic avenue for identifying and addressing the problems. The misconceptions and misunderstandings that characterise many attempts at collaboration in the context of multidisciplinary research centres, for example, are the product of very different paradigmatic conceptions, different problem approaches and strategies, and different research and practice cultures. The mis-representations which characterise cross-disciplinary and cross-research management highlight somewhat different problems with respect to a pervasive nonrecognition of the human domain as a species-specific area of scientific expertise. Another misunderstanding is the unfortunate belief that social science simply equates with tourist behaviour research and/or socioeconomic valuation. The consequences of the above misunderstandings and mistaken identities in terms of missed opportunities are multifold and extensive. They frustrate the potential development of standardised environmental indicators, cross-disciplinary comparisons and cross validations, and genuine integration and synthesis at strategic decision making and policy levels.

WHAT IS MEANT BY SOCIAL SCIENCE?

While there is limited value in debating which disciplines constitute 'social science' most would agree that, historically and academically, core disciplines include anthropology, psychology and sociology. Economics, education, history, political science and human geography are often included under this rubric, along with mixed fields such as cultural studies, leisure studies, urban studies, health sciences, management and planning (see, for example, the Social Sciences Citation Index). It is interesting that the two social sciences most notable by their absence in natural environment research and management in Australia are psychology and sociology, each of which, as a discipline and practice, has well-developed subdisciplinary areas of environmental psychology and environmental sociology (Burdge, 1999; Stokols, 1995), with environmental psychology being particularly prominent as an area of disciplinary and professional specialisation (Bell et al., 1996; Bonnes and Secchiaroli, 1995; Cassidy, 1997; Gifford, 1997; McAndrew, 1993; Stokols and Altman, 1987; Veitch and Arkkelin, 1995).

The substantive issue we are addressing here is that there are simply very few individuals with undergraduate or postgraduate degrees in core social science disciplines, or with reasonable training in these areas, working for, or undertaking research on behalf of, those management agencies, Co-operative Research Centres (CRCs), or government departments which are responsible for protected area management in Australia. At the same time, individuals with natural science qualifications working in or on behalf of such agencies and organisations would, at a conservative estimate, outnumber social science graduates and professionals by a factor of 50 to 1. The dilemma and problem this state of affairs poses and reflects is that there is limited understanding in the natural environment arena of what applied social science areas such as environmental psychology or environmental sociology are or what they have to offer.

WHAT IS THE NATURE AND CHARACTER OF THIS 'DIVIDE' AND WHY IS IT THERE?

It is difficult to describe and explain, in brief terms, the paradigmatic differences or the vastly different assumptive worlds which exist across disciplinary divides (Gibbons et al., 1994; Kuhn, 1970). The core of the problem is in some ways even more basic, however. From a logical and intuitive perspective it is clear that management and protection, in a natural environment context, must be substantially about managing people and minimising negative human impacts in protected areas and ecosystems. The 'protection, preservation and presentation' mantra and mandate of protected areas such as World Heritage Areas further tell us that 'people management' has to do with designing, managing and monitoring the nature and quality of people's transactions with the natural environment. Any consideration of interpretation, education or enjoyment, on the one hand, or community perceptions, attitudes or concerns on the other, underscores the importance of understanding, and if necessary influencing and modifying, psychological and social aspects of environmental experiences and encounters. This in turn requires a modicum of understanding of intra- and inter-individual processes such as human perception, cognition, emotional response, motivation, social dynamics, community dynamics and functioning, and behaviour change.

Certainly such assumptions and inferences are the starting point for a social scientist. In addition, a social science perspective would take it as read that the 'natural environment' and protected areas such as 'national parks' and 'world heritage areas' and 'natural and cultural heritage', are complex social constructions and representations (Berger and Luckman, 1967; Burr, 1995; Semin and Gergen, 1990). These are ideas and notions of interwoven understandings and expectations, as well as behaviour settings and places and physical environments. Indeed, there are few social scientists today who would not also immediately think about and frame the nature of the enterprise as, in part, an exercise in charting the virtual reality and landscape of 'the Wet Tropics' or 'the rainforest' or 'the reef', whether in terms of presentation, promotion, imaging, or 'mapping', and the impacts of these psychological, social and virtual domains on the biophysical 'behaviour setting' (Jagtenberg and McKie, 1997; Rheingold, 1992).

There are several other aspects of a social science approach which are of particular importance and relevance. Many nonsocial scientists would 'understand' a social science approach as being characterised by a focus on perceptions, attitudes, values, and human behaviour. Fewer, however, would appreciate that these notions and variables are essentially theoretical, within-the-person, constructs deemed to be of particular importance in mediating behaviour, and that they are essentially operationalised and measured by psychometric procedures and scales in a reasonably rigorous and systematic way. Rarely would a nonsocial scientist understand that such perceptions, attitudes and values find particular expression and currency in social representations such as discourse, texts, images, and a multitude of cultural products, including entities like a 'World Heritage Area' or a World Heritage convention or charter. The point is that constructs such as values, for a social scientist, *are* constructs. They reflect a reasonably elaborate theoretical housing and operational consensus, and they are understood as residing *in people*, not places or things.

Another important feature of a social science approach is that there is often a focus on social influence and behaviour change, whether in terms of better understanding how change takes place or with respect to being effective agents of change. In an environmental context, influences and 'impacts' are immediately understood as bi-directional and reciprocal, with the impact on the individual person and experience being as important as the impact on the environment, and with this latter immediately including the social as well as the physical environment. This dramatically and profoundly changes how one frames the issues in terms of management and impact assessment, and offers a spectrum of opportunities with respect to social influence and behaviour change. The challenge of mitigating biophysical impacts with respect to the natural environment broadens to include designing and influencing *experiences* and behaviours to bring about more sensitive and ecologically responsible encounters with the natural environment. Finally, 'psychological' and 'social' are not conventionally the same thing in the social science domain when speaking about environments and impacts. 'Psychological' generally pertains to the individual, and individual experience, whereas 'social' relates to the more encompassing social environment, including people in groups and communities as well as social institutions and processes, such as aspects of social exchange as economic benefit and monetary 'value'. 'Psychosocial' is a far better analogue to 'biophysical'. 'Social impact' by itself tends to exclude and marginalise psychological impact and individual experience, as well as relevant disciplinary expertise and relevance.

We are very aware that these comments will seem simplistic and obvious to many, but we have become acutely aware of the tyranny of language in our work across disciplines and agencies and stakeholders. We have also become sensitised to the vagaries and confusing semantic and referential worlds of many forms of 'ecospeak' in the public and scientific domain. We feel strongly that a core issue here, as with many research endeavours, is the challenge of clearly and adequately specifying, both conceptually and theoretically, and operationally and empirically, what it is that we are talking about, researching and measuring. The expression 'world heritage values' is a particularly compelling case in point. Our emphasis here is more particularly concerned with how language is *used* in the more public *discourse* and *decision making* of researchers, management agencies, government organisations and stakeholders, including how the notion 'social science' is employed.

There are many reasons why the divide continues, and why our attempts at collaborations and interdisciplinarity often shift into boundary disputes and the validation of prejudices. Of these, the most important, in many ways, are the different perceptions and understandings of these disciplinary domains and the notions of 'science' and 'scientists' by management, grant agencies and government departments. It is important to appreciate that public understandings of science both reflect and create social representations of areas of expertise. The 'experts' in one domain may well have a lay understanding of other disciplinary domains. Indeed, many understandings of other disciplines and disciplinary practices are very naive and uninformed. Working in a multidisciplinary context may or may not lead to a disabusing of caricatured and incorrect understandings of other fields, with this often depending on whether areas of assumed similarity and common ground are critically discussed and addressed (Salter and Hearn, 1996).

These are not new issues which we are raising but they are not often expressed, discussed, or meaningfully addressed. This is, in part, because of the perceived risks with respect to violating political correctness or tacit understandings between 'the players' regarding the sometimes inchoate state of professional and management discourse and strategic planning in NRM. It is worth noting that anthropology in particular has been very interested in the nature, language and cultural relativity of protected area management discourse, and has found this a rich and fascinating 'nature preserve' (Milton, 1993, 1996; Pannell, 1997; Pannell and von Benda-Beckmann, 1998).

SOME ILLUSTRATIVE EXAMPLES

We have chosen to look briefly at two examples of very different disciplinary understandings within the natural environment management context. These are the notion of 'world heritage values' and the nature of social impact assessment. The assumptions, understandings and use of each of these constructs vary substantially as one examines different discourses and practices. While the same language is being used, the conceptual realities and research and management implications are widely divergent.

Value, Values and Valuing in the World Heritage Arena

The initial example relates to the expression 'world heritage values'. The use and meaning of this expression in the context of the WTWHA of North Queensland, by natural scientists, managers, politicians and journalists, constitutes a sobering example of how a very confused rhetoric and very different understandings are driving arguably questionable procedures, policies and protected area management decisions. There are a number of aspects of this problematic use, but the more important and consequential relate to the nature and status of such 'values', where they are 'located', the nonreflective use and currency of the expression, and how such values are ultimately specified, operationalised and measured.

> The rainforests of Queensland's wet tropics are now recognised to contain the highest concentration of primitive flowering plant families in the world, and are 'recognized internationally as holding important and unique clues to the problem of the origin, evolution and migration of the flowering plants'. *It is these values* which form the basis of the World Heritage list inscription. (Frawley, 1991, p. 221)

A fundamental problem for social scientists encountering the current use of the construct 'values' in protected environment and World Heritage discussions is that this use simply does not make good sense, and is largely inconsistent and incompatible with social science use and conceptual, theoretical and operational elaboration and understanding.

To a layperson the adjective 'environmental' preceding 'values' can suggest that values are literal and intrinsic features of environments, and 'environmental evaluation' can be taken to mean a more economic and monetary valuation of the environment, as well as an evaluation or assessment of the perceived cultural, life-support, leisure, or spiritual value of the environment to the human community. The environmental management and nonsocial science research discourse on Wet Tropics and Great Barrier Reef World Heritage *values* repeatedly locates values *in* the environment. There is a confused doubletalk which takes place whenever the discussion turns to environmental values. Significantly, this does not happen when the expression 'environmental attitudes' is used. There seems to be little awareness that the domain of value inquiry is philosophically and empirically complex, with important distinctions existing between value, values, valuing, kinds of value(s), systems of values, valuation and so on (Bronowski, 1956; Meux, 1998). Quite apart from the more than one hundred year history of axiology, and the fifty year social science history of conceptualisation and measurement (Allport et al., 1951; Baier and Rescher, 1968; Kluckhohn and Strodbeck, 1961; White, 1951), current use of these terms in the Australian World Heritage context is intuitively, logically and methodologically problematic and confusing. It is curious that conventional natural science rigour seems to be abandoned when dealing with issues of methodology and measurement in the domain of values. It is ostensibly possible for scientists to visit a natural area or region, with species and landscape feature list and clipboard in hand, and undertake an audit of world heritage values. Such an endeavour would leave most social scientists speechless.

It is interesting that when one looks to what is actually done or recommended, on the ground, the language often changes, and it is clear that what is undertaken is an inventory of flora, fauna, features, processes and interdependencies.

It is not our intention to enter into long theoretical discussions on the nature of Natural Heritage Values. If, however, they are to be monitored, there has to be a precise understanding of what they are and how they can be measured. This is not simple because the term Natural Heritage Value is used commonly in a nominal sense to refer to classes or categories of characteristics. As such, Natural Heritage Values are not scaleable, measurable or 'mappable' but tend to be general, holistic characteristics expressed only by considering the Wet Tropics as a whole. Natural Heritage *Values* are, in effect, the integrated expressions of a myriad of natural ecological processes, past and present, which are manifested in terms of particular elements which are present within the area and which have significance in relation to the four Natural World Heritage Criteria. It is these component elements which can be measured and monitored within an area (Hopkins and Johnson, 1995).

Notwithstanding such ground-truthing of the language in the case of actual auditing, there is repeated reference to threatened values, impacts on values, protection of values, and changing values, with the reference almost invariably being the attributes, elements, processes or integrity of the ecosystem and area itself. This is a very awkward and cumbersome use of language.

It might be argued that this is really a relatively inconsequential semantic imbroglio, that everyone knows what 'values' mean and where they reside, and that values 'in a natural environment context' are simply synonymous with environmental attributes or qualities of particular significance. It is clear, upon careful reflection, that this is patently not the case, and that glossing over differences in use and understanding here has far-reaching consequences. One can affirm and argue that 'values' reside in people and societies, or that individuals and cultures 'hold' particular values, but values as such do not and cannot reside in natural environments. When it is said that 'the Wet Tropics World Heritage Area has intrinsic value or values' what is meant is that *human society* values this environment, and what it stands for, and its unique qualities and threatened status, for its own sake, as well as in human benefit and economic terms. Yet, language and practice lead managers and nonsocial scientists to try and operationalise and quantify this human value and legislative stance in terms of species lists, vista inventories, monetary valuations of public good benefits in terms of goods and services, and 'willingness to pay' for the continued existence of the 'amenity'. While such dollar-value audits are perhaps necessary in the *realpolitic* of ministerial requirements and policy decisions relating to protected environments, it would seem that a far less tortured and confusing path would be to objectively, transparently and systematically measure, document and monitor community and societal values with respect to World Heritage Areas. This would achieve some semblance of construct validity and reliability, as well as consensual meaning and mutual understanding.

We have not addressed the contested discourse and practice of socioeconomic valuation in this chapter as this is heavily trafficked terrain in which the currency of constructs such as value, values and valuation, and contingent valuation, have been often questioned and debated (Bazerman et al., 1997). Passing reference is, however, necessary as the privileging of this socioeconomic perspective as best practice social science is increasingly being employed in the World Heritage, and protected area, arenas. The touchstone nature and criterion character of *values* and *valuing* in this eco-economics discourse is paramount, if not somewhat confused. Recent and controversial valuing of the planet's ecosystem goods and services (Costanza et al., 1997) is a good example of the valuation argument being a ubiquitous refrain, almost invariably premised on socioeconomic assumptions, constructs, and language.

The issue of valuation is inseparable from the choices and decisions we have to make about ecological systems. Some argue that valuation of ecosystems is either impossible or unwise, that we cannot place a value on such 'intangibles' as human life, environmental aesthetics, or long term ecological benefits. But, in fact, we do so every day . . . Another frequent argument is that we should protect ecosystems for purely moral or aesthetic reasons . . . But there are equally compelling moral arguments that may be in direct conflict with the moral argument to protect ecosystems; for example, the moral argument that no one should go hungry . . . So, although ecosystem valuation is certainly difficult and fraught with uncertainties, one choice we do not have is whether or not to do it. Rather, the decisions we make as a society about ecosystems imply valuations . . . We can choose to make these valuations explicit or not; we can do them with an explicit acknowledgement of the huge uncertainties involved or not; but as long as we are forced to make choices, we are going through the process of valuation. (Costanza et al., 1997, p. 255)

We do not entirely disagree with the sentiments expressed although we have serious reservations concerning the larger enterprise and the set of assumptions which underlie it. What does concern us, though, is how the discussion of economic valuation so often glibly slides from that which is valued to essentialised values:

The environment's services are, without doubt, valuable. The air we breathe, the water we drink, and the food we eat are all available only because of services provided by the environment. How can we transform *these values* into income while conserving resources? (Chichilnisky and Heal, 1998, p. 629)

It is interesting that in the cataloguing and costing of 17 ecosystem services and functions workshopped by Costanza and his colleagues (1997), only two relate to what might be considered direct psychological, social or cultural benefits or domains, with these being 'recreation' and 'cultural'. The exemplar given for the 'cultural' category does, parenthetically, highlight *values* – in contrast to all other categories – with reference to the 'aesthetic, artistic, educational, spiritual, and/or scientific *values* of ecosystems' (Costanza et al., p. 254). We should hasten to add that the whole argument of Costanza and his co-writers is in terms of public good and the '*production* of human welfare' and hence all categories 'have value'. But, equally clearly, valuation and costing are treated as synonymous and indistinguishable, with all of the problems that this entails.

The definitional and meaning issues with respect to world heritage values are in some ways no different from those that plague other expressions of particular importance and currency in today's environmental discourse, for example, with 'sustainable development', 'environmental protection', 'environmental quality' and 'biodiversity' (Caldwell, 1990; Pezzey, 1992; Wilson, 1988). This has been clearly evidenced with respect to 'ecologically sustainable development' in the context of research and management discourse and the Great Barrier Reef World Heritage Area. Indeed it is incumbent on environmental scientists and managers to clearly understand that the very concepts of 'nature' and 'environment' are cultural constructions and cultural meanings which are both product of and precursor to their own models, paradigms and parameters (see Ellen and Fukui, 1996; Everden, 1992; Robertson et al., 1996; Soulé and Lease, 1995).

SOCIAL AND PSYCHOSOCIAL IMPACTS

The second example relates to conventional understandings of social impact in the environmental management arena. While much has now been written on SIA as a component of environmental impact assessment (Barrow, 1997; Burdge, 1998; Taylor et al., 1995; Thomas, 1998), there are few clear and informative guides to the conceptual and theoretical underpinnings of SIA or how it relates to more generic understandings of evaluation research or social measurement. In the environmental management context of the Wet Tropics, social impact is routinely understood as largely socioeconomic impacts on the adjacent communities and region. It is also occasionally used as synonymous with human impacts on the biophysical environment. Our intention is not to debate, from a social science perspective, this problematic use and very selective understanding of social impact as impacts on the surrounding human community, or the narrow spectrum of socioeconomic and demographic parameters typically employed to measure or address 'social impact'. Rather, we would like to point out a number of logical and practical issues and problems from a social science and environmental psychology perspective. These have to do with the nature and notion of 'impact'.

Part of the dilemma for social scientists is that the notion of impact implies a consideration and documentation of change, in this case resulting from an environmental intervention. The prognostic character of an 'Environmental Impact Assessment' itself makes the use of the term impact somewhat incongruous, given that what is attempted is a snapshot of a situation, with extrapolations made to possible future scenarios. Perhaps what is most incongruous, however, is that impact assessment generally, and social impact assessment in particular, appear to be divorced from mainstream evaluation research and thinking, such that little thought is given to policy or programme evaluation or meaningful post-decision and intervention assessment. A more social science focus on issues of measurement, methodology and evaluation would also highlight the inherent reactivity of EIAs and SIAs in polarised communities and/or with respect to controversial proposals. In the context of Wet Tropics research and management in North Queensland the notion of impacts, both biophysical and 'social', drives much decision making and 'monitoring' research. Stakeholders often have their own view of 'impacts', with the tourist industry, for example, feeling that the very term privileges a widespread understanding of impact assessment as being about the documentation of negative biophysical impacts rather than a more balanced consideration of positive and negative biophysical and social impacts. These somewhat different and rather loose understandings of environmental impacts understandably lead to confusion, conflict, and problematic focus.

From an environmental psychological perspective an aspect of impact that is routinely ignored in the protected area context is the *impacts* on those who are visiting and using World Heritage sites. While some aspects of the experience and responses of people in these natural settings are often researched, typically in the context of market research and satisfaction, it is rarely conceptualised as impact. Again, from an environmental psychological, transactional perspective, the impact of the natural environment on individuals who are encountering and experiencing this environment is an intensely interesting and particularly valuable window on the nature and quality of transactions and reciprocal impacts. Such *psychological impact* is central to explorations of interpretation and presentation, and provides a valuable and possible avenue for behaviour change and people management. While any impact assessment is concerned with how changes introduced into the natural system affect ecosystem integrity and functioning, it is clear that visitation and use constitutes a multifaceted, interactive and dynamic set of transactions and impacts, which need to be conceptualised as such.

It is strange that professionals involved in natural resource and protected area management on the one hand, and impact assessment on the other, have not, in their mutually overlapping areas of interest and practice, more seriously considered and addressed psychosocial impact.

DISCUSSION

Where does this take us? What are the implications of this social science perspective for social science and the natural environment? There are, of course, many, but the most critical and pressing, in our view, is that social scientists must better package and communicate who and what they are and what they have to offer in the area of methods, measures and theory. They must strategically foster a culture change in the environmental management and research arenas such that social science is more accurately and clearly represented as a multidisciplinary forum of scientific experts with highly relevant expertise with respect to the 'people management' challenges of protected area management.

The potential cost of the current social science disciplinary drift in the environmental domain, and the ecospeak which characterises the protected area management discourse, is that someone will point out that the emperor is wearing no clothes with respect to such matters as world heritage values and social impact and social indicators. Social scientists will then 'wear' the problematic practices of nonsocial scientists attempting to do social science in the environmental domain. Quite apart from the sense of ironic injustice social scientists might collectively experience, the cause of World Heritage conservation, protection and presentation will have been substantially compromised and frustrated. It is interesting to note that it is precisely social science parameters such as world heritage values and concerns that have become the touchstone and direction of current natural science thinking and practice.

One of the advantages a social science perspective confers is that it allows its practitioners to more easily step back and reflect upon what they are doing as social scientists working in the environmental domain. They have been able to ask larger and, in a sense, more 'ecological', big picture questions about the appropriateness of the questions asked, as well as the methodologies and the measures they are using. They have looked somewhat more intently at the historical, political and cultural contexts that have driven environmental, conservation and protected area agendas. They have put such notions as 'nature', 'sustainability', 'heritage', 'management' and indeed 'reality', 'science' and 'value' on the table and asked what we mean by these notions, how such constructs and understandings drive our disciplinary and social practice, and how we can best move forward (Ellen and Fukui, 1996; Everden, 1992; Milton, 1993; Soulé and Lease, 1995).

Readers of this chapter might get the erroneous impression that it is a fairly straightforward matter to sample the social science literature and find what they need with respect to value measures, social impact scales and social indicators. Unfortunately there are few maps or guidebooks to what is a very complex and continually changing academic and applied landscape. The 'environmental' preface will also ensure that any literature search spans many disciplines, paradigms and levels of expertise. If we look closely at the implications of the value example discussed, even within the social science discourse, the compass of constructs such as 'value' and values are such that it is easy to get lost, nor does there exist an available, standardised, purpose-designed yardstick or set of procedures. The application of value theory to natural resource management requires both systematic development and consensus, as well as clear objectives and analytic clarity with respect to which value domains are being addressed. Ideally a standardised protocol and procedure will be developed which will distinguish between and independently measure knowledge, attitudes, beliefs, values and concerns relating to natural environments, both local and global, with these measures collectively and convergently documenting how *changing* communities see, understand and value their *changing* natural environments. This endeavour would be of particular utility to environmental managers and environmental research, and the measures would greatly assist in the documentation and monitoring of psychosocial as well as biophysical impacts and would constitute excellent *environmental* indicators.

REFERENCES

Allport, G., P. Vernon and G. Lindsey (1951), *A Study of Values*, Boston: Houghton Mifflin.

Baier, K. (1969), 'What is Value? An Analysis of the Concept', in Baier, K. and N. Rescher, (eds), *Values and the Future: The Impact of Technological Change on Human Values*, New York: The Free Press, pp. 33–67.

Baier, K. and N. Rescher (eds) (1968), *Values and the Future: The Impact of Technological Change on Human Values*, New York: The Free Press.

Barrow, C. (1997), *Environmental and Social Impact Assessment: An Introduction*, London: Arnold.

Bazerman, M., D. Messick, A. Tenbrunzel and K. Wade-Benzoni (eds) (1997), *Environment, Ethics and Behavior: The Psychology of Environmental Valuation and Degradation*, San Francisco: The New Lexington Press.

Bell, P., T. Greene, J. Fisher and A. Baum (1996), *Environmental Psychology*, Fourth Edition, New York: Harcourt Brace.

Berger, P. and T. Luckman (1967), *The Social Construction of Reality*, Ringwood: Penguin.

Bonnes, M. and G. Secchiaroli (1995), *Environmental Psychology: A Psycho-social Introduction*, London: Sage.

Bronowski, J. (1956), *Science and Human Values*, New York: Perennial Library.

Burdge, R. (1998), 'The Making of a Discipline: The Evolution of Society and Natural Resources as a Scholarly Journal', *Society and Natural Resources*, **12**, 179–187.

Burdge, R. (1999), *A Conceptual Approach to Social Impact Assessment*, Middleton, Wisconsin: Social Ecology Press.

Burr, V. (1995), *An Introduction to Social Constructionism*, London: Routledge.

Caldwell. L. (1990), *Between Two Worlds: Science, the Environmental Movement and Policy Choice*, New York: Cambridge University Press.

Cassidy, T. (1997), *Environmental Psychology: Behavior and Experience in Context*, Hove: Psychology Press.

Chichilnisky, G. and G. Heal (1998), 'Economic Returns from the Biosphere', *Nature*, **391**, 629–630.

Costanza, R., R. d'Arge, R. deGroot, S. Farber, M. Grasso, B. Hannon, K. Limburg, S. Naeem, R. O'Neill, J. Paruelo, R. Raskin, P. Sutton and M. van den Belt

(1997), 'The Value of the World's Ecosystem Services and Natural Capital', *Nature*, **387**, 253–260.

Ellen, R. and K. Fukui (eds) (1996), *Redefining Nature: Ecology, Culture and Domestication*, Washington: Berg.

Everden, N. (1992), *The Social Creation of Nature*, Baltimore: The Johns Hopkins University Press.

Frawley, K. (1991), 'Queensland Rainforest Management: Frontier Attitudes and Public Policy', *Journal of Rural Studies*, **7** (3), 219–239.

Gibbons, M. et al. (1994), *The New Production of Knowledge: The Dynamics of Science and Research in Contemporary Societies*, London: Sage Publications.

Gifford, R. (1997), *Environmental Psychology: Principles and Practice*, Second Edition, Sydney: Allyn and Bacon.

Hopkins, M. and R. Johnson (1995), *The Development of a Plot-Based Monitoring Strategy for Assessing Changes in World Heritage Values in the Wet Tropics*, A Report Prepared for the Wet Tropics Management Authority, Atherton, Queensland: CSIRO Division of Wildlife and Ecology.

Jagtenberg, T. and D. McKie (1997), *Eco-Impacts and the Greening of Postmodernity: New Maps for Communication Studies, Cultural Studies, and Sociology*, Thousand Oaks: California: Sage.

Kluckhohn, F. and F. Strodbeck (1961), *Variations in Value Orientations*, Row, Peterson, Illinois: Evanston.

Kuhn, T. (1970), *The Structure of Scientific Revolutions*, Chicago: The University of Chicago Press.

McAndrew, F. (1993), *Environmental Psychology*, Pacific Grove: Brooks/Cole.

Meux, M. (1998), 'A Value Agenda for Theoretical Psychology', *American Psychologist*, **53**, 64–65.

Milton, K. (ed.) (1993), *Environmentalism: The View from Anthropology*, London: Routledge.

Milton, K. (1996), *Environmentalism and Cultural Theory: Exploring the Role of Anthropology in Environmental Discourse*, London: Routledge.

Pannell, S. (1997), 'Managing the Discourse of Environmental Management: The Case of Sasi from "Southest" Malulu, Indonesia', *Oceania*, **67**, 289–308.

Pannell, S. and F. von Benda-Beckmann (eds) (1998) *Exploring Issues of Resource Management in Eastern Indonesia*, Canberra: Centre for Resource and Environmental Studies.

Pezzey, J. (1992), 'Sustainability: An Interdisciplinary Guide', *Environmental Values*, **1**, 321–362.

Rheingold, H. (1992), *Virtual Reality*, London: Mandarin.

Robertson, G., M. Mash, L. Tickner, J. Bird, B. Curtis and T. Putnam (eds) (1996), *FutureNatural: Nature/Science/Culture*, London: Routledge.

Salter, L. and A. Hearn (1996), *Outside the Lines: Issues in Interdisciplinary Research*, Montreal and Kingston: McGill-Queens University Press.

Semin, G. and K. Gergen (eds) (1990), *Everyday Understanding: Social and Scientific Implications*, London: Sage.

Soulé, M. and G. Lease (eds) (1995), *Reinventing Nature? Response to Postmodern Deconstruction*, Washington, DC: Island Press.

Stokols, D. (1995), 'The Paradox of Environmental Psychology', *American Psychologist*, **50**, 821–837.

Stokols, D. and I. Altman (eds) (1987), *Handbook of Environmental Psychology*, Vols I and II, New York: Wiley.

Taylor, C., C. Bryan and C. Goodrich (1995), *Social Assessment:Theory, Process and Techniques*, Christchurch: Taylor Baines and Associates.

Thomas, I. (1998), *Environmental Impact Assessment in Australia: Theory and Practice*, Sydney: The Federation Press.

Veitch, R. and D. Arkkelin (1995), *Environmental Psychology: An Interdisciplinary Perspective*, Englewood Cliffs: Prentice-Hall.

White, R. (1951), *Value Analysis: Nature and Use of the Method*, Ann Arbor, Michigan: Society for the Psychological Study of Social Issues.

Wilson, E. (ed.) (1988), *Biodiversity*, Washington: National Academy Press.

4. A Transdisciplinary Framework for the Analysis of Tropical Agroecosystem Transformations

Luis Llambí and Luis Daniel Llambí

INTRODUCTION

Agroecosystems are deliberate manipulations by human populations of the social and biophysical environment to generate flows of products and services for domestic consumption and/or to be exchanged in the market for cash income. This chapter focuses on tropical agroecosystems, and particularly upon those based upon the fragile and resource-poor biophysical and social environments of humid tropical regions.

Different modes of shifting cultivation[1] form part of the agroecological activities and livelihood strategies which have been practised by native populations in these tropical areas for centuries. Slash-and-burn is still the most common technique used by human populations for clearing the forest, followed by short cropping cycles and long fallow periods. The rationale behind these cropping techniques is that, as secondary successions during the long fallow period tend to replenish the soil's nutrient components, the original natural resource base is partially restored and a new cropping cycle can be started. An additional characteristic of these agroecosystems is that of hunting, fishing and gathering. It has been an integral part of the human population's livelihood (Balée and Gély, 1989; Dufour, 1990).

These rather complex agroecosystems are based on two sorts of general conditions. The first is a low population density, relatively stable demographic size, and high spatial mobility of the human population. The second is a subsistence-oriented productive system.

What happens when these conditions are partially disturbed or completely transformed? How can we explain these agroecosystem transformations, and what are the underlying (natural or social) forces driving the whole process? What are the effects of these changes on the natural resource base; on the flow of products and income they intend to produce; and on the welfare conditions of the human populations? Most farm/households in today's tropical ecosystems do more than farm. Therefore, their responses to changes in the biophysical and social conditions cannot be reduced to changes in the agricultural component of their productive systems. To explain the role played by these other components of their livelihood strategy also has to be part of our research inquiries.

Our contention is that, to accomplish these goals, a new conceptual framework is needed. It is based upon two criteria. The first is that the framework should go beyond disciplinary boundaries. This involves identifying a new set of research problems and developing a new set of concepts to map a general line of inquiry to which specific research projects may be related. The second is that it should span multiple spatial and time scales. Agroecosystems are 'open' not only to the biophysical habitat and human-made inputs, but also to the social and cultural environments engendered by human populations. The scope of factors explaining agroecosystem transformations may extend from soil units, to farms, to a regional market and even to the global economy. Furthermore, the changes affecting the system may vary from short-term weather or price fluctuations to long-term natural resource degradation or to a basic U-turn in national macroeconomic policies.

This chapter's objective is to develop a new conceptual framework explaining tropical agroecosystem transformations as embedded within the shifting livelihood strategies of rural farm/households. It is divided into two parts. Part one is a review of the main contributions of agroecology, economics and anthropology to the transdisciplinary framework that we are advocating here. Part two outlines the conceptual matrix for developing such a framework, by focusing first on the short-term responses of farm/households to market signals and policy interventions; and then by developing a long-term dynamic model for jointly explaining changing livelihood strategies and agroecosystem transformations.

THE DISCIPLINARY CONTRIBUTIONS

The complexity of the subject requires inputs from a range of disciplines in the natural and social sciences. Each discipline involves a large and complex literature on which many books and papers have been written. Therefore, a critical analysis of this literature has to be selective. The focus is on identifying the potential contributions of each discipline to the transdisciplinary framework advocated in this chapter. We will summarise these contributions in three broad disciplinary approaches: agroecology, economics and anthropology. [2]

Agroecology

The scientific agenda of agroecology has focused on the description of the structure and functioning of agricultural systems, understood as people-managed ecosystems. Nye and Greenland (1961) were the first agroecologists to identify: (a) the basic demographic and socioeconomic conditions for the functioning of shifting cultivation in 'optimal' conditions;[3] (b) the changes in management practices leading to the 'fallow crisis';[4] (c) the ultimate socioeconomic causes of these changes; and (d) their main unintended socioeconomic effects. Finally, they set up a research strategy to understand these changes and to design alternative solutions having both human goals and environmental concerns in mind. The scientific agenda, as they defined it, was to compare plots of land at different stages of cropping and fallowing to determine the relative efficiency of various shifting cultivation systems in terms of physical yields and economic returns to the farmer.[5]

Based on their fieldwork in sub-Saharan Africa, they developed a theoretical framework which successfully explained the key role played by the nutrient cycle in the restoration of soil fertility during the fallow, the decline in fertility under the cropping period, and the long-lasting effects of changes in management practices when the optimal socioeconomic conditions were modified. Pointing towards the need for developing a transdisciplinary framework, they identified the need to consider not only the biophysical mechanisms underlying the nutrient cycle under shifting cultivation, but also 'the whole social, historical and environmental setting of the people (within the) limits set by custom (and) the desire to acquire rights over land and so forth' (Nye and Greenland, 1961, p. 29). Thus, they set up the strategy for a successful collaboration of different disciplines in understanding agroecosystem transformations.

During the 1970s, Nye and Greenland's research agenda led towards the development of UNESCO's so-called 'Man and the Biosphere' (MAB) programme, and in 1984 to the Tropical Soil Biology and Fertility (TSBF) programme explaining the biophysical determinants of soil fertility in tropical regions. One of the most successful attempts within the MAB programme to integrate socioeconomic variables into the agroecological approach was developed by Ramakrishnan's (1992) study of the Jhum system of shifting cultivation in northeastern India. Ramakrishnan extended Nye and Greenland's approach, allowing the comparison between longer shifting cultivation periods when they are replaced by shortened fallows and, finally, when they are transformed into permanent or sedentary agriculture.

According to Ramakrishnan, when the fallow period is reduced to five years or fewer, a threshold is surpassed and farmers have to rely on expensive chemical and organic fertilisers to compensate for nutrient depletion and yield loss. He also found that, in northern India, the preferred farmers' response to compensate for the decline in yields was to convert forests to farmland in order to meet the requirements of a rapidly growing human population.

Summarising, these different agroecological approaches identify the functional relationships and mechanisms between biophysical variables (natural resource flows as they are manipulated by human agents) and their physical outputs (yields) in agroecosystems. These approaches do not explain, however, why the system works in such a way. In particular, they do not answer why human populations continue practising shifting cultivation in an increasingly market-oriented environment, despite evidence of diminishing yields and decreasing economic returns. In other words, they tend to ignore human agency. As a result, they overlook the proximate and underlying factors explaining why and how agroecosystems are transformed. Might we be assisted by neoclassical microeconomics?

Neoclassical Microeconomics

Neoclassical microeconomics starts where agroecology left the explanation: opening the black box of human decision making and behaviour. Its scientific agenda is focused on explaining the responsiveness of producers and consumers to changes in relative prices, and on prices as the main economic signal to resource allocation decisions. To cope with the decisions that people have to face in the resource-poor and highly constrained environments of most tropical agroecosystems, new neoclassical microeconomic approaches have relaxed traditional assumptions, attempting to provide more realism to their predictions.

Boserup's (1977) theoretical work on agricultural intensification is based on the neoclassical approach. Her interpretation of the historical evidence is that, as population pressure on the land increases, the response of society has been to intensify farm production by increasing both labour and capital productivity.

We do not question that neoclassical microeconomics can provide us with some reasonable expectations of why people may act in a particular way, under axiomatically defined 'ideal' conditions. For example, it can help to explain why farmers shift towards more labour- and/or capital-intensive technologies when the land price rises. That is Boserup's point. Thus, relative factor scarcity and prices may be basic determinants of changes in the agroecosystem. Yet, for a variety of reasons farmers may not have access to sufficient financial capital, appropriate technologies, or knowledge, to make these technical shifts. This is why we have to turn to political economy and institutional approaches (old and new) in search for more thorough responses.

Political Economy

Political economy contributions may be summarised as follows. First, by relaxing the neoclassical behavioural assumption of agents as individual goal-seekers, it frames human decisions within processes in which the interests of individuals and groups may differ. This leads to analysing strategic behaviours in which choices are not made independently of the decisions made by others. The outcomes to these real world situations might involve negotiated and cooperative solutions, or the kind of conflictual solutions which have been formalised by game theory (Baland and Platteau, 1993). Second, taking into account inequalities of power and access to resources in society helps us explain why and how resources (human-created or not) are converted into assets by producers or consumers. This also helps us to explain the functioning of segmented factor and product markets whereby some individuals or groups might be better placed to obtain economic benefits than others. Third, political economy expands the time frame of the explanation. Instead of instantaneous responses to a single choice and immediate stimuli or signals, a more complex decision making process is presumed, involving not only accumulated experiences but also expectations about the future (Eggertsson, 1997).

New Institutional Economics (NIE)

NIE attempts to reconcile the theoretical formality of microeconomic models with the historical richness of details of the old institutionalist school in economics. There are three basic insights of NIE's approach which require explication here.

The first concerns NIE's definition of institutions. Institutions provide the rules which frame the social relations in which most economic decisions are made. Market mechanisms, for instance, are always embedded within a set of formal and informal regulations which set the rules of the game. Market rules are not the only codes of conduct patterning individual decision making and behaviour. Coercive mechanisms, such as public policies and state regulations, and grass-roots collective agreements, are alternative institutions that may frame economic decisions (Grima and Berkes, 1989).

Rules governing economic transactions are particularly important, from the point of view of human/ecosystem relations, because they assign rights of access to resources. Private property is just one possibility. Public property is another. Poorly defined rights of use, or a breakdown in the system of enforcement of rules, may lead to conflicts in the use of scarce resources, and even to a collapse of the system when resources are depleted.

Transaction costs are also an important contribution of NIE to the study of agroecosystems. Access to information, Coase (1960) suggests, is an unevenly distributed asset. Most of the time, people do not make economic decisions with a complete knowledge of their possible options. Moreover, the costs of bargaining, monitoring, coordinating and enforcing contracts should also be accounted for by both producers and consumers in their daily transactions (Bardham, 1989). Thus, transaction costs affect the efficiency of resource allocation. In any society, not only formal contracts but also informal personal arrangements for controlling the use of resources (such as kinship networks) may affect economic decisions, as well as their outcomes (Eggertsson, 1997).

Finally, NIE's concept of social capital is also relevant to our framework. Social capital includes all those social networks providing insurance, coordination, information-sharing and regulation in which people participate and which therefore form part of their collective assets. The main point is that social networks and interlinked markets may play important roles in saving (or increasing) transaction costs as well as partially circumventing incomplete or non-existent markets, particularly in small rural societies (Bardham, 1989).

Cognitive Anthropology

Anthropology in general, and cognitive anthropology in particular, serve to open even further the black box of human decision making in agroecosystems. It is important to distinguish the theoretical contributions of anthropology to the understanding of agroecosystems in general from the specific ethnographic descriptions anthropologists (and human ecologists in particular) make about agroecosystems in subsistence-oriented societies or in groups at the margins of the market economy. Instead of developing formal axiological reasoning, anthropology proposes to bring substantive (that is, ethnographically and historically informed) theorising to the social sciences.

Anthropology's concern with cognition and human values has a longstanding history. It has moved between the emphasis on culture as a structural behavioural concept, to current postmodernist emphases on the multiplicity of value systems and norms. Cognitive anthropology's agenda is to map the symbolic and cognitive order that shapes people's preferences and constrains the strategies they pursue. Ethnoecology, in particular, is concerned with how people's conceptual models of the environment shape the allocation of resources. The 'emic' – the cognitive, valorative, and normative perspective of the agents – as part of the explanation of decision making and behaviour is perhaps anthropology's main contribution to the transdisciplinary perspective in agroecology that we are advocating here.

DEVELOPING A TRANSDISCIPLINARY FRAMEWORK

Each one of the disciplinary approaches intentionally leaves out some crucial pieces of the story. The challenge now is how to add realism to our theoretical framework, and therefore predictive strength, without losing too much of the formal simplicity that the more general and abstract approaches can provide.

We proceed as follows. First, we focus on explaining short-term resource-allocation decisions of farm/households living in sedentary village settlements, whose main livelihood strategy is related to semi-commercial tropical agroecosystems. Second, we turn to explain how livelihood strategies (including agroecosystems) are transformed, due to either the building up of gradual effects or as the result of sudden 'shocks' having long-lasting effects.

Explaining Short-Term Resource-Allocation Decisions

This version of the framework only takes into consideration short-term biophysical fluctuations and economic–political junctures: for example, short-term weather fluctuations and pest oubreaks, economic downturns, and minor · public policy changes. It addresses allocative and investment decisions such as: why has a specific crop or crop mix been selected?; why has a particular combination of resources (assets) been used and how are resource constraints being solved?; when does a particular combination of activities or productive techniques cease to be convenient for the farm/household?; when are other income or investment opportunities besides the agroecosystem being considered by household members?, and, are resource conservation practices considered by the farm/household members (and, if not, why)?

This conceptual model relates five clusters of factors which affect, and in turn are affected by, the farm's/household's resource–allocation and management decisions: (1) farm/household characteristics and assets; (2) biophysical and social conditions; (3) market signals and policy interventions; (4) farm/household welfare and agroecosystem performance; and (5) biophysical and social impacts (see Figure 4.1).

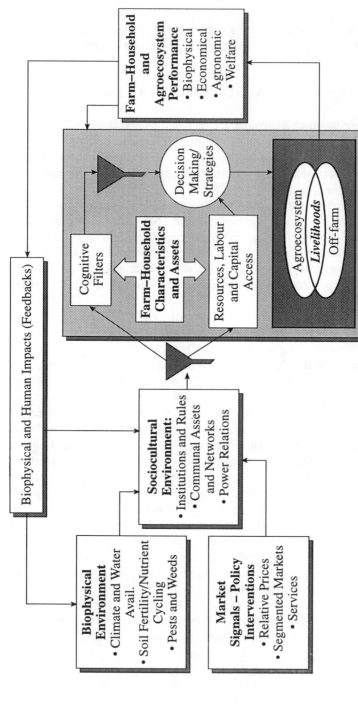

Figure 4.1   Explaining Short-Term Decision Making

Farm/household characteristics and assets

The entry point is the farm/household and its agency. Households differ in the size, type and composition of their labour force. Family size and composition, along with gender roles and kinship relations, determine the amount of household 'domestic' labour available. Farm/households also differ in the amount and type of natural, human and financial resources to which they have access. In particular, natural resources have to traverse two 'filters' to become assets: a social (political economy) filter determining the resources to which they have access; and a cognitive filter determining which resources are valued and the know-how to convert them into productive assets.

Biophysical and social conditions

Farm/households face a set of 'external' (environmental) conditions, which constrain or enable short-term decision making. Resource-allocation decisions are conditioned by complex interactions between these constraints: the natural resource base (NRB), market forces, available technologies, as well as formal (public policy) and informal (social and cultural) rules (Vosti and Reardon, 1997). Local community-owned assets also shape household decisions in two possible ways: (a) the group's productive and social built-in communal assets affect individual access to resources and safety-nets;[6] (b) the group's informal networks (social capital) regulate access to common recourses.

Market signals and policy interventions

Price and non-price incentives (and disincentives) condition the allocation of resources to different farm/household activities, including farm and off-farm income-generating and investment strategies. But it all depends on the existence, structure and performance of the product, input and technology markets. Relative prices also shape the changing technical rates of substitution between farm- or community-owned 'natural' assets (for example, a natural seed) and 'industrial' inputs (such as a high-yielding variety seed). Other household survival strategies, such as the decision to have more children, or to acquire a new skill (for example, to learn a new language) or to participate in collective actions, are also influenced by market forces. Product and factor market segmentations affect the prices and opportunity costs of the foods and other items produced by the household – *vis-à-vis* those that may be purchased in the markets.[7] Relative prices are also influenced by public policies, and by the policy interventions of NGO and grass-roots organisations.

Farm/household welfare and agroecosystem performance
Besides fallow cultivation in semi-commercial tropical agroecosystems, the livelihood strategies of farm/households frequently embody a bundle of other production, consumption, services, and income-generating activities. Farming, wild food gathering and other household activities (artcraft, petty commerce, domestic chores, and so on) are basic components in household livelihood strategies. Since we are focusing here on semi-commercial agroecosystems, it is important to take into consideration that some household production might be destined for domestic consumption; while market-oriented production, services, and other income-generating activities, including wage labour, may also form part of the household's livelihood strategy.

Biophysical and social impacts
Agroecosystems result from the intended results of household practices to generate flows of products and services to satisfy people's needs. Sometimes these practices also produce unintended, and occasionally undesirable, effects on the natural environment and on people's welfare. The point is to determine when people become aware of these negative (or positive) effects, and when these impacts trigger responses from the people that feel their security or livelihood is threatened.

Explaining Long-Term Livelihood Strategies and Agroecosystem Transformations

The dynamic model implicit in most agroecological studies of the humid tropics is based on a three-stage linear path. These stages are: (a) subsistence-oriented shifting cultivation; (b) semi-commercial fallow cultivation; and (c) market-oriented sedentary agriculture. This linear three-stage theoretical transition underpins the two most complete explanations which have been offered so far on the crises and transitions of tropical shifting cultivation systems: Ramakrishnan's (1992) work focusing on agricultural extensification as a solution to the fallow crisis; and Boserup's (1977) approach focusing on agricultural intensification as a result of the food crises engendered by population explosion. Whose interpretation provides the most historically adequate explanation or the best reliable prediction? Our contention is that it all depends on the social conditions under which we can expect that, for a specific group of farmers in a particular juncture, the extension of the agricultural frontier will be more feasible than agricultural intensification. In other words, we contend that these approaches, by narrowing their focus on the agroecosystem component of the farm's/household's livelihood strategies, provide a reductionist and unilinear image of a series of historical transitions that are more complex and variegated.

We propose instead to rework the previous short-term version of the framework now taking into consideration two sorts of outside disturbances: (a) the conditions underpinning the agroecosystem component of the farm/household livelihood strategy; (b) the conditions under which the other production, consumption and income-generating components are based. This leads us to define three hypothetical paths of transition in rural livelihoods and tropical agroecosystems (see Figures 4.2 and 4.3). They are: (1) from subsistence-oriented shifting cultivation, to a semi-commercial short-fallow system, to a market-oriented sedentary agroecosystem; (2) an 'arrested succession' between shifting cultivation and a short-fallow system, in which the farm/household remains basically attached to its semi-commercial agroecosystem; and (3) an 'off-farm' diversification strategy, in which the household no longer depends on the agroecosystem for supplying its basic needs, but increasingly relies on other transactions in the labour and product markets.

The transition from subsistence-oriented shifting cultivation, to a semi-commercial short-fallow system, to market-oriented sedentary agriculture is Boserup's preferred scenario. Increased population growth (via migration or natural growth) leads to higher population density when, parallel to demographic growth, the sedentarisation of a formerly nomadic or semi-nomadic population occurs. In the absence of fertilisers, a fallow crisis ensues, and the shifting cultivation system changes into a sedentary short-fallow agroecosystem. This modified version of the shifting cultivation system is highly unstable, as Ramakrishnan clearly perceived. Thus, in the absence of an extensive margin or other income opportunities, it should lead to agricultural intensification – as Boserup predicted – or to gradual impoverishment and starvation. If the conditions for agricultural intensification are met,[8] and the opportunity costs for farm investments are lower than any other alternative, the farm/household is increasingly locked into a growing dependence on market forces. The end result is 'a farmer', who is now completely reliant on farm product and factor markets for success. Boserup was right, but until when and under what conditions?

The 'Arrested Succession' From Shifting Cultivation to a Longstanding Short-Fallow System

From general ecology we borrow the term 'arrested succession' to characterise a path, whereby the farm/household livelihood strategy remains attached to a short-fallow semi-commercial agroecosystem, but at increasingly higher costs for compensating the soil's nutrient exhaustion

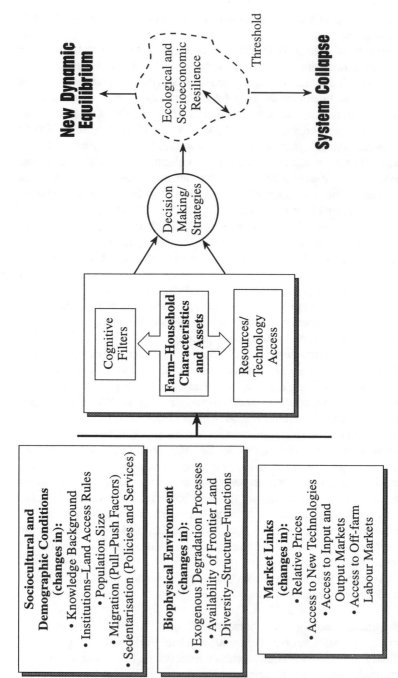

Figure 4.2   Explaining Long-Term Strategies/Responses

64

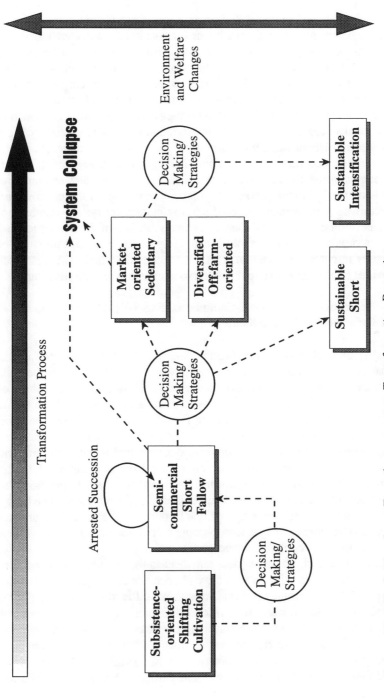

Figure 4.3   Explaining Long-Term Agroecosystem Transformation Dynamics

65

with industrialised chemical and organic subsidies. There are two possible intermediate strategies in this path: one is agricultural extensification, that is to continue into operation by moving 'from the more accessible to increasingly less accessible areas and from the most valuable to the less valuable species' (Grima and Berkes, 1989, p. 51). While some will attempt this strategy, at some point in time the farm/household will reach the end of the available land margin. The second strategy is income diversification, that is to relieve pressure on the land via migration towards places where there are seasonal labour market opportunities, or via some participation in the non-farm product (or service) markets. The succession is arrested, however, if countervailing forces override or conceal the forces of transition from semi-commercial to full market integration. There is no involution, however. A return to a subsistence-oriented shifting cultivation system is ruled out because the farm/household has been already 'locked-in' by market forces.[9] In this case, the farm/household is caught up in a long downward spiral of 'poverty/resource degradation' (Malik, 1998) in which the resources provided by the agroecosystem only serve to maintain its bare subsistence.

The Transition From a Semi-Commercial Short-Fallow System to an Off-Farm Diversification Strategy

Finally, an 'off-farm' diversification strategy may also lead towards a situation in which the semi-commercial agroecosystem is no longer the basis for the farm/household livelihood strategies. In the absence or limited use of fertilisers, nutrient exhaustion results in decreasing yields, and the whole agroecosystem manifests a decreasing factor productivity. When food and income flows are impaired, the farm's/household's subsistence is threatened, triggering some responses. At some point a threshold is surpassed, and the farm/household perceives that its survival is no longer attached to the agroecosystem but to its other off-farm livelihood activities. In this case, the farm/household becomes more a household using all means to survive than a farm. When the threshold is crossed, the labour market and/or other product (and services) markets conditions, become more important for survival than the conditions affecting the agroecosystem.

In the long run, all three paths may lead to the vicious cycle of poverty and resource degradation to which we alluded before. But there are always the possibilities of some virtuous cycles as well. Reardon and Vosti (1995) called them 'sustainable intensification', referring to the investment strategies that farm/households may undertake to enhance their environment.

These theoretical interpretations of historical processes may remain a sketchy image of the world, without a clear specification of the agents and conditions that may fully explain why one particular path has been followed rather than another. Our contention is that to ascertain such explanations, we must ground our theoretical models in detailed historical and fieldwork research.

CONCLUSIONS

This chapter attempted to arrange – into an integrated framework – the complexity of factors affecting the biophysical and social environments in wet tropical regions, when the conditions underpinning human livelihoods and agroecosystems are transformed.

Agroecology accurately defined agroecosystems as people-made environments. Its main agenda has been to map different agroecosystems and to identify how they work. We have argued that this is not enough, that it is as important to explain why a system works in a particular way, how it is transformed, and what other systems might evolve from it. Narrowing our inquiry, however, to processes of change in humid tropical regions involving shifting cultivation has been enlightening because it has permitted us to explore the multiple factors affecting these systems' distinct but related components: farming operations, forest-related activities, and a large bundle of other production and consumption tasks not directly linked to the agroecosystem. This led us to grasp that the way agroecology usually defines and analyses agroecosystems, although still central to our endeavour, is insufficient to understand the complexity of the processes we are dealing with here. Human agency, we realised, and particularly the livelihood strategies of human populations, had to be the focus of analysis.

Neoclassical microeconomics offered an opportunity to open 'the black box' of human agency. It was also useful because most agroecological studies of the humid tropics identify a three-stage transitional path leading from a subsistence-oriented shifting cultivation system, to semi-commercial short-fallow systems, to fully market-oriented sedentary agriculture. But neoclassical microeconomics was also deemed insufficient to explain the conditions under which most tropical agroecosystems are transformed. How, though, do we consider that the allocation of resources by farm/households among different activities depends not only on market-mediated relative prices but also on the rules of access to natural resources, on the existence or availability of particular technologies, on the broader political–economic scenario setting up the opportunities or constraining their choices? Searching for clues to answer this question, we turned to political economy and to new institutional economics. They both had the advantage of restoring 'substantive' (human relations) and 'history' (time-specified dimensions) into theorising, without necessarily denying the predictive strength and formal simplicity of neoclassical microeconomic models.

Attempting to open the black box even further we turned to anthropology to find clues on how to specify human decision making, given that the social environment does not fit the stylised fully competitive market relations assumed by neoclassical microeconomic models. In particular, cognitive anthropology led us to accord a key explanatory weight to the individual's knowledge and skills, and to the group's shared values and norms in shaping human decisions and behaviour *vis-à-vis* the biophysical environment.

Equipped with the conceptual tools provided by these different disciplines, but also aware of their limits, we tackled the goal of developing a framework that might add realism to our theoretical perspective on tropical agroecosystems. The strategy we laid out to accomplish this task was to reduce the parameters affecting farm/household decision making to those relevant only in the short term. We then proposed a multifarious long-term path model, leading from subsistence-oriented shifting cultivation to increased market integration – one contingent on the multiplicity of factors that could affect either the agroecosystem components or the other elements of the farm's/household's livelihood strategies.

The inclusion of policy interventions into the framework is this chapter's incomplete agenda. If the goal is not only to explain and predict, but also to design, new agroecosystems or to make adaptations to old ones, then it is necessary to broaden the framework's scope even more. Targetting specific populations and incorporating policy variables explicitly into the framework, to evaluate their 'efficacy' and to calibrate their effects, should be the utmost priority in our theoretical and research agenda.

ACKNOWLEDGEMENTS

We have benefited from comments by Rafael Herrera, Thomas Reardon and James Copestake on earlier drafts of the chapter.

NOTES

1. Also referred to in the literature as swidden cultivation.
2. Other disciplines such as geography, agronomy and rural sociology (as well as subdisciplines such as human ecology and economic anthropology) have important contributions to make to this or similar frameworks. Space constraints prevent their inclusion in this chapter.
3. With minimum disruptions and external inputs.
4. Defined as falling yields as a consequence of decreasing the length of the fallow period, while maintaining cropping time on the same plot.

5. Other early agroecological studies of shifting cultivation in the humid tropics were Bartholomew et al. (1953), and Ewel (1971) (quoted in Ramakrishnan, 1992).
6. And also exclude non-members from access to these resources.
7. Segmented markets may result in two different types of strategies from producers: strategy A targets consumers based on their price elasticity of demand. Strategy B targets consumers based on volume of demand. In most agricultural markets, the most common strategy is B since consumers (farm/householders) are dispersed, and this results in atomistic demand. When producers select strategy B, they obtain additional profits whereas larger consumers obtain a bigger utility.
8. For example, markets, appropriate technology, technical know-how and other cognitive skills.
9. Or by subsidies provided by the government.

REFERENCES

Baland, J. and J. Platteau (1993), 'Are Economists Concerned with Power?', *IDS Bulletin*, **24** (3).

Balée, W. and A. Gély (1989), 'Managed Forest Succession in Amazonia: the Ka'por Case', in D. Posey and W. Balée (eds), *Resource Management in Amazonia: Indigenous and Folk Strategie, pp.* 129–158.

Bardham, P. (1989), *The Economic Theory of Agrarian Institutions*, Oxford: Clarendon Press.

Boserup, E. (1977), *The Conditions of Agricultural Growth: The Economics of Agrarian Change under Population Pressure*, Chicago: Aldine.

Coase, R. (1960), 'The Problem of Social Cost', *Journal of Law and Economics*, **3**, 1–44.

Dufour, D. (1990), 'Use of Tropical Rainforests by Native Amazonians: These Sophisticated and Complex Agricultural Systems Can Serve as Models of Sustainable Agriculture', *BioScience*, **40** (9), 652–659.

Eggertsson, T. (1997), 'The Old Theory of Economic Policy and the New Institutionalism', *World Development*, **25** (8), 1187–1203.

Grima, A. and F. Berkes (1989), 'Natural Resources: Access, Rights-to-use and Management', in F. Berkes (ed.), *Common Property Resources: Ecology and Community-based Sustainable Development*. London: Belhaven Press.

Malik, S. (1998), 'Rural Poverty and Land Degradation: A Reality Check for the CGIAR', A report prepared for the Technical Advisory Committee of the CGIAR (unpublished material).

Nye, P. and D. Greenland (1961), *The Soil Under Shifting Cultivation*, Farnham Royal, England: Technical Communication No. 51, Commonwealth Bureau of Soils.

Ramakrishnan, P. (1992), 'Shifting Agriculture and Sustainable Development: An Interdisciplinary Study from North-Eastern India', *Man and the Biosphere*, Series No. 10, Paris: UNESCO and The Parthenon Publishing Group.

Reardon, T. and S. Vosti (1995), 'Links Between Rural Poverty and the Environment in Developing Countries: Asset Categories and Investment Poverty', *World Development*, **22** (9), 1495–1506.

Vosti, S. and T. Reardon (eds) (1997), *Sustainability, Growth, and Poverty Alleviation: Policy and Agroecological Perspectives*, Baltimore and London: Johns Hopkins University Press.

5. Integrating Social Sustainability Considerations into Natural Resource Management

Sharon Pepperdine and Sarah Ewing

INTRODUCTION

There has been much discussion about sustainability, but how do we know whether we are shifting towards a more sustainable system? Monitoring can play an important role in providing feedback to aid decision making and inform planning. Since the notion of sustainability embraces ecological, economic and social issues and the complex interdependence between these dimensions, a broad approach needs to adopted at the planning and management level to shed light on this multi-dimensional picture. However, a systematic approach for considering the social dimensions of sustainability is not well developed in Australia, or internationally.

This chapter reviews the relative merit of various approaches to the assessment of sustainability in natural resources management, particularly of *social sustainability*, in a rural, agricultural setting. Many of the approaches considered here, such as State of Environment (SoE) reporting, Sustainable Regional Development (SRD) and community sustainability projects, were established specifically to address sustainability concerns. Others, such as Quality of Life (QoL) studies and community development studies, are derived from diverse areas ranging from assessments of well-being to specific community issues.

COMMUNITY SUSTAINABILITY IN A RURAL CONTEXT

Sustainability is one of the main issues facing agricultural communities today. Rural community sustainability is a relatively recent notion and emerged out of the Brundtland Report (WCED, 1987). Corresponding to the framework of sustainable development, rural community sustainability identifies three main dimensions: social, environmental or ecological, and economic. Figure 5.1 illustrates three different approaches used to represent these dimensions for sustainable development and the interrelated nature of each sphere. It highlights the complexity inherent in the idea of rural community sustainability.

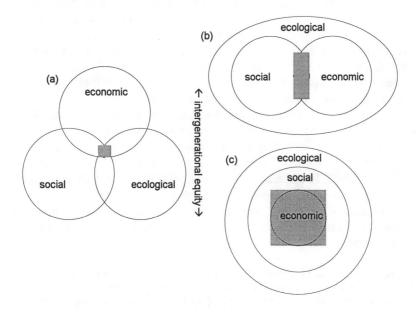

Notes: The sustainability domain is shown as the shaded section: where (a) the three components are largely independent; (b) economic and social dimensions remain largely independent but within an ecological framework; and, (c) economic dimensions sit within the social sphere which is contextualised within an ecological framework.

Source: Adapted from Lowe (1996).

Figure 5.1 Components of Rural Community Sustainability

Discussion on rural community sustainability in the literature can be divided roughly into three themes. The first emphasises the *maintenance* of social (including demographic), ecological and economic aspects; the second is related to the notion of *intergenerational equity*; and the third is concerned with the *intertwined nature* of the social, ecological and economic components of the rural system.

The importance of this latter theme, and the issue of social, economic and ecological viability in rural communities, is captured by Lawrence (1995, p. 32), who suggests that the process of rural community sustainability consists of 'a combination of factors which provides for population growth, economic viability and social development in nonmetropolitan regions ... It fosters a system of production which not only counters environmental degradation but which helps, through new options, to enhance community structures via job growth and regional development.'

The future of rural communities is intimately entwined with ecological, economic and social issues. Increasingly, the importance of social well-being of rural communities to the broader agricultural picture is being recognised (for example, Lawrence, 1995; Pomeroy, 1996; Troughton, 1995). The relationship between sustainable communities and a sustainable agricultural sector has been made explicit by Pomeroy (1997, p. 97), who argues that a 'sustainable agriculture depends [in part] on the social "health" or well-being of those involved in the industry'.

These social dynamics are important not only because they contribute directly to the social fabric of rural regions (Lawrence, 1995), but also because they have been linked to environmental management (Fitzgerald and Carlisle, 1994; Lockie et al., 1999; Vanclay, 1998; Vanclay and Lawrence, 1995). In response to the interdependent nature of environmental and social well-being, Fitzgerald and Carlisle (1994, p. 11) advocate that the inclusion of social indicators in monitoring trends in sustainability is warranted to assist in decision making and planning for natural resource management:

> The maintenance or enhancement of [social] well-being can be seen as one aspect of (or even performance criterion for) environmental management . . . Monitoring of various aspects of [social] well-being or quality of life is therefore a proactive means for the development of timely and appropriate policy interventions, as well as identifying the intended and unintended outcomes of policy, service provision and environmental management decisions.

This relationship between social sustainability and environmental management is particularly relevant in the agricultural sector when we consider the large role agriculture plays in natural resource management. In countries such as Australia and New Zealand, where agricultural land use has such a significant impact on the landscape and influences other land uses, the imperative is even greater (SCARM, 1993). An understanding of social sustainability in the rural sector is thus vital to gain an insight into the sustainability of the agricultural sector and has implications for natural resource management and decision making.

However, there is a lack of adequate research into, and understanding of, the social dimension of rural community sustainability. Gaps have been identified both nationally and internationally (see Lawrence, 1995; Troughton, 1995). In Australia and Canada, for instance, studies of rural communities in terms of the broader issue of sustainability are rare (Campbell, 1994; Troughton, 1995). The dearth of research into the issues of rural social sustainability can be attributed both to the inadequate theoretical development of concepts of social sustainability and to the paucity of detailed community studies in relation to sustainability (Everitt and Annis, 1992; Jones and Tonts, 1995). Further, the level of detail gained from community studies is often limited due to the use of aggregated statistical data (Hudson, 1989).

Social issues need to be investigated and incorporated in systems which represent agriculture in order to understand and address constraints to sustainable agricultural production (Bryant, 1992; Pomeroy, 1997). Social sustainability, or well-being, of rural communities clearly needs to be included in any assessment of sustainability since it reflects, and impacts upon, environmental sustainability (Vanclay, 1998; Vanclay and Lawrence, 1995).

MEASURES OF SOCIAL SUSTAINABILITY

One mechanism which can be employed to generate feedback into decision making and planning, is monitoring. Monitoring, with the aid of indicators, can be applied to the agricultural sector to give a picture of the sustainability of the biophysical, economic and social systems (Pomeroy, 1996; SCARM, 1993). It can aid in establishing baseline information and detecting trends in relation to sustainability, alerting producers and policy makers to problems that may arise from various actions and strategies (SCARM, 1993). Monitoring can also assist in establishing a level of accountability and credibility (Dore and Woodhill, 1999). It is critical, though, as argued earlier, that in designing monitoring systems, attention is given to the measurement not only of biophysical and economic change but also of social trends. These different components and the links between them need to be captured (Dore and Woodhill, 1999; Pomeroy, 1996; SCARM, 1993).

Recently, there has been a resurgence in the use of social indicators to monitor trends in the social environment. There were developments in this area, initially, in the 1960s and early 1970s. In particular, the approach of the Organisation for Economic Cooperation and Development (OECD) to 'social well-being' focuses on the level of the *individual*, not *societal well-being* (OECD, 1976). Furthermore, the focus here was on objective indicators regarding the quality of housing, education, employment, income and health in isolation from institutional structures operating in society, thus providing limited insight into the social system (OECD, 1976). Indicators of this nature, and others (such as measures of Gross National Product), are limited in their utility to current discussions about sustainability. Nowadays, the emphasis in indicator development for sustainability reporting is rather less on gross measures and rather more on measures which are meaningful at the local community scale (see Taylor et al., 2000). This allows local variation to be captured and for the linkages between different dimensions to be identified.

Various approaches that incorporate monitoring are available which could be used to measure trends in social sustainability. Some of the tools that will be considered have been advanced specifically to address sustainability concerns. These include State of Environment (SoE) reporting, a Sustainable Regional Development (SRD) framework recently developed in Australia, and community sustainability projects. Others have been developed in disparate fields ranging from assessments of social well-being in Quality of Life (QoL) research to community aspects in community development studies. The strengths and weaknesses of these approaches for monitoring social sustainability are discussed below.

STATE OF ENVIRONMENT (SoE) REPORTING

There is growing emphasis on SoE reporting in Australia and internationally. SoE reporting has emerged in numerous countries over more than two decades for reporting at national and regional levels. It has been promoted by the OECD, the European Community and the United Nations – giving it widespread exposure. The OECD, for instance, has compiled international SoE reports which cover the member countries since 1979 (OECD, 1979). The objective has been to provide environmental information for member countries and a tool for environmental reporting to 'assist in the definition, implementation and evaluation of environmental policies and . . . [help] to incorporate environmental concerns in decision making' (OECD, 1979, p. 9). It has since been adopted in numerous countries (Parker and Hope, 1992). In Australia, for example, it has been operationalised at state and national levels to monitor both the environment and the appropriateness and effectiveness of programmes and policies in response to Ecologically Sustainable Development (ESD) objectives (Lloyd, 1996). As such, SoE reporting is largely concerned with the collection of biophysical information for natural resource management.

While the initial impetus for SoE reporting was to report on the condition of the biophysical environment, there is now some recognition of the need to incorporate the human dimensions of environment. Parker notes, for example, that in Australia and Canada, practitioners are seeking to go 'beyond measures of environmental quality to also monitor the interaction between human and ecological systems' (1995, p. 53). In the most recent SoE report in Australia, social dimensions are included in the notion of 'environment', as are the linkages between the biophysical and social dimensions in terms of the role social aspects play, not only in the biophysical environment, but also more broadly in sustainable development (SEAC, 1996).

However, despite the stated intentions, the measurement of some aspects of the social system in Australia's SoE reporting remains inadequate; whilst demographic, health and socioeconomic aspects are well represented in the national SoE framework, there is a paucity of other social measures. For example, while 'livability' has been recognised as an important aspect of sustainability, a tool with which to measure it is poorly developed. It has been defined to encompass social amenity (comprising socioeconomic factors), health and well-being including individual and community well-being (SEAC, 1996). However, aspects of well-being are undefined and have been largely neglected. Instead, urban design has been adopted to measure community well-being despite the absence of 'well-developed indicators of community or good urban design' (SEAC, 1996, pp. 3–27). Thus, the current national SoE framework in place in Australia lacks adequate procedures to incorporate social reporting. To be useful for sustainability considerations, social, economic and cultural information needs to be integrated in conjunction with environmental monitoring in SoE reporting systems (see Taylor et al., 2000).

The system for SoE reporting is subject to several other limitations. First among these, is that the use of quantitative indicators simplifies the systems and hence overlooks the complexities and interconnectedness of the systems (Parker, 1995). Secondly, the data used are aggregated to such a level that the information they provide lacks sensitivity to local issues and fails to appreciate linkages between the biophysical and human subsystems (Parker, 1995). These problems for social reporting are inherent in current SoE measures.

SUSTAINABLE REGIONAL DEVELOPMENT (SRD)

A framework for SRD has recently been proposed for regional planning in Australia (Dore and Woodhill, 1999; and see Lawrence, 1998). It promotes a holistic approach to encourage sustainable development and, as such, is concerned with improving outcomes for the regional community, economy and environment in an integrated way.

SRD offers a process-orientated approach. A dynamic model is used which encompasses four main phases: (i) setting up; (ii) planning strategically; (iii) implementing and managing; and (iv) learning and adapting. Monitoring is incorporated in this last 'learning and adapting' stage. The process suggested for monitoring includes: determining success criteria and evaluation needs; establishing indicators; monitoring; critically reviewing progress; and changing in response to the review outcomes from the preceding stage (Dore and Woodhill, 1999).

The SRD framework incorporates an adaptive management approach. Adaptive management relies on feedback to inform decision making through monitoring (Holling, 1978). The process of critical review allows for dynamic feedback and social learning. It permits an iterative system which is flexible, adaptive and responsive to learning from experience. Furthermore, an adaptive management approach is particularly relevant for sustainability considerations as it 'recognises and embraces complexity and the interdisciplinary nature of SRD' (Dore and Woodhill, 1999, p. 371).

Dore and Woodhill (1999) acknowledge that key social, economic and environmental indicators are yet to be established to provide baseline information and longer-term monitoring and, moreover, that the current systems for incorporating such knowledge is lacking. However, the SRD framework, thus far, does not propose any indicators. Rather the SRD approach provides a *system* to guide the process of strategic planning for sustainable development incorporating an adaptive management approach in a regional context. While social aspects are recognised as integral to sustainability monitoring, the authors stop short of saying *how* it might be done or *what* the measures might be. As has often been the case in this field of literature, a strong case is made for the importance of social reporting. However, it falls short of providing specific *procedures* for its measurement.

COMMUNITY SUSTAINABILITY PROJECTS

Another approach which can be used to inform considerations of social sustainability is through the conduct of community sustainability projects. Several examples have been reported in the literature over the past decade. Measures of community sustainability have been constructed specifically for a rural context in North America (Annis, 1990; Dykeman, 1990), Scotland (Copus and Crabtree, 1996; Fife Regional Council, 1995), and New Zealand (Pomeroy, 1997), and are currently being developed in Australia (Lockie et al., 1999; MacGregor and Fenton, 1999; Pepperdine, 1998; Taylor et al., 2000). Urban systems have been the focus of other studies in North America (Sustainable Seattle, 1995), England (Lancashire County Council, 1997) and Australia (Melbourne City Council, 1995; Yiftachel and Hedgcock, 1993). These studies tend to determine issues integral to the sustainability of the system and propose indicators with which to measure them. The outcomes can provide a framework to establish a local information system (LIS) *and* the means to monitor it.

Typically, in both rural and urban settings, these studies have employed participatory strategies to help identify aspects important for local sustainability. Stakeholder involvement is an essential ingredient, for it allows the identification of locally relevant and meaningful indicators and, subsequently, the development of a locally specific information management strategy. This can better assist decision making by providing a framework to enable 'individuals and decision makers to recognise the outcomes of their decisions in terms of their stated sustainability goals' (Parker, 1995, p. 50). An LIS offers a framework to both monitor the environment (social, economic and ecological) and provide feedback in relation to sustainability.

The process of stakeholder consultation and participation offers additional benefits. It is a valuable way to promote local community adoption, empower the community and facilitate education to motivate change and commitment (Parker, 1995). Based on their experience with the Lancashire County Council sustainability indicators project, Macnaghten et al. (1995) argue that public involvement in the process is vital for the results to be accepted by the public. The identification of stakeholder values can assist in decision making by promoting locally significant issues while also encouraging local commitment and credibility.

Five main domains of interest emerge across these studies: (i) biophysical; (ii) economic; (iii) demographic; (iv) social; and (v) political dimensions. However, the emphasis varies between studies. Social and political issues, for example, were found to be the key factors for the sustainability of small rural communities (Everitt and Annis, 1992). A range of social and political issues can be compiled from these studies which include: involvement in decision making; leadership; access to, and availability of, key goods and services including infrastructure, education and information; demographic issues; health and safety; and community support in terms of participation in civic life, community pride and spirit, community cohesion, neighbourliness and cooperation.

While studies like these provide a useful framework for developing a tool to measure social sustainability, they are not without limitations. They suggest a comprehensive list of indicators, but these are typically location-specific. Added to this is the difficulty that they are restricted to the urban or rural system for which they were designed. Even within the same sector, some studies restrict their focus to a particular aspect of the system, for instance socioeconomic issues (see Copus and Crabtree, 1996) and 'capacity for change' (see Lockie et al., 1999; Taylor et al., 2000), rather than encompassing a range of social issues which affect the community. As indicators may be limited to their original context, they need to be developed from the local system. This will promote the identification of indicators germane to the system of interest. Whilst indicators relevant to a particular setting are needed and whilst this has been done for a variety of systems, few have written of the *process* – that is, *how* the issues were identified and *how* the indicators were developed.

QUALITY OF LIFE (QoL) STUDIES

Another approach that could be drawn upon to inform the measurement of social sustainability derives from QoL research. The QoL paradigm has been advanced for considerations of sustainability (Hyman, 1994). QoL research has encompassed measures of social well-being since the 1970s (Andrews and Withey, 1974, 1976). However, studies of QoL offer little for assessments of social sustainability, as they are typically concerned with the individual level rather than that of the community. Likewise, the social indicators developed to measure QoL tend to focus on the subjective well-being of individuals rather than at the societal level (Diener, 1994). Community sustainability, and social sustainability as a component of this, is concerned with a higher level of social needs (for discussion of a hierarchical model of social needs see MacGregor and Fenton, 1999).

COMMUNITY DEVELOPMENT STUDIES

Studies undertaken in the area of community development could aid in the development of a system to measure social sustainability by providing insight into the social functioning of the system. Attributes identified by Warren (1970), for example, in his research of what makes a 'good community' could be used to assist in the development of a conceptual framework for social sustainability. Underlying criteria proposed include: primary group relationships, community autonomy, viability, power distribution, commitment, heterogeneity, neighbourhood control, and conflict (Warren, 1970). Goudy (1983) on the other hand, focused on the desires held for a community by residents. An understanding of what community leaders *and* community members perceive as important could offer a useful basis to the establishment of meaningful sustainability criteria; inconsistencies have been found between community leaders' and residents' perceptions (Allen and Gibson, 1987).

More recent work in the area of community development continues to add insight into community issues. During the 1990s, community development research has focused on a range of community issues including: population trends (migration, ageing); quality of life; financial viability; rural services and infrastructure (such as education and technology including telecommunications); leadership; entrepreneurship;

participation; voluntarism; self-help; cohesion; communication; social networks; diversity; and gender (Community Development Society, n.d.). While such studies provide an understanding of the functioning of communities, they are typically issue-specific and lack an holistic framework.

DISCUSSION

A systematic approach to the consideration of social issues is vital to both inform the social context for decision making and provide feedback on policy outcomes. A system to measure social sustainability could provide valuable information for planning and decision making.

While social dimensions have been recognised as integral to sustainability in SoE reporting in Australia (SEAC, 1996), social assessments as part of this are currently inadequate. Monitoring is also an important element of the SRD framework. But while the framework is conceptually useful, indicators have not yet been developed. Limitations are inherent in QoL reporting because of its focus on well-being at the personal level, rather than at the societal level. Community development and QoL studies both lack an overarching framework for the consideration of the social aspects of community sustainability. Rather than combining issue-specific indicators, meaningful indicators that consider the system as a whole need to be developed.

One strategy which acknowledges the interconnections of the system and which is likely to result in useable, and useful information, builds upon stakeholder participation. Specifically, the development of a local information system (LIS). The outcomes from community sustainability projects could be used to inform the development of an LIS. However, while these projects tend to be locally specific, they offer an in-depth and locally driven approach that allows insight into the social system and the identification of locally meaningful indicators at the community level. This can highlight linkages between subsystems and provide site-specific information to better assist decision making.

Local information systems have been developed from community sustainability projects. However, the disparate and locally specific nature of the case-studies, such as those referred to above, poses difficulties in reconciling the outcomes for application to similar systems in different settings. An approach which incorporates generic indicators while permitting a locally driven process needs to be developed.

A project is underway in rural Victoria, Australia, to identify a series of indicators which measure social issues fundamental to rural community sustainability, as a way to improve the delivery of information for decision making (Pepperdine, 1998). It draws on the approach employed in community sustainability projects. It incorporates issues identified in the literature along with community input, to establish a generic set of indicators which reflect the underlying issues of the social system. This will provide a tool to measure social sustainability that can be applied to other rural systems to assist in the construction of an LIS while allowing the issues to be prioritised to reflect the local context.

CONCLUSION

In the field of natural resource management, considerable attention has been given to the task of reporting on environmental conditions. Typically, the reporting task has focused on an assessment of the biophysical condition of the environment. But, as this chapter has argued, given that natural resource management embraces not only biophysical considerations but also human considerations, our reporting structures should have the capacity to acknowledge and report upon social concerns as well.

The focus here has been upon the relative merit of various approaches to the task of measuring social condition. Of the approaches reviewed, local community sustainability projects were found to have the most promise. The outcomes generated through these projects can be used to inform the development of a local information system (LIS).

An LIS offers a system to incorporate locally meaningful criteria identified through community sustainability studies. It overcomes the constraints inherent in SoE and QoL reporting and community development studies. Potentially, it could be used as part of the monitoring process in the SRD framework to provide feedback of trends in the social system. An LIS has the capacity to embrace the fundamental, intertwined, nature of issues critical to decision making about natural resource management.

ACKNOWLEDGMENTS

The support of the Land and Water Resources Research and Development Corporation, through Project UME 29, is gratefully acknowledged.

REFERENCES

Allen, L. and R. Gibson (1987), 'Perceptions of Community Life and Services: A Comparison Between Leaders and Community Residents', *Journal of the Community Development Society*, **18** (1), 89–103.

Andrews, F. and S. Withey (1974), 'Developing Measures of Perceived Life Quality: Results from Several National Surveys', *Social Indicators Research*, 1, 1–26.

Andrews, F. and S. Withey (1976), *Social Indicators of Well-Being: Americans' Perceptions of Life Quality*, New York: Plenum Press.

Annis, R. (1990), *A Look at Communities Most Likely to Succeed*, Brandon: Westarc Group Inc., Brandon University.

Bryant, L. (1992), 'Social Aspects of the Farm Financial Crisis', in F. Vanclay, G. Lawrence and B. Furze (eds), *Agriculture, Environment and Society: Contemporary Issues for Australia*, South Melbourne: Macmillan, pp. 157–171.

Campbell, A. (1994), *Landcare: Communities Shaping the Land and the Future*, St Leonards: Allen and Unwin.

Community Development Society (n.d.), *Journal of the Community Development Society*, (1990–1998) **21–29**, <http://www.comm-dev.org/journal/>, (6 Dec. 1999).

Copus, A. and J. Crabtree (1996), 'Indicators of Socioeconomic Sustainability: An Application to Remote Rural Scotland', *Journal of Rural Studies*, **12** (1), 41–54.

Diener, E. (1994), 'Assessing Subjective Well-Being: Progress and Opportunities', *Social Indicators Research*, **31**, 103–157.

Dore, J. and J. Woodhill (1999), *Sustainable Regional Development: Final Report: An Australia–Wide Study of Regionalism Highlighting Efforts to Improve the Community, Economy and Environment*, Canberra: Greening Australia.

Dykeman, F. (ed.) (1990), *Entrepreneurial and Sustainable Rural Communities*, Sackville: Rural and Small Town Research and Studies Program, Mount Allison University.

Everitt, J. and R. Annis (1992), 'The Sustainability of Prairie Rural Communities', in I. Bowler, C. Bryant and M. Nellies (eds), *Contemporary Rural Systems in Transition: Volume 2, Economy and Society*, Wallingford: CAB International, pp. 213–222.

Fife Regional Council (1995), *Sustainability Indicators for Fife*, Fife: Department of Economic Development and Planning.

Fitzgerald, G. and A. Carlisle (1994), *An Approach to Implementing Monitoring and the State of the Social Environment in Territorial Local Authorities* (Draft), Christchurch: Christchurch City Council.

Goudy, W. (1983), 'Desired and Actual Communities: Perceptions of 27 Iowa Towns', *Journal of the Community Development Society*, **14** (1), 39–49.

Holling, C. (ed.) (1978), *Adaptive Environmental Assessment and Management*, New York: John Wiley and Sons.

Hudson, P. (1989), 'Change and Adaptation in Four Rural Communities in New England', NSW, *Australian Geographer*, **20** (1), 54–64.

Hyman, D. (1994), 'Toward a Quality-of-Life Paradigm for Sustainable Communities', in D. McSwan and M. McShane (eds), *Issues Affecting Rural Communities*, Townsville: Rural Education and Development Centre, James Cook University, pp. 320–325.

Jones, R. and M. Tonts (1995), 'Rural Restructuring and Social Sustainability: Some Reflections on the Western Australian Wheatbelt', *Australian Geographer*, **26** (2), 133–139.

Lancashire County Council (1997), *Lancaster's Green Audit 2: A Sustainability Report: Local Agenda 21 in Lancashire: Lancashire's Key Environmental, Social and Economic Indicators, Their Inter-Relationships and Trends*, Preston: Heckford Advertising and Print.

Lawrence, G. (1995), *Futures for Rural Australia: From Agricultural Productivism to Community Sustainability*, Rockhampton: Central Queensland University.

Lawrence, G. (1998), 'The Institute for Sustainable Regional Development, Central Queensland University', in J. Grimes, G. Lawrence and D. Stehlik (eds), *Sustainable Futures: Towards a Catchment Management Strategy for the Central Queensland Region*, Rockhampton: Institute for Sustainable Regional Development, pp. 6–8.

Lloyd, B. (1996), 'State of Environment Reporting in Australia: A Review', *Australian Journal of Environmental Management*, 3 (3), 151–162.

Lockie, S., S. Coakes and M. Fenton (1999), '"Capacity for Change" in the Fitzroy Basin: Integrating the Social in Natural Resource Monitoring and Planning', in *Country Matters*, 20–21 May 1999, Canberra: Bureau of Rural Science.

Lowe, I. (1996), 'Performance Measurement', in Fenner Conferences on the Environment (ed.), *Sustainability: Principles to Practice: Fenner Conference on the Environment: Proceedings, 1994*, 13–16 November 1994, Canberra: Department of the Environment, Sport and Territories.

MacGregor, C. and M. Fenton (1999), 'Community Values Provide a Mechanism for Measuring Sustainability in Small Rural Communities in Northern Australia', in *Country Matters*, 20–21 May 1999, Canberra: Bureau of Rural Science.

Macnaghten, P., R. Grove-White, M. Jacobs and B. Wynne (1995), *Public Perceptions and Sustainability in Lancashire: Indicators, Institutions and Participation*, Preston: Lancashire County Council.

Melbourne City Council (1995), *Creating Prosperity: Victoria's Capital City Policy: Annual Review, 1994–95*, Melbourne: Department of Planning and Development, Melbourne City Council.

OECD (Organisation for Economic Cooperation and Development) (1976), *Measuring Social Well-being: A Progress Report on the Development of Social Indicators*, Paris: OECD.

OECD (Organisation for Economic Cooperation and Development) (1979), *The State of the Environment in OECD Member Countries*, Paris: OECD.

Parker, C. and C. Hope (1992), 'The State of the Environment: A Survey of Reports from Around the World', *Environment*, 34 (1), 18–20.

Parker, P. (1995), 'From Sustainable Development Objectives to Indicators of Progress: Options for New Zealand Communities', *New Zealand Geographer*, 51 (2), 50–57.

Pepperdine, S. (1998), 'Making Peoples' Values Count: Measuring Rural Community Sustainability', paper presented at the 18th Annual Meeting of the International Association for Impact Assessment: Sustainability and the Role of Impact Assessment in the Global Economy, 19–24 April 1998, Christchurch.

Pomeroy, A. (1996), *Ambiguous Territory: 'Social Indicators' in the Context of Sustainable Agriculture*, Wellington: Ministry of Agriculture.

Pomeroy, A. (1997), 'Social Indicators of Sustainable Agriculture', *Situation Outlook for New Zealand Agriculture*, Wellington: Ministry of Agriculture, pp. 97–100.

SCARM (Standing Committee on Agriculture and Resource Management) (1993), *Sustainable Agriculture: Tracking the Indicators for Australia and New Zealand*, Standing Committee on Agriculture and Resource Management Report No. 51, East Melbourne: Council for Scientific and Industrial Research Organisation.

SEAC (State of the Environment Advisory Council) (1996), *Australia: State of the Environment 1996*, Collingwood: Council for Scientific and Industrial Research Organisation.

Sustainable Seattle (1995), *Indicators of Sustainable Community: A Status Report on Long-Term Cultural, Economic, and Environmental Health*, Seattle: Sustainable Seattle.

Taylor, B., S. Lockie, A. Dale, R. Bischof, G. Lawrence, M. Fenton and S. Coakes (2000), *Capacity of Farmers and Other Land Managers to Implement Change*, Technical Report, Theme 6, Fitzroy Implementation Project, National Land and Water Resources Audit, Centre for Social Science Research: Central Queensland University.

Troughton, M. (1995), 'Presidential Address: Rural Canada and Canadian Rural Geography – An Appraisal', *The Canadian Geographer* **39**, (40), 290–305.

Vanclay, F. (1998), 'Inclusion of Social Data in the National Land and Water Resources Audit', *Rural Society*, **8** (1), 40–48.

Vanclay, F. and G. Lawrence (1995), *The Environmental Imperative: Eco-social Concerns for Australian Agriculture*, Rockhampton: CQU Press.

Warren, R. (1970), 'The Good Community – What Would it Be?', *Journal of the Community Development Society*, **1**, 14–23.

WCED (World Commission on Environment and Development) (1987), *Our Common Future*, Oxford: Oxford University Press.

Yiftachel, O. and D. Hedgcock (1993), 'Urban Sustainability: The Planning of an Australian City', *Cities*, **10** (2), 139–157.

6. The Influence of Social Eco-Logics in Shaping Novel Resource Governance Frameworks

David J. Brunckhorst and Phil Coop

INTRODUCTION

As nature retreats from human pressure and the earth's resources diminish, the divergence of human social systems and ecological systems grows. There are strong signs of functional problems in the operation of many ecological systems. Declining productivity, land salinisation, and blue-green bacterial blooms in rivers and dams are symptoms of breakdown of ecosystem processes and function.

The continuance of ecological processes and functions across multiple spatio-temporal scales provides the foundation for a sustainable future (Brunckhorst, 1998, 2000; di Castri, 1995; Forman, 1995; Norton and Ulanowicz, 1992; Noss, 1983). Species alone cannot maintain ecosystem function (De Leo and Levin, 1997; Naeem et al., 1994; Walker, 1995). It is also becoming evident that actions to sustain ecological systems, flows and functions must be integrated across regional landscapes. Such regions encompass natural areas, human living places (that include rural or oceanic production), and a mosaic of other land uses (Brunckhorst and Bridgewater, 1994, 1995; Hobbs, 1993; Leopold, 1949; Noss and Cooperrider, 1994; Slocombe, 1993). Consequently, there is increasing interest in broader ecosystem concepts – 'greater-ecosystems', landscape ecology, eco-regions, and bioregional planning and management concepts (Brunckhorst, 1995, 2000; Brunckhorst et al., 1997; Kim and Weaver, 1994; Forman, 1995; Forman and Godron, 1986; Noss, 1983, 1993; Slocombe, 1993).

Current institutions seem to be a long way from dealing with these extremely difficult issues but, while scientific knowledge is inadequate, urgency is growing (Brussard, 1995; Lovejoy, 1995). Our understanding of political economies and economic 'growth' appears to undermine moves towards an economically and ecologically sustainable society. The model most frequently used in decision making gives predominance to an economic rationale, arguing that the environment can be 'looked-after' when the economy is good.

We affirm that the economy-driven model is fundamentally flawed and the inverse is required (see discussions by Brunckhorst, 1998; Harpham and Boateng, 1997). The required model for decision making must view economics as a subset of society, which in turn is a part of the biosphere. Securing the quality of life for future generations is one of the key goals of ecologically sustainable development (di Castri, 1995). Securing the ongoing functional processes of ecosystems and landscapes is a necessary condition for maintaining biodiversity, sustainable resource use, economies and human quality of life. Little research effort has focused on understanding the relationship between society (or local communities) and ecosystems at the scale of regional landscapes (for example, bioregions).

Whatever it may be, future sustainability will depend on a system of land management that mediates the relationship between society (including the economy), and endurance of ecosystem function across human dominated landscapes (Brunckhorst, 1998; Harpham and Boateng, 1997). A socially eco-logical framework for natural resource planning and management is one that is a logical and pragmatic, spatio-temporal, matching of social functions and ecological functions operating across regional landscapes.

SOCIAL ECO-LOGICAL FUNCTION AND INSTITUTIONAL BARRIERS

Many authors now consider that sustainability objectives need to be planned at the scale of landscapes and regions (see Courrier, 1992; De Leo and Levin, 1997; Forman, 1995; Forman and Godron, 1986; Kim and Weaver, 1994; Norton and Ulanowicz, 1992; Noss and Cooperrider, 1994). To be effective in achieving sustainable resource use, resource governance systems have to be compatible with the character and dynamics of the ecosystems involved, and with the social, cultural and institutional norms of the society to which resource users belong. Multi-scale and cross-scale spatial and temporal elements of ecological and social functions and their influence on the landscape need to be analysed together. Where resources are a part of broader scale systems, the above features and activities might be organised in an operational hierarchy where the scale of governance is matched to the scale of the resource, ecosystem function and associated externalities – the essence of adaptive management (see Walters, 1986; Walters and Holling, 1990).

The landscape–regional scale draws together the variety of attributes that individually occupy a confined space in nature or society, but which have wider influences, so that human needs and activities are reconciled and integrated with ecological processes. We refer to this scale of management as a 'bioregion' (but not bioregionalism). It is a large area exhibiting 'soft perimeters' characterised by its drainage, flora and fauna, climate, geology, human culture and land use. Hence, a practical and operational bioregion, or 'biocultural landscape', integrates human governance within ecological law.

Practical solutions to the sustainable use of natural resources are constrained by institutional impediments, narrowly focused scientific research and entrenched or compartmentalised government systems, and other institutionalised constraints such as the market, property rights and land ownership and use (Caldwell, 1970; Holling and Meffe, 1996; Kim and Weaver, 1994; Ostrom, 1990; Slocombe, 1993). Ecosystem management approaches are not simply impeded by a lack of knowledge of ecosystems and their function at various scales, but a lack of research and development to applications of existing data (Brunckhorst, 1995; Brunckhorst and Bridgewater, 1994). Barriers to integration and communication across institutions, to the rural community and other land managers, and to the general public, often stem from inflexible or narrowly-focused management cultures and jurisdictional barriers (Brunckhorst, 1995, 2000; Caldwell, 1970; Hobbs and Humphries, 1995). Enormous benefits and efficiency gains are likely to accrue through better communication and information transfer, a freeing up of institutionalised domains and programmes and improved cross-jurisdictional responsibility for land use management (Brown and MacLeod, 1996; Saunders, 1990).

Institutional inadequacy stems from relying on entrenched institutional forms to solve new classes of problems. For example, in Australia and the US, inherited European styles of agriculture and institutions, such as property rights, do not match the biophysical and climatic nature of these lands. Property rights and ownership issues in industrial nations are also major barriers to the pursuit of sustainability at the necessary, cross-jurisdictional, landscape scale (Bird, 1987; Ostrom, 1990). There is a dualism within rural areas. Agricultural land with freehold title, is a commodity on one hand, and a set of interconnected ecosystems functioning across a landscape with no regard to ownership boundaries, on the other (see Reeve, 1992, 1997).

SOCIETY AND CIVIC INFLUENCE

Social systems are not only complex but also convoluted in terms of scale issues. Many societal elements such as families, corporations and government agencies predominantly operate in a top-down hierarchical manner. One basic building block in society is still generally considered to be the family. Social norms are then built around the home environment and then a widening circle of interactions with friends/neighbours, education/communication, citizenry/government and work/land use. These might be influenced by a variety of factors such as a set of spiritual beliefs, the neighbourhood, peers, behavioural norms, and a sense of community built. A simple example of a few of these and their spatial nesting is given in Figure 6.1. However, contemporary society is influenced and built by a much greater range of factors often operating horizontally (Meidinger, 1997).

Globalisation in all forms, including trade and powerful multinational companies, contribute to the shape of social systems. Multiple layers of government, administrative arrangements and infrastructure (roads, urban services) are probably the main cause of convolutions and overlapping (or competing) institutional requirements (Bromley, 1991; Brunckhorst, 1998; Caldwell, 1970; Ostrom, 1990). These top-down political structures again give rise to problems of policy coordination across levels, fragmented sectoral-based resource management (Brunckhorst, 2000).

We all play some role in creating the social configuration within which we also live. Some features of 'social identity' are difficult to represent spatially because of their cognitive and interpretive nature, but they do affect human value systems, issues of equity and how we identify with and interpret our surroundings, our sense of 'place', and resource management. Various case studies suggest that 'policy communities' or 'communities of common concern', which are loosely organised, local–regional, social networks allow innovation for development of new institutional forms and organisational arrangements to pursue social and ecological sustainability (Gunderson et al., 1995; Shannon, 1998). Most of these features have a spatial context in which they sit and, indeed, often have a wider area of influence on both social and ecological processes (Brunckhorst and Rollings, 1999; Meidinger, 1997). These can be mapped in multiple layers on a Geographical Information System (GIS). Similarly, the zone or extent of regulatory mechanisms and administrative arrangements can also be spatially represented (Rollings and Brunckhorst, 1999). Social processes can take a variety of forms and occur at a variety of scales – for example their strength and direction, weakening or spreading, and rate of change or cycling through time. Data that are gathered by a population census might help to spatially frame a social context. Mapping of land use, rural social networks and personal feelings of some identity with landscape features are equally important.

The structure and function of spiritual beliefs (Figure 6.1) may be difficult to represent spatially because of their cognitive and interpretive

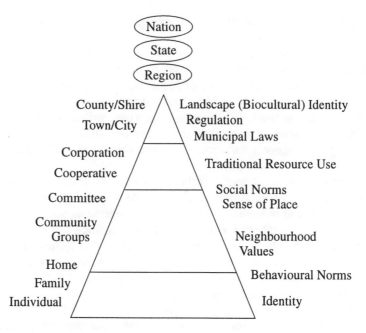

Source: Brunckhorst and Rollings (1999).

*Figure 6.1   Generalised Nesting of Structural and Functional Components
of Social Institutions*

nature, but they do affect human value systems and how we identify with
and interpret our surroundings. Most if not all such features have a spatial
context in which they sit and often a wider area of influence (Slocombe,
1993). These can be mapped in multiple layers together with the known or
assumed sphere of influence across a landscape or urban setting.

Similarly, the zone or extent of regulatory mechanisms and administrative
arrangements can also be spatially represented. It is at the scale of
landscapes that humans and society have the greatest interaction and
influence. This understanding can provide an integrated (cultural)
bioregional context to plan and manage for integrated conservation and
sustainable resource use (Brunckhorst, 1995; Brunckhorst and Bridgewater,
1994, 1995; Brunckhorst et al., 1997). Policies and institutions for natural
resource management might then be planned and integrated for appropriate
configurations (Armitage, 1995; Holling and Meffe, 1996; Norton and
Dovers, 1996).

SPATIAL AND INSTITUTIONAL REQUIREMENTS FOR LAND RESOURCE MANAGEMENT

Sustainability of resource use ultimately depends on the system of resource governance that mediates the relationship between the citizenry and the economy on one hand, and continuance of ecological functional processes on the other. Advances have been made in sociology (Lawrence, 1987; Hannigan, 1995), geography (Powell, 1976), resource economics (Young, 1992), institutional economics (Bromley, 1991, 1992) and latterly, regional approaches to resource planning and management (Brunckhorst, 1995, 1998; Brunckhorst and Bridgewater, 1994, 1995; Forman, 1995; Noss, 1983, 1993; Noss and Cooperrider, 1994; Slocombe, 1993). However, consideration of the critical interplay between ecosystem function, institutional forms and functions, culturally defined land tenure, land use and resource governance has been lacking in theoretical and applied research.

Community, civic and institutional adaptation to a system of ecologically sustainable land management will determine whether the functioning of the economy and actions of people erode the natural processes on which society relies, or remain within the limits necessary to sustain the functional integrity of ecosystems and ecological processes (see Bromley, 1991, 1992; De Leo and Levin, 1997; Ostrom, 1990; Reeve, 1997; Young, 1992;). It is apparent from this developing body of work that, to ensure resources are used sustainably, land management systems must have a number of key capacities (adapted after Ostrom, 1990; Reeve, 1997).

Spatial Information – the ability to spatially define ecosystem structure and the way in which ecosystem processes provide resource-capability function across landscape regions.

Functional Influences – the ability to identify/monitor, in a spatial context, the interaction between resource use, the social system and ecosystem functional processes in terms of their extent, magnitude and direction.

Coordinated Land Management Policy – the ability of the local community or citizenry to arrive at rules for resource use through some form of collective action, which is based on a spatial understanding of landscape ecological functioning across their bioregion.

Flexible Adaptation – the ability to adapt these rules in response to new knowledge about the ecosystems, to changing demand for resources originating from exogenous economic forces, and to climatic and other biophysical sources of stress.

Enforcement by Community Established Governance – the ability to ensure that the rules for sustainability within the functional capacity of bioregions are adhered to by resource users.

The above attributes are manifested differently according to the social, cultural, institutional and historical differences in the societies to which resource users belong. In contemporary Australian society, while some institutional adaptation has occurred towards improved land management (for example, development of leasehold tenure, participatory catchment management, and concepts of native title) the pace of institutional adaptation falls far short of what is needed to deal with the forms of land degradation that have emerged in the last few decades. There is seen to be an urgent need, particularly in rural areas, to increase the pace of institutional adaptation to encourage the development of sustainable systems of resource governance (see Fitzhardinge, 1994; Hobbs, 1993; Holmes, 1994; Lawrence, 1987; Martin, 1991; Reeve, 1992; Vanclay and Lawrence, 1995).

There appear to be two fundamental obstacles to achieving this. First, little recognition is given to the need for resource governance systems to be crafted to fit both the biophysical and socioeconomic contexts within which they must function. This is perpetuated by the current system of governance where political expedience and bureaucratic inertia favour the modification of existing institutional forms rather than developing new ones (see Caldwell, 1970; Norton and Dovers, 1996).

The second obstacle is an inability, or failure, to recognise the need to combine three types of spatially-distributed information that are essential building blocks for the design of resource governance systems (Brunckhorst, 1998). These are: influence of institutional structures; the distribution of social, environmental and political values held by those with interest in particular resources; and ecological connectivity between landscape components (Brunckhorst and Rollings, 1999).

Spatial information is required to examine the influence that institutional structures have on the landscape. Geographic Information Systems that map biophysical characteristics are increasingly common (Brunckhorst and Bridgewater, 1994; Thackway and Cresswell, 1993) but the use of such systems for institutional mapping has yet to be realised. This is due, in part, to the natural evolution of spatial information systems. Spatial information is required on the distribution, magnitude and direction of social, environmental and political values held by those parties with interest in particular resources. Knowledge of these values, together with various ways of framing resource issues, are essential in determining to what extent land management can depend on social and cultural norms to provide monitoring and enforcement capabilities, and to what extent these capabilities may have to be established by the state or other institutional entities at the regional level (Reeve, 1992, 1997).

Spatial information is also required on the extent of functional, ecological connectivity between landscape components (see Brunckhorst, 1995, 1998; Forman, 1995; Forman and Godron, 1986). In the case of dryland salinity, for example, a landscape component in a discharge area would carry information on which land elements in recharge areas had the potential to affect the level of the water table below that land element. This type of information, which essentially maps the extent of the externalities of land use or sphere of functional influence, is essential to determining which landholders should participate as stakeholders in particular land management systems. We refer to the spatial extent of functional influence that might be mapped for both ecological functions and social functions (Rollings and Brunckhorst, 1999). The total influence will provide a spatial context for sustainable resource management (constrained by ecosystem function) and principles and options for resource governance (in that cultural–biophysical context). This final requirement leads us to the design of land management systems that support the requirements of society but also match and sustain the functioning of ecological processes and services at the scale of regional landscapes (Figure 6.2).

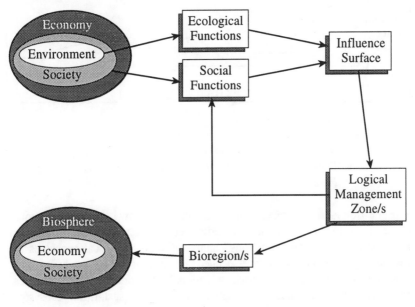

Figure 6.2   An Operational Framework for Future Sustainability

THE INFLUENCE OF SOCIAL AND ECOLOGICAL SYSTEMS ON LANDSCAPES

The goal is to maintain ecological and social systems across regional landscapes. The objective for bioregional planning and management is to facilitate the development of culturally appropriate local and regional systems of resource governance that match resource exploitation to the bioregional capacity to provide resources and ecosystem services. A simplified example of one kind of landscape–functional influence and the requirement for land resource governance is given in Figure 6.3.

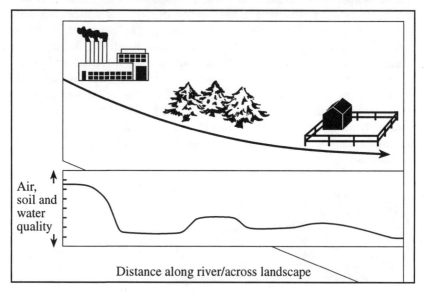

Source: Brunckhorst (1998) Reeve (1998).

Figure 6.3   A Landscape Functional Element that has Magnitude and Direction: A Simplified Example – Factories, Forests and Farms

The question is, therefore, can an understanding of how landscape ecological processes transmit costs and benefits between resource users, and an understanding of social functions, catalyse the sociopolitical processes for resource governance that are needed to establish and adapt to new institutions? We therefore need a rationale to identify socioecological management zones that make sense in terms of sustaining ecosystem function across landscapes, with which local citizens feel they can identify (see Brunckhorst, 1995; Brunckhorst and Bridgewater, 1995; Walton and Bridgewater, 1996).

Previous attempts to understand landscapes have taken either a structural approach or a functional approach (De Leo and Levin, 1997; Forman, 1995). Structural approaches are concerned with biophysical inventories of populations, species and communities. Under these circumstances the loss of a structural component to the landscape will cause a loss of integrity of that landscape. Functional approaches seek to study production and consumption within landscapes. Under these circumstances the loss of a functional component of the landscape will cause a loss of integrity of that landscape.

Maintenance of ecological function across regional landscapes has been identified as a major requirement of sustainability. Ecosystem function itself stems from the interaction within and between structural components of the landscape that is driven by inputs. An integration between these components will provide flexibility with regard to structural and functional redundancy and landscape integrity (see De Leo and Levin, 1997). When combined with social functions across the landscape, such a method may be employed to identify landscape associations that will form the basis for restructuring land management.

If we consider a landscape in terms of its structural and functional components, a hierarchy of landscape components or members can be defined (Figure 6.4). From a structural perspective we can define a fundamental building block for landscapes termed a structural unit, which is an area of uniform physical characteristics such as slope, aspect and parent material. Correspondingly, each structural unit will have a series of processes attached to it, which may operate within the unit itself, or influence other units. By combining structural units, based on uniform land cover, we can derive structural elements. The influences emanating from the structural element will be the sum of the influences of the constituent units. We can then define a (multi-scale) hierarchy of structure and function shown in Figure 6.4.

Elements combine into associations, the functional equivalents of which are ecosystems. Associations can be integrated into landscapes, which correspond in scale to functional landscapes (Forman, 1995). At the scale of functional landscapes, functioning refers to gross indicators such as productivity. This is the critical level at which to reconcile ecological functioning with social institutions if we are to approach sustainability (see Brunckhorst, 1995; Forman, 1995; Kim and Weaver, 1994). The hierarchy continues through Functional Regions, Continental Ecoregions, Biomes and, ultimately, the entire Biosphere.

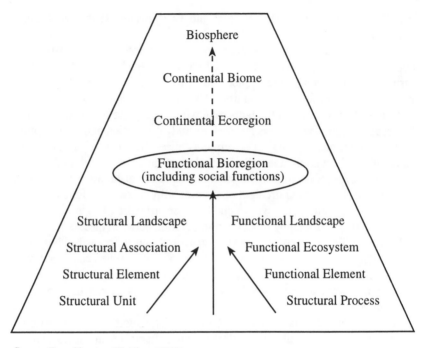

Source: Brunckhorst and Rollings (1999).

Figure 6.4   Hierarchy of Structural and Functional Components

In essence, this model follows previous classifications that are based on spatial hierarchies (see Forman, 1995; Forman and Godron, 1986; Miller, 1978). At each level of the hierarchy we can define the spatial extent, magnitude and direction of the relationship that exists within, and between, structural components. This then provides a vehicle to integrate structure and function at fine scales into landscape-scale processes that reflect its gross capability, which may then be reconciled with new governance models which the citizenry is capable of adopting and willing to adopt. This is the scale of the bioregion (Brunckhorst, 2000). Thus we potentially have the ability to move between spatial scales ranging from global issues down to management at the paddock level. Any phenomenon identifiable at one scale must necessarily find expression at other levels.

INFLUENCE FUNCTIONS: SPATIAL DIMENSIONS

Influence functions describe the relationship within and between structural elements of the landscape. Influence functions are spatio-temporally variant surfaces that describe the spatial extent, magnitude and direction of influence one landscape component has over another. By integrating these influence functions through the various scales of the hierarchy we can derive the sphere of influence attributed to functional ecosystem processes (Brunckhorst and Rollings, 1999). From an analytical viewpoint, influence functions are ideally suited to raster data models in geographic information systems and can be visualised as a three dimensional surface, its spatial characteristics defined by strength (height) and the extent and direction of the influence surface (Figure 6.5).

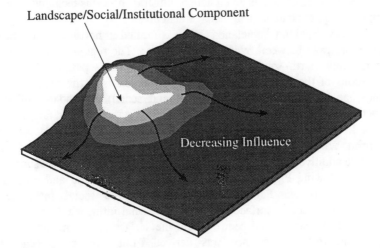

Source: Rollings and Brunckhorst (1999).

Figure 6.5   Three Dimensional Surface Representing a Hypothetical Influence Function

The role of influence functions is in linking structure and function at all levels by establishing the spatial relationship between structure and function. Concomitant to the influence function is the receptor function. The receptor function governs how a landscape component will react when under the influence of one or more influence functions. Receptor functions are used to modify the shape of the influence function so that it more closely represents reality. By summing all influence functions and their corresponding receptor functions we can build a model of total influence on any landscape element. The same approach may be used to map institutional and social influences on landscape components.

The influence function does not describe ecosystem function. It is a model that describes the influence one component (at any scale) will have on another, be it ecological, social or institutional (Figure 6.5). By modelling influence functions our aim is to identify regions that share similar ecosystem and social influences across landscapes.

APPLICATION OF INFLUENCE FUNCTION SURFACES: AN EXAMPLE

Influence functions provide a method to visualise the influence that social, ecological and institutional processes have on components across landscapes. An example is given here to illustrate how this technique may be employed to delineate logical management areas.

The New England Tablelands (NET) is located in north-east New South Wales, midway between Sydney and Brisbane. The region is characterised by a major north–south trending escarpment that separates the higher elevations of the NET from the lower coastal plains to the east. For each landscape component (both ecological and social) a standard influence function can be assigned, in this case a simple distance squared function was used. In the first instance, ecological processes and social processes are mapped. When all influence functions are assigned they are combined using a simple additive or multiplicative model to generate an influence surface.

The following Figures (6.6, 6.7) consist of both social and ecological influence surfaces. For illustrative purposes the social influence is represented by social surface contours. The social influence decreases with distance from each social centre where the surface is at a maximum. The ecological influence surface was derived from broad-scale vegetation communities. The ecological surface represents high functional capacity (influence strength) in the darker areas and decreases with distance to the highly modified systems represented by the lighter areas.

These surfaces represent the total influence exerted by all component influences. At any stage, however, it is possible to refer back to an individual component's influence function if necessary. The method is very flexible and standard influence functions can be assigned at any scale in the hierarchy, or they can be generated from influence functions assigned at lower levels in the hierarchy. Social influence functions operate in a similar fashion to ecological influence functions except that they depict zones that reflect the spatial extent and magnitude of biocultural identity with a landscape/region; and, social institutions, jurisdictions and their spatial influence.

When the surfaces for social and ecological functions have been generated they are coupled to generate a combined surface that links ecologically functional regions with identifiable socially functioning, human communities.

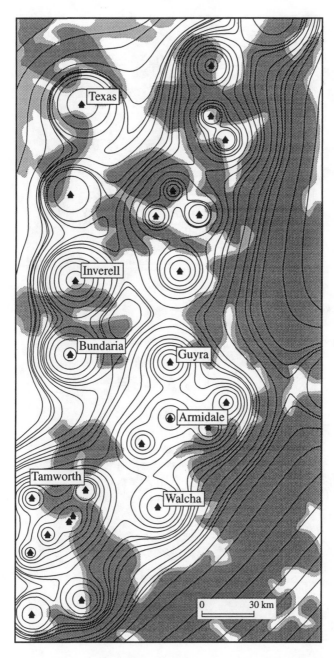

Figure 6.6   Social Surface (Represented as Contours) and Ecological Influence Surface

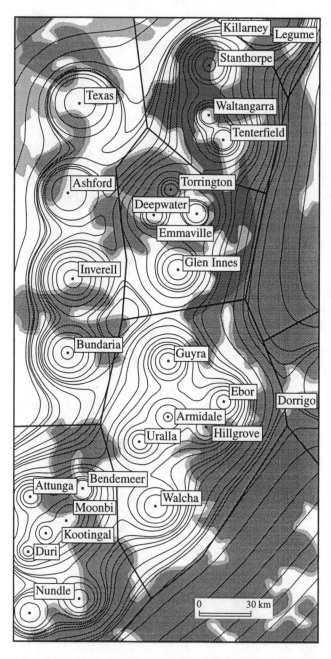

Figure 6.7   Bioregions Within a Broader Spatial Hierarchy (Ecoregions)

The social influence surface may also represent the degree to which communities associate with their surroundings. This type of information provides an opportunity to spatially define management areas based on the collective views expressed by participating communities.

Figure 6.7 depicts the social and ecological influence surfaces and identifies potential management areas that were delineated according to socially defined variables. In this example, management area boundaries are defined according to biocultural identity. By examining the community 'nestings' with the physical, geological and ecological characteristics of the New England Tablelands, it would appear that pragmatic 'regional'-scale management zones could match up both ecological functions and social functions (including common communities) as shown diagrammatically in Figure 6.7.

There are many economic, ecological and social benefits. It provides a logical operational framework for local government and for services, environment reporting, vegetation strategies, bush fire strategies, threatened species, health and so on.

SUMMARY AND CONCLUSIONS

Studies of landscape ecosystems must address not only biophysical relationships, but also social and institutional processes and functions that cause anthropogenic impacts which ultimately manifest themselves in socioeconomic consequences. This might best be accomplished if social science and policy studies are conducted in tandem with large-scale ecological research.

We have outlined a theoretical model and research framework that seeks to spatially couple the influences of ecological functions and social functions across regional landscapes to identify an appropriate regional context to facilitate the emergence of more sustainable systems of land management. The model is concerned with direct and indirect influences of changes in ecosystem function on economies and communities, in particular, how criteria for maintaining ecological processes across landscapes and regions might direct the local and civic capacities for resource governance at the scale of regional landscapes. It should help elucidate the linkage between ecological processes, perceived ecosystem change, responses by institutions and organisations, and formal decision processes that may or may not appropriately interpret these changes and initiate planning to improve the pattern of human-influenced ecosystem changes.

Application of the theoretical model provides insight into management regimes that utilise a nested approach to resource management in order to cope with the broader-scale issues of environmental management where problems may be physically beyond the capacity of any one management area (Ostrom, 1990). A social–ecological influence function approach to resource management therefore provides opportunities to better match social and ecological processes within a bioregional (biocultural) framework, enhancing the opportunities for sustainable outcomes (Brunckhorst, 2000).

Preliminary application of the model suggests this ambitious approach holds promise. Its application in discussions on local government amalgamations and boundary changes has demonstrated its practical application. Such a process involving stakeholders might actually effect change or adaptation towards new institutional forms for a sustainable future.

REFERENCES

Armitage, D. (1995), 'An Integrative Methodological Framework for Sustainable Environmental Planning and Management', *Environmental Management*, **19** (4), 469–479.

Bird, E. (1987), 'The Social Construction of Nature: Theoretical Approaches to the History of Environmental Problems', *Environmental Review*, Winter, 255–264.

Bromley, D. (1991), *Environment and Economy: Property Rights and Public Policy*, Oxford: Basil Blackwell.

Bromley, D. (1992), *Making the Commons Work: Theory, Practice and Policy*, San Francisco: Institute for Contemporary Studies Press.

Brown, J. and N. MacLeod (1996), 'Integrating Ecology into Natural Resource Management Policy', *Environmental Management*, **20** (3), 289–296.

Brunckhorst, D. (1995), 'Sustaining Nature and Society – A Bioregional Approach', *Inhabit*, **3**, 5–9.

Brunckhorst, D. (1998), 'Comment on "Urban Governance in Relation to the Operation of Urban Services in Developing Countries" by Trudy Harpham, and Kwasi A. Boateng', *Habitat International*, **22** (1), 69–72.

Brunckhorst, D. (2000), *Bioregional Planning: Resource Management Beyond the New Millenium*, Amsterdam: Harwood Academic, Gordon and Breach.

Brunckhorst, D. and P. Bridgewater (1994), 'A Novel Approach to Identify and Select Core Reserve Areas and to Apply UNESCO Biosphere Reserve Principles to the Coastal Marine Realm', in D. Brunckhorst (ed.), *Marine Protected Areas and Biosphere Reserves: Towards a New Paradigm*, Canberra: UNESCO/ANCA, pp. 12–17.

Brunckhorst, D. and P. Bridgewater (1995), 'Coastal Zone Conservation – Sustaining Nature and Society', in O. Bellwood, H. Choat and N. Saxena (eds), *Recent Advances in Marine Science and Technology '94*, PACON International and James Cook University, pp. 87–94.

Brunckhorst, D. and N. Rollings (1999), 'Linking Ecological and Social Functions of Landscapes: I. Influencing Resource Governance', *Journal of the Natural Areas Association*, **19** (1), 34–41.

Brunckhorst, D., P. Bridgewater and P. Parker (1997), 'The UNESCO Biosphere Reserve Program Comes of Age: Learning by Doing, Landscape Models for a

Sustainable Conservation and Resource Use', in Hale and Moritz (eds), *Conservation Outside Reserves*, Brisbane: Centre for Conservation Biology, University of Queensland Press, pp. 176–182.

Brussard, P. (1995), 'The President's Column – Critical Issues', *Society of Conservation Biology Newsletter*, **2** (1).

Caldwell, L. (1970), 'The Ecosystem as a Criterion for Public Land Policy', *Natural Resources Journal*, **10** (2), 203–221.

Courrier, K. (ed.) (1992), *Global Biodiversity Strategy: Guidelines for Action to Save, Study and Use Earth's Biotic Wealth Sustainably and Equitably*, Washington, DC: WRI, IUCN, UNEP.

De Leo, G. and S. Levin (1997), 'The Multifaceted Aspects of Ecosystem Integrity', *Conservation Ecology*, **1** (1), 3, URL: <http://www. consecol.org/vol1/iss1/art3>

di Castri, F. (1995), 'The Chair of Sustainable Development', *Nature and Resources*, **31** (3), 2–7.

Fitzhardinge G. (1994), 'An Alternative Understanding of the Relationship Between the Ecosystem and the Social System: Implications for Land Management in Semi-arid Australia', *Rangelands Journal*, **16** (2), 254–264.

Forman, R. (1995), *Land Mosaics: The Ecology of Landscapes and Regions*, New York: Cambridge University Press.

Forman R. and M. Godron (1986), *Landscape Ecology*, New York: J. Wiley and Sons.

Gunderson, L., C. Holling and S. Light (eds), (1995), *Barriers and Bridges to the Renewal of Ecosystems and Institutions*, New York: Columbia University Press.

Hannigan, J. (1995), *Environmental Sociology: A Social Constructivism Perspective*, London and New York: Routledge.

Harpham, T. and K. Boateng (1997), 'Urban Governance in Relation to the Operation of Urban Services in Developing Countries', *Habitat International*, **21** (1), 65–77.

Hobbs, R. (1993), 'Effects of Landscape Fragmentation on Ecosystem Processes in the Western Australian Wheatbelt', *Biological Conservation*, **64**, 193–201.

Hobbs R. and S. Humphries (1995), 'An Integrated Approach to the Ecology and Management of Plant Invasions', *Conservation Biology*, **9** (4), 761–770.

Holling, C. and M. Meffe (1996), 'Command and Control and the Pathology of Natural Resource Management', *Conservation Biology*, **10** (2), 328–337.

Holmes, J. (1994), 'Changing Values, Goals, Needs and Expectations of Rangeland Users', *Rangelands Journal*, **16** (2), 147–154.

Kim, K. and R. Weaver (eds) (1994), *Biodiversity and Landscapes: A Paradox of Humanity*, New York: Cambridge University Press.

Lawrence, G. (1987), *Capitalism and the Countryside: The Rural Crisis in Australia*, Sydney: Pluto.

Leopold, A. (1949) (commemorative edition 1989), *A Sand County Almanac – And Sketches Here and There*, New York: Oxford University Press.

Lovejoy, T. (1995), 'Will Expectedly the Top Blow Off? Environmental Trends and the Need for Critical Decision Making', *Bioscience Supplement – Science and Biodiversity Policy*, 3–6.

Martin, P. (1991), 'Environmental Care in Agricultural Catchments: Toward the Communicative Catchment', *Environmental Management*, **15** (6), 773–783.

Meidinger, E. (1997), 'Organizational and Legal Challenges for Ecosystem Management', in K. Kohm and J. Franklin (eds), *Creating a Forestry for the 21st Century: The Science of Ecosystem Management*, Washington, DC: Island Press.

Miller, D. (1978), 'The Factor of Scale: Ecosystem, Landscape Mosaic and Region', in K. Hammond, G. Macinko and W. Fairchild (eds), *Sourcebook on the*

Environment: A Guide to the Literature, Chicago: University of Chicago Press, pp. 63–88.

Naeem, S., L. Thompson, S. Lawler, J. Lawton and R. Woodfin (1994), 'Declining Biodiversity Can Alter the Performance of Ecosystems', *Nature*, **368**, 734–736.

Norton, B. and R. Ulanowicz (1992), 'Scale and Biodiversity Policy: A Hierachical Approach', *Ambio*, **21** (3), 244–249.

Norton, T. and S. Dovers (1996), 'Uncertainty, Ecology, Sustainability and Policy', *Biodiversity and Conservation*, **5**, 1143–1167.

Noss, R. (1983), 'A Regional Landscape Approach to Maintain Diversity', *Bioscience*, **33** (11), 700–706.

Noss, R. (1993), 'A Conservation Plan for the Oregon Coast Range: Some Preliminary Suggestions', *Natural Areas Journal*, **13** (4), 276–290.

Noss, R. and A. Cooperrider (1994), *Saving Natures Legacy: Protecting and Restoring Biodiversity*, Washington, DC, Island Press.

Ostrom, E. (1990), *Governing the Commons. The Evolution of Institutions for Collective Action*, Cambridge: Cambridge University Press.

Powell, J. (1976), *Environmental Management in Australia, 1788–1914. Guardians, Improvers and Profit: An Introductory Survey*, Melbourne: Oxford University Press.

Reeve, I. (1992), 'Sustainable Agriculture: Problems, Prospects and Policies', in G. Lawrence, F. Vanclay and B. Furze (eds), *Agriculture, Environment and Society: Contemporary Issues for Australia*, Melbourne: Macmillan, pp. 208–223.

Reeve, I. (1997), 'Property and Participation: An Institutional Analysis of Rural Resource Management and Landcare in Australia', in S. Lockie and F. Vanclay (eds), *Critical Landcare*, Wagga Wagga: Centre for Rural Social Research, pp. 83–96.

Reeve, I. (1998), 'Commons and Coordination: Towards a Theory of Resource Governance', in R. Epps (ed.), *Sustaining Rural Systems in the Context of Global Change. Proceedings of the Conference of the Joint IGU Commission for the Sustainability of Rural Systems and the Land Use–Cover Change Study Group*, Armidale: University of New England, pp. 54–65.

Rollings, N. and D. Brunckhorst (1999), 'Linking Ecological and Social Functions of Landscapes: II. Scale and Modelling of Spatial Influence', *Journal of the Natural Areas Association*, **19** (1), 42–50.

Saunders, D. (1990), 'The Landscape Approach to Conservation: Community Involvement, The Only Practical Solution', *Australian Zoologist*, **26** (2), 49–53.

Shannon, M. (1998), 'Understanding Social Organizations and Institutions', in R. Naiman and R. Bilby (eds), *River Ecology and Management: Lessons from the Pacific Coastal Ecoregion*, New York: Springer Verlag, pp. 529–551.

Slocombe, D. (1993), 'Implementing Ecosystem-based Management: Development of Theory, Practice and Research for Planning and Managing a Region', *BioScience*, **43** (9), 612–622.

Thackway, R. and I. Cresswell (1993), *Environmental Regionalisations of Australia: A User-oriented Approach*, Canberra: Environmental Resources Information Network, Australian National Parks and Wildlife Service.

Vanclay, F. and G. Lawrence (1995), *The Environmental Imperative: Eco-social Concerns for Australian Agriculture*, Rockhampton: CQU Press.

Walker, B. (1995), 'Conserving Biological Diversity through Ecosystem Resilience', *Conservation Biology*, **9** (4), 747–752.

Walters, C. (1986), *Adaptive Management of Renewable Resources*, New York: Macmillan.

Walters, C. and C. Holling (1990), 'Large-scale Management Experiments and Learning by Doing', *Ecology*, **71** (6), 2060–2068.

Walton, D. and P. Bridgewater (1996), 'Of Gardens and Gardeners', *Nature and Resources*, **32** (3), 15–19.

Young, M. (1992), *Sustainable Investment and Resource Use: Equity, Environmental Integrity and Efficiency*, Paris and Carnforth: UNESCO and Parthenon.

PART II

Planning and Impact Assessment

7. Democratising Environmental Assessment: The Relevance of Deliberative Democracy for Environmental Decision Making in Western Australia

Tabatha Jean Wallington and Ian Barns

INTRODUCTION

Over the past two decades or so in Australia, as elsewhere, opportunities for public involvement have become institutionalised in the environmental assessment process. In Western Australia, this commitment to public participation is formalised in the *Environmental Protection Act* 1986 (the Act). The Act envisaged a forum in which the developmentalist agenda of governments, historically oriented toward the exploitation of the state's natural resources, could be challenged.

The promise of this forum was short-lived. Since 1993, following the election of a Liberal–National Party State Government, the opportunities for public participation in environmental assessment have been significantly weakened. In part, these changes reflect the strong developmentalist priorities of the present state government. However, it is argued that the erosion of these democratising initiatives reflects the pervasive influence of an instrumentalist rationality entrenched within the system of government and political culture in Australia, such that public participation is viewed as dispensable.

This chapter contends that understanding the vulnerability of formal commitments to public participation requires an appreciation of the political philosophies that underpin the institutionalised practice of environmental assessment. As Isaiah Berlin (1962, cited in Bernstein 1976, p. 57) instructs:

> The first step to understanding [people] is the bringing to consciousness of the model or models that dominate and penetrate their thought and action . . . The

second task is to analyse the model itself, and this commits the analyst to accepting or modifying or rejecting it, and in the last case, to providing a more adequate one in its stead.

Following Berlin, this chapter will examine the way that the model of liberal democracy, informed by a regime of instrumental rationality, inhibits effective public participation in environmental assessment. It will be argued that an alternative regime of deliberative rationality would provide a firmer foundation for more meaningful public participation in environmental decision making. To begin, the limited and tokenistic nature of formal provisions for public participation in environmental assessment will be briefly described.

FORMAL COMMITMENTS TO PUBLIC PARTICIPATION IN ENVIRONMENTAL ASSESSMENT

Environmental impact assessment represents 'a fundamental change in perceptions of how propositions regarding society's environmental future should be evaluated and how political and economic decisions affecting the future should be made' (Caldwell, 1989, p. 7). Therefore, beyond the development of science-based procedures to inform decision makers of the likely consequences of their actions, environmental assessment was intended as a means to 'the protection and improvement of the environmental quality of life' (Caldwell, 1989, p. 9). Unfortunately, this larger political purpose has been largely displaced by a preoccupation with technique (Lawrence, 1997).

In Western Australia's system of environmental assessment, the limited commitment to public process betrays the dominance of a procedural approach. The main opportunity for public participation is formal public review of the proponent's environmental report and presentation of written submissions to the Environmental Protection Authority (EPA). The following examples illustrate that while the administrative procedures serve to legitimise public involvement, the constrained opportunities for public participation simultaneously stifle community debate about the public issues to be decided.

The first restrictive feature is the late stage of public participation in environmental assessment, which formally limits the public's role in setting the agenda for addressing environmental concerns. Public review of the completed environmental report occurs after the major development decisions have already been made (Ortolano and Shepherd, 1995; Poisner, 1996). The significance of agenda-setting is that the definition of an issue essentially determines its solution (Barber, 1984). Therefore, this process explicitly discounts the value of public lay knowledge in environmental decision making.

A second limiting feature is the form of communication enabled by public review, which is essentially one-way information exchange. This diminished 'monological' conception of communication is reinforced by the fact that 'public' review of the environmental report generally occurs in private. In effect, the provisions for public involvement serve to privatise, and thus to depoliticise, environmental values. In contrast, the negotiations between the EPA and the proponent, and the deliberations characteristic of joint ministerial decision making, are explicitly dialogical. However, these elitist negotiations 'behind closed doors' prevail at the expense of inclusive and open processes of community debate.

These restrictive tendencies are compounded with recent Act amendments that aim to reduce avenues for public involvement, justified by the time delays and uncertainty – in effect, the efficiency – of the assessment process *for developers*.[1] This focus reflects a distinct reorientation of government purposes away from citizens, and toward a new set of 'clients': namely, private industry. This shift is significant, pointing as it does to the co-option of public processes by the larger technocratic agenda of government.

INSTRUMENTAL RATIONALITY AND ITS EFFECT ON PROCESSES OF PUBLIC PARTICIPATION

In the discussion that follows, it will be argued that the increasingly restricted public access to the environmental assessment process reflects, at a fundamental level, a regime of instrumental rationality that informs the structures and practices of liberal democracy. Instrumental rationality is 'the capacity to devise, select, and effect good means to clarified ends' (Dryzek, 1990, p. 4). It is an approach which, while appropriate to the implementation of policy, 'destroys the more congenial, spontaneous, egalitarian and intrinsically meaningful aspects of human association' necessary to the creation of policy goals (Dryzek, 1990, p. 4).

Instrumental reason has become the major concept of reason to make sense in modern society (Bernstein, 1983). Informed by this rationality, governmental decision making is oriented to the solution of technical problems rather than to the realisation of practical goals. Thus, the aim of government has been reduced to referring 'as many social and political decisions as possible to the realm of administrative decision making, where they can be redefined and processed in technical terms' (Fischer, 1990, p. 43). The effects of instrumental rationality on the processes of public participation in environmental assessment are manifested in three important areas of liberal democratic governance: public administration, technology management and public life.

Public Administration and the Formal Separation of Political and Technical Phases of Environmental Assessment

A significant feature of the present system of representative government and cabinet government is the concentration of formal decision making power in the hands of ministers and the formal separation of the political and technical dimensions of policy development (Marsh, 1995). This system frames the structures and practices of environmental assessment, where the administration of the technical phase (the analysis of information to develop ministerial policy advice) is a function of the Department of Environmental Protection (DEP), and the political phase begins with ministerial attention to implementation. Public input to this process is thus conceived within the technical phase of decision making, the political phase being the domain of the public's agent, the minister.

This *formal* separation of the technical and political phases of policy development is of course a myth; however, this normative framework does have very real results in the processes designed to facilitate public policy making. Until quite recently, this separation has been reflected in the ethic of impartiality governing the public service, which was meant to express a broad commitment on the part of the professional civil service to serve the good of the community as a whole and not just the interests of a particular party.

This notion of public-spirited professionalism has been weakened as the result of ongoing managerialist reforms in Australia, where the broader commitment to 'the public good' has given way to the application of administrative and managerial skills based on a means/ends technical rationality. This 'new managerial' model thus replaces the language of political choice by that of management, supplanting the substantive ends of public service by the 'apologetics of "efficiency"' (Hirst, 1996, p. 97). As Yeatman (1987, p. 349) warns, 'it is a small and easy step to take for granted that the tasks of the public sector and public service must be framed not only to accommodate but to foster privately-oriented economic activity as the only type of genuine economic activity'. Hence, it is in the context of these reforms that we may understand recent arguments of efficiency in environmental assessment, and the consequent redefinition of the DEP's role as one of facilitating private sector economic development.

An Instrumentalist View of Technology

The second important context of environmental governance is that of institutionalised approaches to technology choice, management and assessment. Environmental assessment is part of a broader task of the public management of dynamically evolving technological systems, the implementation and operation of which necessarily impacts on natural and social environments.

Unfortunately, in the narrow perspective of an instrumental rationality, such technologies are generally viewed as 'tools' that are more or less productive and efficient in achieving the economic and social goals they are meant to serve. However, we actually experience technologies as much more than mere tools, and technological change as much more than mere cause-and-effect. As Winner (1986, p. 6, 9) comments, technologies are ways of building order in our world: 'technologies are not merely aids to human activity, but are also powerful forces acting to reshape that activity and its meaning . . . as technologies are being built and put to use . . . [n]ew worlds are being made. There is nothing "secondary" about this phenomenon.'

Recognition of the inherently social and political process of technological development means that the costs associated with technological systems cannot be approached in narrow technical terms. Rather, they must be seen contextually, as socially negotiated processes.

In environmental assessment, however, the social commitments embodied in our existing technological systems are unwittingly reproduced as criteria for existing projects are invoked to guide future environmental reviews (Wood and Bailey, 1994). Of course, this attention to maintaining and progressing the modern trajectory of techno-economic development is a fundamental characteristic of liberal democracy. But it is an approach that poses strong barriers to any attempt to think about the public dimensions of technological choice (Winner, 1993, p. 55).

Technological change, defined as 'progress', is seen as an ineluctable process in modern history. To encourage progress is to encourage private inventors (entrepreneurs) to work unimpeded by state interference. As later theorists in the liberal tradition modify this understanding, they notice 'market externalities' that cause stress in the social system or environment. This does not alter the fundamental attitude toward economic and technical choices. The burden of proof rests on those who would interfere with the beneficial workings of the market and processes of technological development. The public must assume the burden of proof and provide grounds for objection to development proposals in environmental assessment – only there is less and less opportunity to do so. In effect, '[t]here is no moral community or public space in which technological issues are topics for deliberation, debate, and shared action' (Winner, 1993, p. 56).

The Procedural Nature of Liberal Democracy, and the Dominance of Interest-Based Politics

The technically oriented nature of environmental assessment processes and the instrumentalist approach to technologies are sustained by the 'thin' proceduralist politics of a liberal democratic political order, which is an approach that privatises and depoliticises as it simultaneously reinforces elitist decision making. Public claims are privatised in liberal democracy because they are defined as expressions of private interests, or preferences. Because preferences are assumed to be formed in private – which by definition is a realm outside the influence of the public sphere of politics – they are simply taken as given. Politics is then defined as the aggregation of interests because, given that we all have conflicting interests and values, it is considered to be the least controversial way to ensure that our personal interests are equally recognised while avoiding public moral conflict (Gutmann and Thompson, 1995).

A fundamental problem with the interest perspective of collective choice is that conflicts of interest, whilst subject to bargaining, are finally intractable because 'my interest and your interest are separated forever by the particularity of me and you' (Barber, 1984, p. 201). The appeal to self-interest thus denies the possibility of the existence or creation of shared values with respect to public goods such as the environment.

Despite the primacy of private interests in justifying the procedural framework of liberal politics, the theory of liberal democracy has little to say about how we are able to form opinions about public issues in isolation. Nevertheless, the assumption that our preferences are formed in private does embody an important message. It defines people as mere bundles of preferences waiting to be expressed; as isolated beings whose values and beliefs are purely the product of self-interest; and as incapable of learning and development. This message must prompt the conclusion that the core assumption of liberal democracy is infeasible, unworkable and destructive to political reality. Indeed, it must be argued that the commitments to environmental protection and public participation embodied in environmental legislation express a common perception of ourselves and the values we stand for as a moral community – they are not intended to satisfy personal preferences (Barns, 1995; Sagoff, 1988).

THE RELEVANCE OF DELIBERATIVE DEMOCRACY FOR ENVIRONMENTAL ASSESSMENT

To this point, it has been argued that the institutions of liberal democratic governance, informed by an instrumental rationality, fail to provide a meaningful role for citizens in ongoing environmental decision making. If democracy is to be redeemed from its presently diminished status as the instrumental calculation of votes on election day, a re-democratisation of political structures and practices is required. In other words, there is a need to strengthen the legitimacy of representative government with ongoing public involvement to ensure that representation is informed by an active citizenry.

To this end, a number of contemporary theorists have argued for a deliberative approach to environmental decision making (see Barns, 1995; Bloomfield et al., 1998; Hayward, 1995; Poisner, 1996). This approach embodies a politics which emphasises public purposes over private interests; shared understanding over adversarial bargaining; transformative capacity over static choice; social and political process over instrumental calculation; and inclusive over elitist decision making.

The following discussion will consider three features of deliberative democracy which aim to counter the problematic features of liberal democracy identified earlier. The implications of deliberative democracy for environmental assessment and public participation will be outlined in the final section of this chapter.

A Political Culture of Public Deliberation Based on Active Citizenship

A key aspect of change required to redeem politics from technocratic democracy is a retrieval of the sphere of politics based on active citizenship. Deliberative democracy responds to the public nature of citizenship by encouraging active citizen participation in public forums oriented to negotiating the common good. This approach embodies the capacity to enrich liberal democracy through its concern with substantive social and political *process* – which would take precedence over instrumental procedure – because it recognises that all institutions influence how judgements are made.

Deliberative democracy thus recognises that the process by which citizens are invited to express their preferences can have an enormous effect on such preferences (Barber, 1984; Miller, 1992; Warren, 1996).[2] Individuals do not simply *have* opinions, they *form* opinions, which necessarily involves a process of testing these opinions in a forum where there is a genuine encounter with differing opinions (Bernstein, 1983).

Political judgement then requires a kind of 'representative thinking' that takes other perspectives into consideration. The ability to make effective public judgements is cultivated in the public forum of debate by the process of political learning (Healey, 1997, p. 238): 'the giving of rights to be heard goes with the responsibility to listen, to give respect, and to learn, through procedures which foster mutual learning about the concerns of others, and which draw on the knowledgeability of all members of a political community'.

The deliberative approach thus aims for values we can respect rather than values we can agree on (Parker, 1995). This is in contrast to 'non-social instrumental action and social strategic action, both of which are oriented toward success' (Bernstein, 1983, p. 185).

The mutual respect encouraged by deliberative democracy is more likely to be engendered when the aim of the process is to find a working consensus in *new* areas of shared meaning. For this reason, deliberative democracy aims to include a wider variety of 'publics' in the process, embracing a broadening of the knowledges and values that are brought to bear on decision making – a situation which provides a space for new 'lines of consensus' to be formed (Bloomfield et al., 1998). In this way, a political culture of deliberative rationality provides the potential to overcome the vicious circle created when instrumentalist institutions oriented to private interests engender an adversary politics that encourages privately oriented behaviour. In contrast, deliberative institutions would provide the potential for a virtuous circle: when new public values are created through dialogue and debate, new social and political spaces are also created in which new rights and responsibilities can emerge. These may encourage the democratic renewal of existing political structures and practices (Bloomfield et al., 1998).

A More Constructive Approach to Technology Assessment

A second key feature of a political culture of deliberative rationality is its capacity to recognise and address the broader social and cultural meanings associated with technological systems. An approach that attempts to respond to these issues has been developed in recent times in the concept of 'constructive technology assessment' (CTA), which 'strives to envision alternative technological futures that might serve alternative configurations of human values and commitments . . . framing assessments in such a way as to address real choices among alternative "forms of life"' (Tatum, 1995, p. 120; see also Rip et al., 1995). The evolution of CTA from the impact assessment model suggests a number of lessons for environmental assessment, in particular with respect to the uncertainty characteristic of many contemporary environmental issues.

The instrumental response to uncertainty is the call for more information, which obscures the fact that problems do not just exist 'out there', waiting to be solved. Problems are subject to conflicting interpretations, so that we essentially 'create' the problem with its definition. As Wynne (1992) and Forester (1993) argue, the problem has been misinterpreted – what we face is not uncertainty, but ambiguity, which requires a quite different response. The political, normative and 'value' questions that arise with ambiguity – with the conditional nature of knowledges and the contested nature of truth claims – requires negotiation and learning about the social commitments and relations embodied in the technologies themselves.

A more constructive approach to environmental assessment would also recognise the problematic emphasis on nature as outside human experience – as the external 'environment' – that reproduces the dualistic nature/culture framing of many environmental issues. Transcending this dualism requires a more practical approach that considers the world-creating nature of technological decision making: 'The future is not a pre-existing land towards which we are all moving, and which it is our task to discern through the mist and prepare for, but something which is created and shaped through all the decisions we make' (Szerszynski et al., 1996, p. 10). Therefore, the inherently political and cultural task of environmental assessment in developing, assessing and regulating technologies requires the facilitation of a public process of articulating and debating the shared conditions for the kind of world we would like to create.

A Facilitative Role for the Public Service

In the context of the public service, both market-oriented reforms and the push for active citizenship evident in Australia encourage a move away from a rationale of public service defined in terms of the provision of technical advice to the minister and toward more active engagement with civil society. However, while the former encourages the facilitation of private sector economic development, the latter demands a more proactive facilitation of democratic civic participation and deliberation. The public service thus represents a highly significant site for contesting the nature of governance in a liberal democratic society.

Indeed, it is suggested here that the current 'crisis' evident in Australia's public sector (Yeatman, 1998) provides a 'window of opportunity' because it betrays a disruption of bureaucratic inertia, opening the way to a number of possible futures. From the perspective of deliberative democracy, the public service needs to be redefined in terms of the concept of 'facilitative governance'. As Yeatman (1998, p. 141) emphasises, '[i]f governments are to do what they should be doing, their role is to specify, insitutitionalise and resource individualised capacities for *citizen* choice and voice'. This requires the intentional design of public institutions that will help to build the circumstances for politics as deliberative practice.[3]

Facilitating Public Deliberation in Environmental Assessment

This chapter has argued that an effective system of public participation in environmental assessment requires the development of an alternative culture of deliberative rationality in public life that takes seriously the cultural significance of technology in approaches to technology choice, assessment and management and which sustains a more 'facilitative' public sector. Although the systematic implementation of such deliberative principles in the environmental assessment process is beyond the scope of this chapter, the example of the deliberative public inquiry – exemplified by the Berger Inquiry – illustrates the practical possibilities of a more facilitative public process that would help to reorient environmental assessment in a more deliberative direction.

The Berger Inquiry was a social and environmental assessment of the proposal for a natural gas pipeline in Canada in the 1970s, and has been described as an accessible and inviting public learning process that valued the 'expert' scrutiny provided by all citizens at least equally to the testimony of technical experts (Gamble, 1978). The explicit involvement of lay citizens meant that the Berger Inquiry was inevitably political, and thus did not attempt to privatise what are in fact public environmental issues. The inclusion of a broader range of knowledges early in the process encouraged participants to take a broader view of the issues, so that cultural and political issues and questions of the 'public good' were considered, including renewable resources, the cultural identity of native peoples and cooperative enterprise (Torgerson, 1986). Further, public values were *created* when the focus of the debate broadened from the pipeline development itself to participants' aspirations about the whole pattern of future development in the area – about the kind of society they wanted to build. In this way, participants were able to redefine the agenda, and to redirect the focus from 'impacts' to the social relations of the proposed technology. The deliberative approach thus holds the potential to reorient the development of technology to public purposes.

CONCLUSION

The central concern of this chapter has been to advocate a more deliberative political practice of environmental decision making. This concern is driven by the current vulnerability of the public institutions of environmental assessment in Western Australia, which has been exacerbated with recent trends toward government facilitation of private sector development. This denigration of the notion of 'public service' shows scant regard for the proper role of government in enabling the creation and sustenance of shared values and public purposes, and ultimately places the integrity and legitimacy of liberal democratic governance at risk.

There is, however, a 'window of opportunity' in the current period of transition being experienced by the public sector in Australia, through which government action might be reoriented toward the facilitation of civic deliberative processes about economic and technological development. The theoretical resources of deliberative democracy serve to remind us that issues about our common environment require a process of collective reasoning based on the assumption that we are indeed capable of creating public purposes. These public values may then provide a normative framework for the creation and renewal of those social relations and public institutions that sustain our natural environment, and for legitimate government action.

The deliberative approach to environmental assessment advocated in this chapter would enable a clear recognition of the essentially ambiguous nature of environmental decision making, which demands a process of learning and negotiation about the social commitments of our technological decisions. Consequently, a deliberative public process of environmental assessment would seek to question the social commitments embodied in the technologies we seek to build, so that we might also build shared circumstances that we can live with.

NOTES

1. See Edwardes (1997) for proposed Act amendments and their justification.
2. An influential account of deliberative democracy is Habermas's (1991) notion of an ideal deliberative procedure, based on norms of communicative rationality. Two broad critiques of Habermas's communicative process ideal are exemplified by Dryzek's (1990) 'discursive democracy' and Young's (1992) 'communicative democracy'. For a useful typology of recent approaches, see Blaug (1996).
3. This task has been embraced by Dryzek (1990), who seeks to show that incipient forms of 'discursive design' already exist in such forms as alternative dispute resolution procedures and policy dialogue. The interest in deliberative mechanisms is evident in the increasing assessments (Renn et al., 1995; Davison et al., 1997) and empirical case studies (Stewart et al., 1994; Coote and Lenaghan, 1997; Kuper, 1997) of innovative institutions such as consensus conferences, citizens' juries, planning cells and regulatory negotiation.

REFERENCES

Barber, B. (1984), *Strong Democracy: Participatory Politics for a New Age*, California: University of California Press.

Barns, I. (1995), 'Environment, Democracy and Community', *Environmental Politics*, **4** (4), 101–133.

Bernstein, R. (1976), *The Restructuring of Social and Political Theory*, Oxford: Basil Blackwell.

Bernstein, R. (1983), *Beyond Objectivism and Relativism: Science, Hermeneutics, and Praxis*, Philadelphia: University of Pennsylvania Press.

Blaug, R. (1996), 'New Theories of Discursive Democracy: A User's Guide', *Philosophy and Social Criticism*, **22**, 49–80.

Bloomfield, D., K. Collins, C. Fry and R. Munton (1998), 'Deliberative and Inclusionary Processes: Their Contribution to Environmental Governance', paper presented at a conference on Environmental Governance: Responding to the Challenge of Deliberative Democracy, University of London, 17 December 1998, Available on the World Wide Web (accessed 8 June 1999) <http://www.gcog.ucl.ac.uk/csru/dip/pub/dipfrm.html>.

Caldwell, L. (1989), 'Understanding Impact Analysis: Technical Process, Administrative Reform, Policy Principle', in R. Bartlett (ed.), *Policy Through Impact Assessment: Institutionalised Analysis as a Policy Strategy*, New York, Connecticut and London: Greenwood Press, pp. 7–16.

Coote, A. and J. Lenaghan (1997), *Citizens' Juries: Theory Into Practice*, London: Institute for Public Policy Research.

Davison, A., I. Barns and R. Schibeci (1997), 'Problematic Publics: A Critical Review of Surveys of Public Attitudes to Biotechnology', *Science, Technology and Human Values*, **22** (3), 317–348.

Dryzek, J. (1990), *Discursive Democracy: Politics, Policy and Political Science*, Cambridge: Cambridge University Press.

Edwardes, C. (1997), *Amendments to the Environmental Protection Act 1986: A Public Discussion Paper*, Perth, Western Australia: Office of the Minister for the Environment.

Fischer, F. (1990), *Technocracy and the Politics of Expertise*, Newbury Park, California: Sage.

Forester, J. (1993), *Critical Theory, Public Policy, and Planning Practice: Toward a Critical Pragmatism*, Albany: State University of New York Press.

Gamble, D. (1978), 'The Berger Inquiry: An Impact Assessment Process', *Science*, **199**, 946–952.

Gutmann, A. and D. Thompson (1995), 'Moral Disagreement in a Democracy', in P. Frankel, F. Miller and J. Paul (eds), *Contemporary Political and Social Philosophy*, Cambridge, New York and Melbourne: Cambridge University Press.

Habermas, J. (1981), *The Theory of Communicative Action*, Cambridge: Polity Press.

Hayward, B. (1995), 'The Greening of Participatory Democracy: A Reconsideration of Theory', *Environmental Politics*, **4** (4), 215–236.

Healey, P. (1997), *Collaborative Planning: Shaping Plans in Fragmented Societies*, Basingstoke: Macmillan.

Hirst, P. (1996), 'Democracy and Civil Society', in P. Hirst and S. Khilnani (eds), *Reinventing Democracy*, Oxford: The Political Quarterly Publishing, pp. 97–116.

Kuper, R. (1997), 'Deliberating Waste: The Hertfordshire Citizens' Jury', *Local Environment*, **2** (2), 139–153.

Lawrence, D. (1997), 'The Need for EIA Theory-Building', *Environmental Impact Assessment Review*, **17**, 79–107.

Marsh, I. (1995), *Beyond the Two Party System: Political Representation, Economic Competitiveness and Australian Politics*, New York: Cambridge University Press.

Miller, D. (1992), 'Deliberative Democracy and Social Choice', *Political Studies Special Issue: Prospects for Democracy*, **40**, 54–67.

Ortolano, L. and A. Shepherd (1995), 'Environmental Impact Assessment', in F. Vanclay and D. Bronstein (eds), *Environmental and Social Impact Assessment*, Chichester, New York, Brisbane, Toronto and Singapore: John Wiley and Sons, pp. 3–30.

Parker, J. (1995), 'Enabling Morally Reflective Communities: Towards a Resolution of the Democratic Dilemma of Environmental Values in Policy', in Y. Guerrier, N. Alexander, J. Chase and M. O'Brien (eds), *Values and the Environment: A Social Science Perspective*, Chichester, New York, Brisbane, Toronto and Singapore: John Wiley and Sons, pp. 33–50.

Poisner, J. (1996), 'A Civic Republican Perspective on the National Environmental Policy Act's Process for Citizen Participation', *Environmental Law*, **26**, 53–94.

Renn, O., T. Webler and P. Wiedemann (1995), *Fairness and Competence in Citizen Participation: Evaluating Models for Environmental Discourse*, Dordrecht, Boston and London: Kluwer Academic Publishers.

Rip, A., T. Misa and J. Schot (eds) (1995), *Managing Technology in Society: The Approach of Constructive Technology Assessment*, London: Pinter.

Sagoff, M. (1988), *The Economy of the Earth*, Cambridge: Cambridge Univerity Press.

Stewart, J., E. Kendall and A. Coote (1994), *Citizens' Juries*, London: Institute of Public Policy Research.

Szerszynski, B., S. Lash and B. Wynne (1996), 'Introduction: Ecology, Realism and the Social Sciences', in S. Lash, B. Szerszynski and B. Wynne (eds), *Risk, Environment and Modernity: Towards a New Ecology*, London: Sage, pp. 1–26.

Tatum, J. (1995), 'Social and Philosophical Constructions of Technology', *Research in Philosophy and Technology*, **15**, 103–115.

Torgerson, D. (1986), 'Between Knowledge and Politics: Three Faces of Policy Analysis', *Policy Sciences*, **19**, 33–59.

Warren, M. (1996), 'What Should We Expect from More Democracy?', *Political Theory*, **24** (2), 241–270.

Winner, L. (1986), *The Whale and the Reactor: A Search for Limits in an Age of High Technology*, Chicago: University of Chicago Press.

Winner, L. (1993), 'Citizen Virtues in a Technological Order', *Inquiry* **35**, 341–361.

Wood, C. and J. Bailey (1994), 'Predominance and Independence in Environmental Impact Assessment: The Western Australian Model', *Environmental Impact Assessment Review*, **14**, 37–59.

Wynne, B. (1992), 'Risk and Social Learning: Reification to Engagement', in S. Krimsky and D. Golding (eds), *Social Theories of Risk*, Westport, Connecticut and London: Praeger.

Yeatman, A. (1987), 'The Concept of Public Management and the Australian State in the 1980s', *Australian Journal of Public Administration*, **XLVI** (4), 339–352.

Yeatman, A. (1998), 'Trends and Opportunities in the Public Sector: A Critical Assessment', *Australian Journal of Public Administration*, **57** (4), 138–147.
Young, I. (1992) 'Communication and the Other: Beyond Deliberative Democracy', in C. Mouffe (ed.), *Dimensions of Radical Democracy: Pluralism, Citizenship, Community*, London: Verso, pp. 134–152.

8. Science and Advocacy in Natural Resource Management: Boundary-Work in Environmental Disputes

Emma Jakku

INTRODUCTION

When studying natural resource management it is crucial to place the scientific component of this process in its broader social and political context (Harding, 1998). Buttel and Taylor (1992, p. 214) highlight the significance of this when they argue that the 'construction of environmental issues is as much or more a matter of the social construction and politics of knowledge as it is a straightforward reflection of biophysical reality'.

Examining the social processes by which scientific knowledge is produced and drawn on as a source of authority in conflict situations has been a central theme within environmental sociology and the sociology of science (Jasanoff, 1990; Wynne, 1992). It is within this theoretical space that concepts such as social constructionism and 'boundary-work' have much to offer. The special authority that is often granted to scientific knowledge, and the way that scientists seek to maintain their role as legitimate interpreters of the natural world, are key themes within the social constructionist perspective on boundary-work (Gieryn, 1999; Moore, 1996). One boundary that has been explored within the literature is the demarcation between science and other forms of cognitive authority (Jasanoff, 1990). However, far little attention has been devoted to the boundary-work between science and advocacy. This relatively under-researched area of boundary-work was the focus of an earlier study upon which this chapter is based (Jakku, 1998).

The aim of this chapter is to analyse the ways in which scientists in a dispute over natural resource management negotiated the boundaries between science and advocacy. After a brief discussion of the term advocacy, the theory of social constructionism and the concept of boundary-work will be outlined. Some brief background information on the case study and research methodology will then be offered before moving onto a broad overview of the study's main findings.

SCIENCE AND ADVOCACY IN ENVIRONMENTAL DISPUTES

A review of the pertinent literature demonstrates tensions between science and advocacy. This literature clearly indicates the place of advocacy in discourses surrounding the involvement of scientists in particular environmental disputes. Some scientists argue that advocacy undermines the objectivity of science and results in 'bad science'. For instance, in the proceedings of a conference on science and natural resource management in the Great Barrier Reef, Cullen (1997, p. 9) describes 'advocacy science' as 'a prostitution of science that does not contribute to wise solutions of problems, nor to the professional standing of science'. Similarly, Wiens (1997, p. 2) associates the effect of advocacy on science with 'pathological science'. Pitelka and Raynal (1989) raise similar themes in their discussion of the roles of science and scientists in the environmental problems of acid rain and forest decline in Europe and North America.

Others argue that advocacy can be facilitated by scientists maintaining their 'neutral' position. This point is developed in Salzman's (1995) study of the controversy over gill netting in central California. In this case, the Point Reynes Bird Observatory (PRBO), a local scientific organisation, is presented as a study of the ways in which a scientific organisation can be involved in 'successful advocacy'. For Salzman (p. 35), the key to the PRBO's success was its 'ability to maintain an objective position in the eyes of the participants'. According to Salzman (1995, p. 37) this is because the PRBO's approach was one of 'focused advocacy', which he defines as 'reporting data and pressing to insure that the information is interpreted correctly and acted upon'.

In this study, the term advocacy is used to refer to adopting a position on an issue, and working towards achieving a particular outcome with respect to that issue. This is a starting point to explore the diversity of meanings given to the concept of advocacy. The next section develops a theoretical framework for analysing these various understandings of the relationship between science and advocacy.

BOUNDARY-WORK: A SOCIAL CONSTRUCTIONIST FRAMEWORK

Studies at the interface between the sociology of science and environmental sociology have highlighted the ways in which environmental disputes 'throw issues about science and scientific knowledge into particularly sharp relief' (Yearley, 1995, p. 478). Social constructionism has been a key theme for many studies within this area (Barnes et al., 1996; Yearley, 1995), and is the underlying approach of this chapter.

Social Constructionism and the Sociology of Science

Four key elements of social constructionism are: a critical stance towards taken-for-granted knowledge, an emphasis on the historical and cultural specificity of knowledge, a recognition of the importance of social processes and interaction for the construction of knowledge, and an understanding of the link between knowledge and social action (Burr, 1995). Combined, these assumptions highlight the importance of meaning, interaction, values and beliefs (May, 1996). Knowledge is viewed as the product of social relations, dependent upon and negotiated in social and historical settings by people trying to make sense of the world (Gergen, 1985; Lupton, 1994; Sarbin and Kitsuse, 1994).

A social constructionist perspective questions many taken-for-granted assumptions about science. In abandoning the notion of science as a straightforward representation of objective reality, the social constructionist approach has opted for 'a closer inquiry into the social processes by which scientific knowledge is produced or "constructed"' (Jasanoff, 1990, p. 12). The underlying assumption here is that the production of science and technology is a social process (Hess, 1995). This means that science is not seen to be directly given by nature, but rather is the product of a web of conventions, practices, social relations, understandings and negotiations which mediate scientists' accounts of the natural world and their evaluation of the technical evidence (Martin and Richards, 1995; Wynne, 1995; Yearley, 1988). Rather than seeing science as a single and authoritative account of the world, the sociology of science emphasises the diverse and heterogeneous nature of both the knowledge and institutions of science (Irwin, 1995).

The social constructionist approach to science also highlights the contextualised nature of scientific knowledge claims and their implementation. A central argument here is that 'perceptions of scientific "reality" are always influenced by contextual factors such as the scientists' professional, institutional, political, and cultural affiliations' (Jasanoff, 1990, p. 37). Thus, a key task for social constructionist studies of science is to carefully investigate particular sciences and their relations with surrounding social contexts (Irwin, 1995; MacKenzie, 1981). Furthermore, social constructionists emphasise the lack of demarcation between science and non-science (Buttel and Taylor, 1992). This issue of demarcation underlies the concept of 'boundary-work'.

Boundary-Work

One of the key distinctions that can be made among theoretical approaches to science is that between essentialist and constructionist perspectives (Gieryn, 1995). The issue of demarcation has been a central concern in philosophical analyses of science, and in some sociological approaches as well. According to Woolgar (1988), the question here is what is it about science that distinguishes it from other activities and makes it a more reliable form of knowledge? For instance, Popper's criterion of demarcation was falsification, while Merton's ([1942] 1973) account used the scientific community's normative structure to distinguish science from non-science (see Gieryn, 1983). However, Gieryn (1995) describes these approaches as essentialist, because they attempt to identify unique, essential and invariant features of science that set it apart from other cultural practices. In contrast, the social constructionist perspective on boundary-work treats the issue of demarcating science from other intellectual activities as a practical problem for scientists and other stakeholders in credibility contests (Gieryn, 1983, 1999). Rather than defining science in terms of trying to answer the question 'What is science?', the focus of the social constructionist approach shifts to examining how (and sometimes why) the boundaries of science are drawn, defended and reinforced in particular contexts (Cozzens and Gieryn, 1990; Moore, 1996).

The theory of boundary-work is a sub-topic of the social constructionist perspective on science. Boundary-work is a useful conceptual tool when analysing the authority of science and the role of science as an arbiter in environmental disputes. Central to the idea of boundary-work is the tension between the argument on the one hand that science is socially constructed, and the recognition on the other that science is nonetheless successful in maintaining significant authority (Gieryn, 1995; Jasanoff, 1990).

This approach highlights the negotiated character of science, seeing the separation between science and non-science as a 'contextually contingent and interest-driven pragmatic accomplishment' (Gieryn, 1995, p. 393).

Boundary-work is thus understood as a strategy through which diverse interests 'contend for, legitimate, or challenge' the authority of science and the 'credibility, prestige, power, and material resources that attend such a privileged position' (Gieryn, 1995, pp. 405, 436). The social constructionist perspective that underpins the theory of boundary-work recognises that the way science is constructed will depend upon the players and stakeholders involved in each dispute over the territory of science. Since boundary-work is understood as a strategic and practical action, it is important to examine how various social groups, each with competing goals and interests, attempt to draw the borders of science in ways that further these goals and interests.

Also, it is crucial to be sensitive of the way that boundary-work occurs in a variety of institutional settings, since different contexts will create different forms of boundary-work (Gieryn, 1999).

Examining science as a cultural space and analysing the way that the borders and territories of science are contested involves a focus on actors' understandings of their social world. The boundary-work perspective also adds a better understanding of the diversity of meanings that are attributed to 'science'.

THE PROPOSED MAGNETIC KEYS MARINA DEVELOPMENT

The controversial Magnetic Keys marina development was to be constructed at Nelly Bay, Magnetic Island, which is located 8 km north of Townsville, within the Central Section of the Great Barrier Reef Marine Park, in North Queensland, Australia (see Figure 8.1). Nelly Bay is a residential community on the south east of Magnetic Island (Bugler, 1991).

A development lease for the proposed marina was taken out in 1983. The concept originally included a 239-room hotel and 16 home units on the 1.8 hectares of freehold land at Bright Point, initially owned by Magnetic Keys Limited. A further 29.8 hectares of Crown leasehold land were proposed as the site of a commercial centre of shops, restaurants and commercial premises, along with a holiday village, backpackers' accommodation, resort apartments, home units, a sports centre and tavern (Whitehouse, 1992). Within the Great Barrier Reef Marine Park, the proposed project involved the excavation of a marina basin, the construction of break walls and the excavation of an access channel to the marina (Whitehouse, 1992).

Subsequently, the project was handled by a number of developers and an assessment process which stretched over four years, including at least five separate environmental assessments under both State and Commonwealth legislation (Inglis, 1997). Finally, on the 28 October 1988 a permit was issued to Magnetic Keys Pty Ltd, allowing construction of the marina and associated infrastructure in Nelly Bay. After a series of appeals and stoppages, site works ceased in December 1990 when the developer went into receivership. In 1993, expressions of interest were sought from private developers to complete the project. Another draft Environmental Impact Statement (EIS) for a smaller residential and marina development was prepared in 1995 and a supplementary EIS was released in October 1997.

With the final EIS released in March 1999 and the Queensland Environmental Protection Agency and Environment Australia due to complete a joint assessment report in late 1999, a decision on the future of the site is expected to occur sometime in 2000.

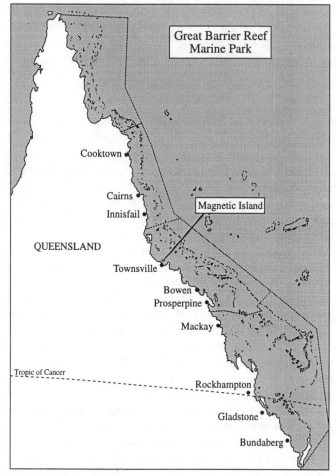

Source: Whitehouse (1992).

Figure 8.1   Location Map for Magnetic Keys

Major Issues in the Magnetic Keys Dispute

From its inception, the proposed marina development was controversial, with some local residents strongly opposing the development and others strongly in favour. An important part of the controversy was conflict over the potential impact on the natural environment of Nelly Bay. Of particular concern were Nelly Bay's fringing reef and adjacent coral reef areas. Other issues related to the risk of localised water pollution, and whether it was acceptable to use Bright Point to provide rock for the breakwaters and a site for a resort hotel (Bugler, 1991; Inglis, 1997).

The Great Barrier Reef Marine Park Authority's (GBRMPA) decision to issue a permit for the marina proposal was challenged in the Administrative Appeals Tribunal,[1] and Whitehouse (1992) carried out an independent review for the Commonwealth government. Whether the GBRMPA had properly considered the environmental effects of the marina and whether suitable management strategies were in place to mitigate these impacts framed the core of the objections. Debate over the issuance of the permit tended to concentrate on the adequacy of biological information in the Public Environment Reports (Inglis, 1997).

Local concern about the transformation of the community centred on the question of what constituted an appropriate level of development for Nelly Bay. There were differing views on whether the potential socioeconomic impacts would be largely positive or negative, and whether private development on a public beach was appropriate. There were a number of additional concerns as well: visual quality and amenity issues, town planning aspects of the proposal, changes to the character of Nelly Bay and the lifestyle of Nelly Bay residents and whether there was a need for a safe harbour (Bugler, 1991; Senate Standing Committee on the Environment, Recreation and the Arts, 1992; Whitehouse, 1992).

METHODOLOGY

This study of the Magnetic Keys dispute was designed as a qualitative analysis, with the aim of collecting a substantial amount of 'rich' data to explore in detail how scientists viewed and dealt with the relationship between science and advocacy.[2] The major data collection method was a case study approach. Using the Magnetic Keys dispute as a case study enabled the exploration of substantive instances of the ways in which different groups perceived and dealt with the tensions between science and advocacy in this particular controversy. Qualitative in-depth interviews were held with 26 people involved in the Magnetic Keys project.

As Table 8.1 shows, the main group in this sample was scientists, situated both on the 'inside' and 'outside' of the formal scientific work involved in the environmental assessment of the marina development. While the main focus was the analysis of scientists' perspectives on the issues, qualitative data were collected from interviews with a variety of key players in the

Magnetic Keys dispute, with the aim of ensuring that the varying perspectives in the debate were represented. The interviews were semi-structured and, except for one interview by email, all were taped (with participants' consent) and later transcribed. Thematic analysis was used to analyse the data.

Table 8.1   Outline of Participants

Category	Number of participants
'Insider' scientists[a]	12
'Outsider' scientists[b]	5
Environmental managers[c]	4
Residents/conservationists opposed to Magnetic Keys[d]	4
Residents/developers supporting Magnetic Keys	1

Notes:
a   Scientists and one engineer involved in different aspects of the scientific work used for the environmental assessment of the Magnetic Keys development.
b   Scientists involved in the Magnetic Keys dispute outside of the formal scientific assessment process.
c   Great Barrier Reef Marine Park Authority staff who held environmental management positions throughout the Magnetic Keys dispute, as well as one scientist who was employed by the Marine Park Authority at that time.
d   Members of Island Voice, the community group formed by residents and conservationists opposed to the Magnetic Keys development.

BOUNDARY-WORK IN THE MAGNETIC KEYS DISPUTE: NEGOTIATING THE LINE BETWEEN SCIENCE AND ADVOCACY

The relationship between science and advocacy in environmental disputes leads to many instances of boundary-work. The metaphor of 'the boundary' in relation to science and advocacy, and the need for caution when dealing with the line between science and advocacy, were recurring themes throughout the interviews. Adrian ('insider' scientist)[3] expressed concern about scientists 'moving outside the bounds' of their 'mandate', while Brad ('outsider' scientist/resident opposed) referred to walking 'a very fine line' in terms of science and advocacy. Comments such as these implicitly highlight the importance of boundary-work in environmental disputes. However, respondents differed about where the line between science and advocacy could be drawn, and if it could be drawn at all. For instance, Mark ('outsider' scientist/conservationist) also used the idea of boundary-work quite explicitly, although his comments highlight the way that some scientists are less concerned about maintaining a strict boundary between science and advocacy. Here in relation to the boundaries between different scientific disciplines, he argued that

> all of these areas of artificial boundaries between things are nonsense and . . . in fact it was . . . one of my examiners [laughs] . . . who was warning me that I would come up against the 'boundary riders' of the discipline. And I have, I've spent my life coming up against the boundary riders of particular disciplines and so on, and I just think we need to think much more broadly.

Mark also used the idea of boundary-work quite explicitly when discussing the relationship between science and advocacy:

> some scientists feel that once you go into advocacy you cross some kind of Rubicon and it's not science any more, it's naughty. I don't actually conceive it like that at all . . . I think it's critical to get out there . . . If people can do that well, I think it's very valuable . . . And I disagree totally with people who say this is all the profession actually is, this core . . . and people outside are actually not scientists but [hand action and laughs]. Have you got that bit?

While Mark refers to the way in which some scientists see science and advocacy as divided by a strict boundary, he rejects this approach. Instead, Mark's approach illustrates how some scientists attempt to redefine the boundaries of science, expanding what it means to be a scientist.

Nevertheless, other players in the Magnetic Keys dispute adopted a different approach to boundary-work. For instance, other scientists took the notion of a boundary more seriously. The next sections will highlight some of the different versions of boundary-work that were evident in the case study. For instance, the depiction of scientists as independent information providers was a recurring theme throughout the interviews. Adam ('insider' scientist) emphasised on numerous occasions that his role in the Magnetic Keys project was one of 'providing information'. He stressed that there was 'an onus on researchers' to make sure that they 'provide the information as honestly, and independently and unbiasedly as possible'. Many of the other 'insider' scientists also characterised their role in this way. For example, Adrian said that his role in the Magnetic Keys project was to 'provide quality information on what was actually happening', while Ian pointed out that 'we were meant to be "impartial" fact-finders'.

Disputed Territory: Scientists and Independence

The above comments portraying the role of scientists as providers of independent information underline how the disinterestedness of scientists is often seen as vital to their credibility (Barnes and Edge, 1982). This has important implications for the perceived authority of science in environmental disputes, since, as Irwin (1995, pp. 27–28) points out, one of the key issues in the 'disputed territory over expertise' is whether or not the information offered is biased. Moore's study of scientists involved in 'public interest' issues reinforces the significance of this by showing how scientists' 'political and professional legitimacy depends on a widely accepted vision of nonpartisanship' (1996, p. 1616). Therefore, an important form of boundary-work in the Magnetic Keys project centred on either defending or undermining the role of 'insider' scientists as independent information providers.

All the 'insider' scientists presented their role as providers of independent information. Paul articulated this in the following way:

> as I explained to the various people from both sides of the fence who came and shrieked at me during this debate, the position I'm in now is to try and deliver you with sort of reasonably unbiased and unambiguous information, and the advocates on each side can use that as they see fit, but if they start misusing that, then I'll jump up and down.

Paul's comment reinforces the notion that one way scientists negotiate the tensions involved in applied settings is to 'stick to the provision of "facts"' (Moore, 1996, p. 1616). This idea of providing the 'reasonably unbiased' information to the different parties in environmental disputes is a key way that scientists defend their image as providers of independent information.

While there was unanimous agreement that an important role for scientists was that of independent information providers, there were a range of views as to whether this was the actual role that scientists played in the Magnetic Keys dispute. As Gieryn (1995, p. 436) points out, 'the "social construction" of the science/politics border is a crucial strategy through which distinctive interests of diverse players are advanced or thwarted'. In contrast to how the 'insider' scientists portrayed their role, Ben (resident/developer) saw the scientists as being manipulated by the conservationists. Similarly, from the opposite perspective, the conservationists and some of the 'outsider' scientists saw the scientists as merely saying what the developers wanted them to. The environmental managers saw themselves as being in the middle of all this and, among other things, having to juggle what the scientists had to say with how other groups perceived the issues and the roles of the scientists. These different views highlight the way that 'the recognition of technical expertise . . . is fraught with political significance' (Barnes and Edge, 1982, p. 9). This is an important link to the next section, which explores how the idea of being independent information providers relates to the issue of advocacy.

DISTANCING SCIENCE AND ADVOCACY

Moore (1996, p. 1620) argues that the source of scientists' 'real political utility' is their 'claim that scientific evidence is untainted by political interests'. For scientists keen to be seen as independent, the dangers of being politically tainted by adopting an advocacy role are very apparent. One way that the scientists interviewed dealt with this issue was to emphasise the need for scientists to distance themselves from advocacy. The following comment by Adam ('insider' scientist) clearly illustrates this theme: 'given the role that we had as essentially information providers in that context, we sought to distance ourselves as much as possible from the proponents and the opponents'.

This attempt to distance their science from the political positions of other groups was the key to the 'insider' scientists' boundary-work in the Magnetic Keys dispute. Adam later explained the importance of this, commenting that if he entered an environmental dispute advocating the position of the proponents, or the management agency, or the environmental group 'then essentially I think that I will pretty much exclude myself from the role of information provider in any sense in an independent way in the future, because at least two out of those three groups will probably write me off as being completely biased'.

Other scientists interviewed agreed that advocacy was something that scientists should strive to avoid, with many of them quick to point out the 'dangers' associated with adopting an advocacy role.

Tainted Science: Scientists and the Tensions Between Objectivity and Subjectivity

Objectivity and value-neutrality are central to what Irwin (1995, p. 47) refers to as the '"enlightenment" view of science'. These are key terms in long-standing debates over the culture of science (Proctor, 1991). The issue of objectivity underlies the view that science and advocacy must be kept separate. James (environmental manager) commented that if scientists 'adopt an advocacy role they can no longer perform as scientists. They're not seen as objective any more.' Takacs (1996) interviewed conservation biologists and found that the tension between objectivity and subjectivity was a very important issue. He interpreted this as a concern that if the 'values informing their work or advocacy are revealed, then some may question scientists' status as objective arbiters in societal or environmental debates' (Takacs, 1996, p. 166). In this study, Paul ('insider' scientist) reinforced this notion by remarking that if scientists 'become an advocate at the same time for more general causes' they 'taint . . . the objectivity of the scientific evidence'.

The fear that science could be 'tainted' by advocacy highlights what Gieryn (1995, p. 436) describes as the need for scientists 'to keep the fence on their "politics" frontier well mended'.

Such a statement support Gieryn's (1995, p. 436) argument that an important element of scientific input into environmental decision making is 'its putative objectivity or neutrality'. Awareness of the political significance of objectivity explains why many of the scientists were emphatic about keeping science and advocacy separate. However, many 'outsider' scientists represent the exceptions to this approach and are discussed in the next section.

Linking Objectivity, Science and Advocacy

Another form of boundary-work involved arguing that objectivity, science and advocacy are *not* mutually exclusive. This was especially significant for the 'outsider' scientists who were attempting to maintain their role as independent information providers. For instance, Jason described his role in the Magnetic Keys dispute as follows: 'It's interesting actually. I wanted to come in as the objective scientist, but I ended up being brought in by the local conservation group. And I still tried to maintain the role as the independent scientist in my testimony.'

He later expanded on this theme by commenting that 'you can be an advocate for something on entirely objective grounds . . . that's not necessary advocacy, but it's putting the cards on the table in ways that people can understand'.

Similarly, Tom, another 'outsider' scientist who donated his expertise to one of the conservation groups, emphasised that 'I had no qualms about was I being an objective scientist, I felt certainly I was.' Like Jason, Tom argued that 'while I'm acting as an advocate . . . my opinion that I give is still an objective and professional opinion, that might not otherwise be put on the table if I wasn't willing to do that'.

Here, the boundaries of objectivity, science and advocacy are merged. Jasanoff's (1995, p. xv) point that the boundaries of science are 'highly contested' and 'negotiable' was thus apparent in the Magnetic Keys dispute. Not only was the defence of the demarcation between objectivity, science and advocacy clearly manifest, but the boundaries themselves were negotiated and redrawn in sophisticated forms of boundary-work. Moore's (1996) study of public interest science organisations is particularly relevant here. Just as Jason and Tom dealt with their role as 'outsider' scientists by linking objectivity, science and advocacy, Moore found that controversy over scientists' obligations regarding public interest issues involves complicated forms of boundary-work. Moore (1996, p. 1593) argues such boundary-work is important for scientists who seek to 'maintain credibility simultaneously as objective scientists and as political actors serving the public good'.

CONCLUSION

The boundary-work that was involved in the Magnetic Keys controversy highlights how the political significance of being seen as independent is crucial for many scientists. This explains their caution about becoming involved in advocacy. Thus, maintaining a separation between science and advocacy is an important part of scientists' boundary-work. The creation of such boundaries is often vital to both the political acceptability of scientific advice and to scientists' professional credibility (Jasanoff, 1990; Moore, 1996). This relates to the extent to which the perceived objectivity and neutrality of scientific knowledge is central to scientists' role as independent information providers in natural resource management (Gieryn, 1995). In order to maintain their position as experts, scientists engage in boundary-work to convince various parties of the unique and distinctive features of science (Moore, 1996). This is especially important in politically contentious areas, because scientists' role in environmental disputes is reduced if they are seen as just another interest group (Gieryn, 1995). Thus, the authority of scientific expertise is based on the assumption that it should be untainted by political bias.

Boundary-work is understood as a strategy used by diverse interests to affirm, compete for, or question the authority accorded to scientific expertise. Crucial to this are the ways in which scientists protect the borders constructed around science and advocacy, demarcating science from non-science in the process and thus maintaining traditional images of scientific rationality and independence. Furthermore, conflict among different parties over the boundaries of science is an important element of environmental disputes. Negotiating the boundaries between science and advocacy is therefore a shared problem for the various scientists involved in environmental disputes such as the one surrounding the Magnetic Keys development.

The contextualised nature of boundary-work highlights the importance of a need to be reflective about the use of this theory as a framework for analysing environmental disputes. When using the idea of boundary-work, it is important not to reify or dehumanise the concepts being studied. As suggested above, scientists in different situations dealt with the boundaries between science and advocacy in a variety of ways. It is therefore vital to understand how science and advocacy have different meanings and implications depending on the social context in which scientists dealing with them exist.

The notion of boundary-work provides a conceptual link to help understand how different scientists construct and defend their identities in environmental disputes. Analysing the boundary-work involved in how different groups in the Magnetic Keys dispute maintained, shifted or challenged the boundaries between science and advocacy suggests that these boundaries are socially constructed, and that their contested nature is a significant part of such controversies.

ACKNOWLEDGEMENTS

I would like to thank Dr Jan Elder, Associate Professor David Burch, Professor Roy Rickson, and Dr Sally Rickson as well as members of the PhD discussion group, for their comments and support.

NOTES

1. The Administrative Appeals Tribunal is defined by the Administrative Review Council (1987, p. 3) as 'a general appeals tribunal capable of reviewing on their merits decisions taken under Commonwealth legislation by decision makers of almost any status'. Island Voice (the resident's group opposed to the development) initiated an action in the Administrative Appeals Tribunal against the Great Barrier Reef Marine Park Authority's decision to affirm the permit issued to Magnetic Keys. Although preliminary hearings were held in October 1989, Island Voice withdrew its appeal in March 1990 when the hearing was brought forward and moved to Brisbane (Whitehouse, 1992).
2. By 'rich' data, I am referring to what Maxwell (1996, p. 95) describes as data that are 'detailed and complete', such as verbatim transcripts of interviews. The aim is to build a 'full and revealing picture of what is going on'. In doing so, Maxwell argues that using rich data is one way to address issues of validity for qualitative research.
3. All names have been changed to ensure anonymity. See Table 8.1 for an outline of the various categories of participants in this study.

REFERENCES

Administrative Review Council (1987), *Report to the Attorney General. Constitution of the Administrative Appeals Tribunal. Report No. 29*, Canberra: Australian Government Publishing Service.
Barnes, B. and D. Edge (eds) (1982), *Science in Context. Readings in the Sociology of Science*, Milton Keynes: Open University Press.

Barnes, B., D. Bloor and J. Henry (1996), *Scientific Knowledge. A Sociological Analysis*, Chicago: University of Chicago Press.

Bugler, M. (1991), *Reasons for Decision of Granting Permit G90/494*, Townsville: Great Barrier Reef Marine Park Authority.

Burr, V. (1995), *An Introduction to Social Constructionism*, London: Routledge.

Buttel, F. and P. Taylor (1992), 'Environmental Sociology and Global Environmental Change: A Critical Assessment', *Society and Natural Resources*, **5**, 211–230.

Cozzens, S. and T. Gieryn (1990), 'Introduction: Putting Science Back in Society', in S. Cozzens and T. Gieryn (eds), *Theories of Science in Society*, Bloomington: Indiana University Press, pp. 1–14.

Cullen, P. (1997), 'Science Brokering and Managing Uncertainty', in *The Great Barrier Reef: Science, Use and Management – People and the Reef*, <http://www.gbrmpa.gov.au/~crcreef/6conference/conference1/volume1/s5_2.htm l>

Gergen, K. (1985), 'The Social Constructionist Movement in Modern Psychology', *American Psychologist*, **40** (3), 266–275.

Gieryn, T. (1983), 'Boundary-work and the Demarcation of Science from Non-science: Strains and Interests in Professional Ideologies of Scientists', *American Sociological Review*, **48**, 781–795.

Gieryn, T. (1995), 'Boundaries of Science', in S. Jasanoff, G. Markle, J. Petersen and T. Pinch (eds), *Handbook of Science and Technology Studies*, Thousand Oaks, London and New Delhi: Sage, pp. 393–443.

Gieryn, T. (1999), *Cultural Boundaries of Science: Credibility on the Line*, Chicago and London: The University of Chicago Press.

Harding, R. (1998), *Environmental Decision-making: the Roles of Scientists, Engineers and the Public*, Sydney: The Federation Press.

Hess, D. (1995), *Science and Technology in a Multicultural world. The Cultural Politics of Facts and Artifacts*, New York: Columbia Press.

Inglis, G. (1997), 'Science and Tourism Infrastructure on the Great Barrier Reef: Learning from Experience or Just "Muddling Through"?', in *The Great Barrier Reef: Science, Use and Management*; <http://www.gbrmpa.gov.au/~crcreef/6conference/conference1/volume1/s5_2.html>

Irwin, A. (1995), *Citizen Science. A Study of People, Expertise and Sustainable Development*, London and New York: Routledge.

Jakku, E. (1998), 'Science and Advocacy in Environmental Disputes: Boundary-work in the Magnetic Keys Marina Development', Honours Thesis, Townsville: School of Psychology and Sociology, James Cook University.

Jasanoff, S. (1990), *The Fifth Branch. Science Advisers as Policymakers*, Cambridge and London: Harvard University Press.

Jasanoff, S. (1995), *Science at the Bar: Law, Science, and Technology in America*, Cambridge and London: Harvard University Press.

Lupton, D. (1994), *Medicine as Culture: Illness, Disease and the Body in Western Societies*, London: Longman.

MacKenzie, D. (1981), *Statistics in Britain 1865–1930. The Social Construction of Scientific Knowledge*, Edinburgh: Edinburgh University Press.

Martin, B. and E. Richards (1995), 'Scientific Knowledge, Controversy, and Public Decision Making', in S. Jasanoff, G. Markle, J. Petersen and T. Pinch (eds), *Handbook of Science and Technology Studies*, Thousand Oaks, London and New Delhi: Sage, pp. 506–525.

May, T. (1996), *Situating Social Theory*, Buckingham, Philadelphia: Open University Press.

Maxwell, J. (1996), *Qualitative Research Design: an Interactive Approach*, London and New Delhi: Thousand Oaks.

Merton, R. ([1942]1973), 'The Normative Structure of Science', in R. Merton and N. Stover (eds), *The Sociology of Science. Theoretical and Empirical Investigations*, Chicago: University of Chicago Press.

Moore, K. (1996), 'Organising Integrity: American Science and the Creation of Public Interest Organisations, 1955–1975', *American Journal of Sociology*, **101** (6), 1592–1627.

Pitelka, L. and D. Raynal (1989), 'Forest Decline and Acidic Deposition', *Ecology*, **70** (1), 2–10.

Proctor, R. (1991), *Value-free Science?: Purity and Power in Modern Knowledge*, Cambridge: Harvard University Press.

Salzman, J. (1995), 'Scientists as Advocates: The Point Reyes Bird Observatory and Gill Netting in Central California', in D. Ehrenfeld (ed.), *Readings from Conservation Biology. The Social Dimension: Ethics, Policy, Law, Management, Development, Economics, Education*, Massachusetts: Blackwell Science and the Society for Conservation Biology, pp. 28–36.

Sarbin, T. and J. Kitsuse (1994), 'A Prologue to Constructing the Social', in T. Sarbin and J. Kitsuse (eds), *Constructing the Social*, London: Sage, pp. 1–18.

Senate Standing Committee on the Environment, Recreation and the Arts (1992), *The Australian Environment and Tourism Report*, Canberra: Commonwealth of Australia.

Takacs, D. (1996), *The Idea of Biodiversity. Philosophies of Paradise*, Baltimore: The Johns Hopkins University Press.

Whitehouse, J. (1992), *Review of the Magnetic Island Marina Development*, Canberra: Australian Government Publishing Service.

Wiens, J. (1997), 'Scientific Responsibility and Responsible Ecology', *Conservation Ecology* [online] **1**(1) 1–3; <http://www.consecol.org/Journal/ vol1/iss1/art16>

Woolgar, S. (1988), *Science: the Very Idea*, Sussex, London and New York: Ellis Horwood Ltd and Tavistock Publications.

Wynne, B. (1992), 'Carving Out Science (and Politics) in the Regulatory Jungle', *Social Studies of Science*, **22**, 745–758.

Wynne, B. (1995), 'Public Understanding of Science', in S. Jasanoff, G. Markle, J. Petersen and T. Pinch (eds), *Handbook of Science and Technology Studies*, Thousand Oaks, London and New Delhi: Sage.

Yearley, S. (1995), 'The Environmental Challenge to Science Studies', in S. Jasanoff, G. Markle, J. Petersen and T. Pinch (eds), *Handbook of Science and Technology Studies*, Thousand Oaks, London and New Delhi: Sage, pp. 457–479.

Yearley, S. (1988), *Science, Technology and Social Change*, London: Unwin Hyman.

9. Resource Community Formation and Change in New Zealand: A Framework for Social Assessment

Nick Taylor, Gerard Fitzgerald and Wayne McClintock

INTRODUCTION

Since the 1980s, there has been ongoing work by social scientists relating to resource communities. Some has been done as basic research – in resource management, geography, planning, sociology, and anthropology. Other work has been more commercial and applied, particularly social assessments of proposals for resource developments by private firms. There has even been an interest in wind-downs and closures, most often from employment and community development agencies, local government and community groups. For the most part, the lines between basic research and applied and commercial work have been artificial – and between the two sources we find ourselves with a body of information and knowledge about communities and resource sectors that can be drawn upon for social assessments. This body of knowledge is, however, incomplete. Most importantly for social assessment, there has been only limited longitudinal research and some development of broad conceptual frameworks for understanding the processes of community formation and change.

There is therefore a need to develop the conceptual basis for social assessment, especially in relation to the notion of 'community'. Despite many different sociological perspectives on community, and applications that vary from the ideological to the practical, it remains a key analytical focus for sociology (Wilkinson, 1991) and for social assessment (Taylor et al., 1995). It also continues to be an important, yet sometimes carelessly-defined, level of organisation for social and economic development and social action. An understanding of community, of the types of social groupings and relationships that operate, and the dynamics of change brought about by internal and external factors, is essential to social assessment. Such knowledge is typically applied in comparative analysis for the projection of effects, and is integral to the social assessment process, including public consultation and participation (Burdge, 1998; Taylor et al., 1995).

The research programme reported in this chapter has been funded by the New Zealand Foundation for Research Science and Technology over a four-year period since 1996.[1] The aim has been to provide baseline data and an understanding of community formation and change in rural New Zealand. The focus of the research is on communities that depend on the primary production or processing of natural resources. These we refer to as resource communities (Taylor and Fitzgerald, 1988). It is intended that the programme should assist social assessment and planning for sustainable development in New Zealand through increased knowledge and understanding of the processes of social change in communities that depend directly on the primary production or processing of natural resources.

The findings will be applied to the development of natural resources policies and plans, and the assessment, monitoring and evaluation of resource consent applications as required under the New Zealand Resource Management Act, 1991 (RMA). The research is providing a better appreciation of sustainability issues, and the relationship between people and communities and their natural resource base – as recognised in the RMA. Central and local government and private sector providers will be able to apply the results in their planning and implementation of social services for communities. Social assessment practitioners and social researchers will benefit from substantive baseline information for future social assessments in the case study areas, as well as an improved understanding of the processes of community formation and change in these types of communities.

In this chapter we examine how the resource communities framework has developed through previous research. The methodology of the research is presented briefly, followed by key findings from the community case studies and comparative analysis of a wide range of communities from different resource sectors. The findings point to clear cycles of growth and decline in employment and population, and some common patterns, including persistent periods of relative economic disadvantage. The conceptual framework is then refined to emphasise the importance of locality within wider mosaics of social and economic relationships and linkages.

THE RESOURCE COMMUNITIES FRAMEWORK

The present research into resource community formation and change in New Zealand has developed since the early 1980s. There had of course been relevant previous community studies, such as the farming community of Oxford (Somerset, 1974 – first published in 1938), the hydroelectricity construction town of Roxbrough (Burch, 1969) and the pulp and paper towns of Tokoroa (Chapple, 1976) and Kawerau (James, 1979). Then, in the early 1980s, Taylor and colleagues at the Centre for Resource Management[2] undertook a series of case study analyses of the characteristics of resource communities – including hydroelectricity construction towns (Taylor and Bettesworth, 1983), forestry communities (McClintock and Taylor, 1983) and farming communities (Taylor and Abrahamson, 1987). This work fed into a series of papers covering broad concerns for social research and resource planning, including rapid population growth in rural areas (Taylor and McClintock, 1985). Some of this work was commissioned by state agencies responsible for central planning and development,[3] and was used to advocate for anticipatory and proactive social impact assessment (Conland, 1985).

A paper by Taylor and McClintock (1984) synthesised conceptual developments, looking in particular at communities involved in the first stages of exploitation of natural resources – the planning and development stage. At the time, NZ was in the throes of a national development strategy (dubbed 'Think Big') – with large-scale developments occurring in energy, petrochemicals and metal processing. The paper noted that the kinds of social changes that attended large scale developments in rural areas had not been adequately documented in NZ, and needed to be understood in a regional context, and in the terms of those people affected by the changes. The intention was to develop a model for analysing boom towns and their host regions. Drawing on development and world systems theory (Wallerstein, 1979), the paper noted how resource development decision making, and the economic benefits from developments, are centralised while the negative impacts of changes and the social costs arising from the developments are substantially borne by the regions and communities in which the resource development activities are located. The previous lack of regional level analysis could itself be understood because planning and research tended to be controlled from the centre, and focused on national benefits.

In terms of shaping communities, the paper by Taylor and McClintock noted the key influences of, and close alliance between, the interests of multinational capital and the state in resource development, the role of technological change (and imported technology) and its influence on work and its organisation, and the power of the corporates to restructure local society. These interacting, extra-local influences, when focused on resource exploitation, bring changes to regional and local communities and their physical environments which are not anticipated or always welcomed. Conflicts result. The writers argued that understanding the changes at a regional level, and the forces behind them, 'can be used to help in the negotiation of outcomes from any new project or industrial restructuring' – that is, it has strategic value (Taylor and McClintock, 1984, p. 389).

In tandem with this work, an increasing number of social impact assessments were being carried out by social scientists on individual, large-scale developments – including hydroelectricity dams, petrochemical developments, coal and gold mining and processing, forest production and processing, and agricultural development. These assessments provided a further body of community studies and a basis for examining the responses of communities and agencies to rapid social change, including 'wind-downs' resulting from the conclusion of construction work and reduction in workforces. Research on resource communities, experience in social impact assessment in individual communities, and experience in monitoring and managing change, were drawn together in a number of publications (for example, Conland, 1985). This represented a collective effort by researchers, social assessment practitioners, planners and policy analysts working under the banner of the Social Impact Working Group. The observed similarity of the social changes associated with different resource developments, and similar experiences in countries such as Australia, fed into social impact assessment theory and practice (Taylor et al., 1995).

An overview of NZ experience and conceptual development in relation to resource communities, one which sought to move from a 'boom-town' model to a resource community model, was provided by Taylor and Fitzgerald (1988). By the late 1980s the projects of the 'think big' era were over and resource communities had experienced project wind-downs and their social effects. Also, under the banner of the new right, the central government had embarked on deregulating the economy and reducing the size of the state (shedding its direct involvement in resource ownership and development and restructuring social services). Social scientists and planners were grappling with how to deal with the effects of these wind-downs and closures.

Taylor and Fitzgerald (1988) expanded on critiques of the 'boom-town' model by writers such as Wilkinson et al. (1982) and advocated linking social research and the results of individual social assessments to natural resource policy. They noted the need to draw on historical and environmental analysis and to compare individual cases of change in resource communities, arguing that similar patterns of social change arise at different times, places and in different social economic and cultural environments for different projects. The central element of this framework was therefore the proposition, based on analyses of New Zealand resource communities and overseas experience (see Wenner, 1984), that the circumstances of resource communities are typically cyclical (Figure 9.1). Integrated natural resource policy – away from sector specific approaches – was advocated along with the strategic utility of social assessment in policy and planning.

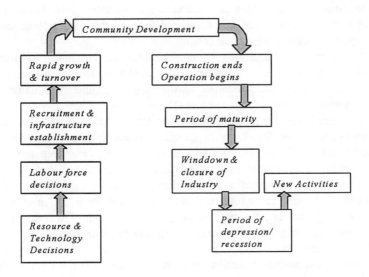

Figure 9.1   The Resource Community Cycle

In the early 1990s there were few resources to systematically pursue the question of resource communities on a broad research front, although substantial work has been done on aspects of tourism and farming. However, social assessment work has continued to stimulate and feed into thinking about resource communities (see Taylor et al., 1995) including assessments as part of resource consent applications in tourism, forestry and mining developments. The current study therefore builds on an extensive base of data and conceptual development.

METHODOLOGY

Tykkylainen and Neil (1995, p. 31) emphasise the need for a comparative approach for an analysis of the restructuring of resource communities and this approach has been the principal feature of the study. In the first phase, in 1996–98, the research examined community formation and change in the three sectors of forestry, mining and agriculture. In the current phase of work (1998–2000) the sectors of fishing, energy and tourism are being examined. In each phase there have been four major sets of tasks:

- documented experiences of resource communities in New Zealand and overseas were reviewed and compared for evidence and explanations of cycles of social and economic change;
- the international and New Zealand contexts for community formation and change in each of the six resource sectors, including processes such as capital formation, the role of the state, technological change and commodity price cycles;
- communities in the resource sectors were selected (58 in total across the six sectors) on the basis of previous research efforts and existing knowledge of the sectors, and brief profiles were prepared using secondary data sources, including comparative census statistics;
- more detailed comparative case studies were made of three communities per sector (four for agriculture) and the results from the first 10 case studies (phase 1) have been written up in a series of working papers made available to the study communities and social assessment practitioners;
- comparative statistical analysis was undertaken of 175 communities from the six sectors using social variables available from 1986 and 1996 census data. In contrast with the brief profiling exercise above, these communities were selected purely on the basis of the sectoral distribution of the labour force as recorded in the 1996 Census of Population and Dwellings.

KEY FINDINGS FROM THE CASE STUDIES AND COMPARATIVE ANALYSIS OF THE COMMUNITIES

Resource Sector Cycles, Technological Change and Restructuring

The research has shown that commodity price cycles have major social and economic effects on the communities that rely on them for primary production or processing. Furthermore, major technological changes have increased labour productivity considerably, both in primary production and processing. Employment opportunities have been reduced, especially for unskilled (often older) workers. These changes are shown in Figure 9.2. There were substantial losses of employment in several resource sectors, but this change was uneven. Employment in the agriculture, forestry, coal mining and energy (electricity and oil and gas) and fishing sectors were all down, but metal rock mining (mainly gold) and tourism were up in the period 1986–96. Across most primary sectors, full-time employment gave way to part-time employment.

Technological change, improved transport systems, and increased capital demands have led to amalgamations and centralising of processing plants, such as timber mills, dairy and meat processing. While a few processing plants have expanded, there have also been communities that have experienced plant closures.

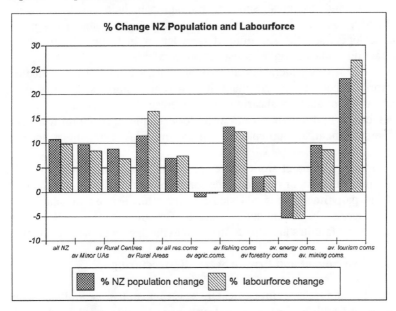

Figure 9.2   Percentage Change in NZ Population and Labourforce

Illustrations of these processes have been found in the case studies. For example, the dairy processing plant at Clandeboye has experienced considerable growth as one of the major South Island dairy processing factories, while plants have closed in surrounding communities in South Canterbury and also in Southland (including the case study community of Otautau) while dairy farming activity has increased in these areas. In the long-established coal mining areas around Runanga on the South Island

West Coast, small mines have all but disappeared, while one large new mine opened (and subsequently closed) and another is planned. At Waihi in the North Island, two large gold mines opened in the last decade, and one subsequently closed.

A further change observed is that the workforces for expanded plants do not necessarily live in the local resource community. Many have been recruited from other labour pools such as farming. Workers commonly commute from larger centres, or from areas with lifestyle blocks developed on farm land, attracted by stronger property markets, educational and other facilities there. Conversely, unemployed people in the traditional communities often do not have the technical skills to work the new technology, or are seen by management to have work attitudes, such as to demarcation or shift work, that are 'outdated'.

Changes in the way work is organised has seen moves to subcontracting of labour and technical support. Examples include mine companies contracting out all heavy earthwork, forestry logging and trucking by contract operators, the shedding of farm labour in favour of agricultural contracting, and catering for construction workforces.

There is also considerable evidence for increased flexibility and mobility of workers between employment in different sectors, sometimes on a seasonal basis (such as shearing or meat processing to forestry). Another new factor is multiple, part-time work; for example, agricultural work plus self employment in agricultural contracting plus work in a tourism business.

The new patterns of work and employment have affected older people, who either shift out, or remain in the community unemployed or sometimes working part time. The social statistics show an increase in numbers of elderly across the communities studied. Depopulation by working–age, child-rearing families has also contributed to the ageing of the populations.

Other Government and Private Sector Restructuring

Since the mid 1980s, in particular, government has centralised social services in health, education, social welfare and employment, leading to a loss of local services and employment opportunities. Local government reform was accompanied by the closure of local depots and rationalising of service centres, leading to further losses of employment from many small centres. The people who subsequently left were often professional and administrative workers and their families who had contributed heavily to the running of community organisations.

Other private sector rationalisation has included banks, mercantile firms and general retailing. These activities have been concentrated increasingly in regional centres with attendant closure of local branches. Government restructuring and private sector rationalisation therefore caused people to withdraw from rural economies, leading to a multiple effect on local economies. Local spending was reduced and shifted to regional centres and their centralised retailing and servicing facilities. Some communities were struck by the multiple effects of restructuring across several sectors, such as agriculture, forestry and mining in Western Southland. These changes are reflected in changes in the total labour force of resource communities 1986–96 that closely reflect those in the total population (Figure 9.3).

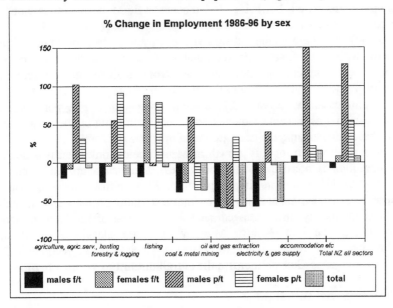

Figure 9.3   Percentage Change in Employment 1986–96 by Sex

The data across the resource community sectors show that, overall, the populations and total workforces of the resource communities have grown less than New Zealand as a whole. This change is uneven between communities and sectors: agriculturally-based communities have declined slightly overall, energy-based communities have declined markedly, forestry-based communities have grown slightly, while fishing and tourism communities have shown marked growth. It should be noted here that there is a close sectoral linkage between fishing and tourism in many coastal communities (such as Picton, Kaikoura and Havelock), and it appears that the tourism sector is influencing growth in these places. The case studies also showed that in some towns, such as Southland's Ohai for example, employment in the 'traditional' sector (in this case coal mining) could fall substantially, but be replaced by employment in another sector (in this case agriculture services) with the town becoming a regional shearing base over the last 20 years.

An Increase in Maori Population

The loss of employment from resource sectors, local government, transport, post office and other government and private-sector services has led to lower-cost housing being available to newcomers. The new arrivals are often characterised by being low-income welfare beneficiaries, single parents, unemployed or unskilled, and Maori (the indigenous people of New Zealand). The case studies identified that in many resource communities there has been an increase in the number of Maori as a proportion of the population, markedly greater than the strong national growth rate for Maori. Between 1986 and 1996 the growth in Maori population in the 175 communities analysed was 60.7 per cent, compared to 27.9 per cent for New Zealand as a whole. Some sectors, such as mining and tourism, with low base numbers, experienced growth of over 100 per cent.

One explanation for this growth in Maori population is that it is due to immigration by non-local *iwi* (outside tribes). These outsiders often lack the support of their extended kin group and local *marae* (tribal meeting place). Recent national-level analysis shows that the Maori population is socially and economically disadvantaged relative to the rest of the New Zealand population (Te Puni Kokiri, Ministry of Maori Development, 1998). Movement to areas that are already socially and economically disadvantaged is likely to increase the overall disparity.

Relative Social Disadvantage

The analysis of the social indicators presented above shows that resource communities in New Zealand appear to be structurally different from the 'mainstream'. In Table 9.1 a number of variables are used as indicators of systematic disadvantage. It can be concluded from these figures that in 1996 there was a picture of relative disadvantage in these communities. Here it has to be emphasised that these are averages for the 175 resource communities and that, while some were experiencing a period of relative growth and affluence, the weight is still heavily towards relative disadvantage. Some individual communities were identified as being very disadvantaged relative to the total New Zealand population. Many of these communities have relatively low personal and household incomes as a

Table 9.1 Resource Communities and New Zealand Comparative Social Indicators, 1996

Comparative indicators 1996	Percentage population change 1986–96	Maori as percentage of population	Persons on income support	No academic qualifications	Personal income <$30000	Adults not in the labour force	Women as percentage of labour force	Solo parent households	Households living in temporary dwellings
All NZ	10.9	15.1	37.5	34.7	76.2	34.6	45.7	14.8	1.6
Averages for resource communities	6.9	20.8	41.2	42.9	83.5	35.0	39.0	11.1	6.2
Comments	Slower growth	More Maori	More income support	Lower academic qualifications	More on low incomes	Adults not in labour force not much difference	Fewer women in labour force	Fewer solo parent households	Many more households in temporary dwellings

result of the income structure of their resource-dependent industries. Further, low-income people are also attracted to these areas and their cheap housing, despite otherwise limited economic opportunities there.

Impacts of Recent Changes on Community Life

As discussed above, many of the resource communities experienced a loss of population between 1981 and 1991. Most importantly, they lost many key people from the 'middle management' level, who previously played strong roles in local community organisation.

In the past decade, communities have become more diverse socially, culturally and economically, with greater levels of disadvantage and disparities of wealth both within and between communities. Locality-based social relations, previously focused around school and hall, and in many cases a dominant workplace, are becoming wider social networks that link to urban areas, with consolidation of activities such as sport teams around regional centres or larger towns, and the demise of many 'traditional' organisations.

Economic Diversification as a Buffer to the Impacts of Resource Cycles

The case studies showed that some communities were buffered from resource cycles by diversity in their local economy, particularly when they had tourism as a major activity, or an economic activity that was not resource dependent, such as manufacturing, or the development of retirement and lifestyle settlements. An example was the community of Katikati and its neighbouring areas, which have become retirement centres for the Waikato–Bay of Plenty region.

Based on earlier research, our initial hypothesis was that diversity of the economic base helps to stabilise and sustain a local economy (Taylor and McClintock, 1985). It is now evident that economic development activity needs to develop alternatives that are not directly resource-based and vulnerable to related cycles. For example, in the late 1980s, agriculture, forestry and coal mining all experienced major restructuring and a simultaneous downturn in commodity prices. Towns such as Ohai, for example, experienced contractions in coal mining and agriculture – with closure of most shops and services.

In the 1990s these trends continued, with further contraction in mining (including gold) and also for a time in tourism. In this respect tourism is far from a panacea, despite considerable growth since a downturn in the late 1980s. Similarly, added value should ideally be based on several sectors, and preferably on moving products as far from the influence of commodity prices as possible – for example, undertaking furniture manufacture instead of simply milling timber. Information technology, alongside transport and services developed for tourism, will be another factor allowing rural areas to promote themselves as attractive for information-intensive development, along with an outdoor lifestyle.

REFINEMENT OF THE CONCEPTUAL FRAMEWORK

The research project has indicated some key aspects to the conceptual framework of 'resource community' that need to be redefined.

Communities – A Redefinition

Community continues to be an important level of analysis for understanding the relationships between society and natural resources. It lies between the individual and household, and wider contexts such as the district region, nation and world system (Beckley, 1998). Machlis and Force (1988, p. 221), when considering timber-dependent communities, identify three major issues arising from the literature – 'How is the community defined? What is meant by "community stability"? And, how is timber-dependency measured?' Like many writers on this topic, they draw on Wilkinson, who considers three elements of community (Wilkinson, 1986, pp. 3–5):

- a local ecology that designates the community as a collective through which residents of a small territory meet their daily needs;
- an organisation of social life that contains sufficient structures such as groups, enterprises, social agencies and facilities to meet all daily needs;
- a field of collective actions to solve local problems and express local identity and solidarity.

Social scientists face problems in the analysis of community through the use of different levels of analysis and interdependent relationships between these levels (Beckley, 1998; Machlis and Force, 1988). For future social assessments a broad and dynamic concept of community is needed, one that can continue to embody Wilkinson's key elements.

Tykkylainen and Neil (1995, pp. 31–32) point out that a resource community may be a compact village, a scattered village, a commune or town, or a subdivision of one of these. It may also consist of a network of localities. Our case studies confirm that communities can represent complex and less obvious social forms than previously found at the locality level. For example, in many places a number of old localities have merged into a new community form, characterised by the loss of old community features, such as local authorities and pest destruction boards, and services, such as post offices, schools and pubs. There may be new organisations that become the basis for community actions, such as sports teams amalgamated from a wider catchment area, or a new land care group.

Tykkylainen and Neil (1995, p. 32) also point out that a 'rural region is a set of various kinds of resource communities' and that 'in many rural areas, the rural space, the countryside, consists of a mosaic of primary production communities and a network of villages and towns processing raw material'. The capacity of a region to survive processes of growth and decline, without undergoing major community formation or deformation, may depend on the nature of its particular mosaic and the ability of its population and workforce to draw on more than one natural resource type. Another crucial factor may be the size and composition of the population that must maintain the social organisation necessary to sustain social life (and collective action).

The Poverty Issue

The features found in localities dependent upon natural resources, of relatively low personal and household incomes, and immigration of low-income people despite limited economic opportunities, have been noted by Nord (1994). In effect, resource dependency and welfare dependency have become interchangeable in many New Zealand communities, and are also found in Australian cases (Lane et al., 1997). Freudenburg and Gramling (1994) examine the issue of poverty and natural resource based communities. The central problem, they argue, is the long-term decline in agricultural employment, and also in the comparative rate of employment in logging, fishing, mining, and oil and gas extraction. These latter industries traditionally offered higher wages than agriculture or tourism. Experience has shown, however, that resource-based 'development' does not necessarily influence other sectors or contribute to overall regional development. Centre–periphery dependence prevails in place of wide and uniform economic growth. Furthermore, as Freudenburg and Gramling point out, it is now evident that some of the worst examples of rural poverty can be found in towns and communities that were previously homes to extractive industries which have either died out or have moved on. They highlight the point that extractive industries such as logging and mining have experienced decreases in employment along with agriculture, as has occurred in New Zealand. Resource-based industries are not the panacea often argued for rural economies, for resource-dependent communities show instability and volatility in employment, resulting in periods of unemployment and relative poverty. These cycles are shown in Figure 9.4.

Model of Resource Community Cycles

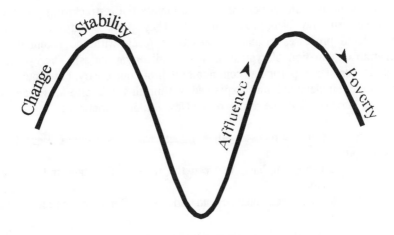

Figure 9.4   Model of Resource Community Cycles

Freudenburg and Gramling (1994) call for a more critical view of the positive relationship often advanced about the link between prosperity and resource extraction. They argue that it is insufficient for communities to wait for prosperity associated with possible resource price rises. In the meantime, extraction may shift elsewhere (nationally and globally) due to factors relating to capital, political context, environmental policy or labour costs – as previously observed and argued for New Zealand communities (Taylor and Fitzgerald, 1988). Also, in a later study of the oil industry in Louisiana, Freudenburg and Gramling (1998) found that in a period of decline or 'bust' in the early 1980s, linked industries experienced a decline in employment along with the employment decline in extractive industries. Examples in New Zealand include the loss of employment in transport as a result of a downturn in several resource sectors, which in turn hastened the centralisation of cartage contracting into regional centres.

The Importance of Extra-Local Linkages: The State, Private Capital and Technology

Tykkylainen and Neil (1995) review a number of prevailing approaches and determine that a new conceptual framework is needed for understanding the wider processes in which resource communities are located. 'Although there are general processes prevailing in the communities, theories of development as such do not explain sufficiently the restructuring process' (Tykkylainen and Neil, 1995, p. 42). They propose, in effect, four interrelated processes or conceptualisations (each with the potential to generate explanation of typical as well as divergent cases). The cyclical experiences of any particular community will of course vary, but should be able to be understood and explained within this framework, which is adapted here to reflect the results of the New Zealand experience.

- general (macro) processes that affect resource communities. For example,
    - shifting emphasis between the roles of the state and private sector
    - technological change and radically different communications systems
    - global product markets and price cycles
    - trade patterns and reform
    - transport systems and energy trends
    - capital markets and investment patterns
- sector-specific processes. For example,
    - sector product markets and product cycles
    - sector research and development and innovation
    - labour, skills and training
    - capital – investment and disinvestment
    - ownership and control
- local processes. For example,
    - social organisation and cultural patterns
    - personal work histories
    - local and regional labour market
    - settlement and commuting patterns
    - social services and infrastructure
    - levels of local government, community development

- policy-related processes (central, regional and local government). For example,
  - monetary policy
  - tariffs and trade
  - sector-specific policies and regulations
  - research and development
  - education, training and business development
  - environmental policy and resource management
  - social policy and community development.

Natural processes could be added to these. For example, Cloke (1996) has found, in a revised analysis of New Zealand's agriculture sector, that changes at the level of productive units (farms) have been due to changes in the role of the state in the resource sector, as well as national economic policy, world market processes and trade policy, and natural cycles such as the weather.

CONCLUSIONS

Resource communities in New Zealand are less clearly defined today as small localities. They consist, instead, of networks of localities and are more complex and less obvious forms of social organisation than previously found at the locality level. A broad and dynamic concept of community is needed, one that accounts for mosaics of primary production activity and social relationships in a network of physical settlements.

The research has strengthened the model of resource cycles in communities, adding an understanding of the interconnections between sectors at local and sub-regional levels. It shows few rural communities in New Zealand are totally dependent on a single resource sector. The research confirms a need to consider both 'macrostructural forces such as a region's position in the world system' and local, regional and resource-specific factors, as identified through community case studies and longitudinal research (Freudenburg and Frickel, 1994, pp. 283–284). This is a more sophisticated model than the limited one with which the research started.

The work provides a stronger conceptual and empirical basis for social assessment and resource planning in New Zealand, especially in communities that depend directly on the primary production or processing of natural resources. It also contributes to the development of more sophisticated frameworks for the analysis of resource community change internationally. These frameworks may contribute to future social assessment that has stronger conceptual and analytical rigour.

NOTES

1. Funding from the Public Good Science Fund, contracts TBA601 and TBA801.
2. At Lincoln College – now Lincoln University.
3. Support and funding from the Town and Country Planning Directorate, Ministry of Works and Development, was of particular importance.

REFERENCES

Beckley, T. (1998), 'The Nestedness of Forest Dependence: a Conceptual Framework and Empirical Exploration', *Society and Natural Resources*, **11**, 102–120.

Burch, W. (1969), 'The Nature of Community and a Case Analysis of Failure', in J. Forster (ed.), *Social Process in New Zealand*, Auckland: Longman Paul, pp. 84–101.

Burdge, R. (1998), 'The Social Impact Assessment Model and the Planning Process', Chapter 3 in *A Conceptual Approach to Social Impact Assessment*, Middleton, Wisconsin: Social Ecology Press.

Chapple, D. (1976), *Tokoroa: Creating a Community*, Auckland: Longman Paul.

Cloke, Paul (1996), 'Looking Through European Eyes? A Re-evaluation of Agricultural Deregulation in New Zealand, *Sociologica Ruralis*, **36** (3), 307–330.

Conland, J. (ed.) (1985), *Social Impact Assessment in New Zealand – A Practical Approach*, Wellington, Town and Country Planning Directorate, Ministry of Works and Development.

Freudenburg, W. and S. Frickel (1994), 'Digging Deeper: Mining-dependent Regions in Historical Perspective', *Rural Sociology*, **59** (2), 266–288.

Freudenburg, W. and R. Gramling (1994), 'Natural Resources and Rural Poverty: a Closer Look', *Society and Natural Resources*, **7** (1), 5–22.

Freudenburg, W. and R. Gramling (1998), 'Linked to What? Economic Linkages in an Extractive Economy', *Society and Natural Resources*, **11**, 569–586.

James, B. (1979), *A Report to the Kawerau Community*, Hamilton: Department of Sociology, University of Waikato.

Lane, M., H. Ross and A. Dale (1997), 'Social Impact Research: Integrating the Technical, Political and Planning Paradigms', *Human Organisation*, **56** (3), 302–310.

Machlis, G. and J. Force (1988), 'Community Stability and Timber–Dependent Communities', *Rural Sociology*, **53** (2), 220–234.

McClintock, W. and C. Taylor (1983), 'Pines, Pulp and People: A Case Study of New Zealand Forest Towns', *Information Paper No. 2*, Centre for Resource Management, University of Canterbury and Lincoln College.

Nord, M. (1994), 'Natural Resources and Persistent Rural Poverty: In Search of the Nexus', *Society and Natural Resources*, **7**, 205–220.

Somerset, H. (1974), *Littledene: Patterns of Change*, Wellington: New Zealand Council for Educational Research.

Taylor, C. and C. Bettesworth (1983), 'Social Characteristics of New Zealand Hydro Towns: A Case Study', *Information Paper No. 1*, Centre for Resource Management, Lincoln College.

Taylor, C. and G. Fitzgerald (1988), 'New Zealand Resource Communities: Impact Assessment and Management in Response to Rapid Economic Change', *Impact Assessment Bulletin*, **6** (2), 55–70.

Taylor, C., C. Goodrich and C. Bryan (1995), *Social Assessment: Theory, Process and Techniques*, Christchurch: Taylor Baines and Associates.

Taylor, N. and M. Abrahamson (1987), *Social Assessment of Rural Change: Implications for Integrated Rural Policy*, paper presented at the 49th ANZAAS Congress, New Plymouth, 26 January.

Taylor, N. and W. McClintock (1984), 'Major Resource Development Projects in a Regional Context: A Framework for a New Zealand Analysis', *The Australian and New Zealand Journal of Sociology*, **20** (3), 377–392.

Taylor, N. and W. McClintock (1985), *Rapid Growth and Resource Development: Social Issues and Strategies for Coping*, a report to the Town and Country Planning Directorate, Ministry of Works and Development.

Te Puni Kokiri (1998), *Progress Towards Closing Social and Economic Gaps Between Maori and Non-Maori*, a report to the Minister of Maori Affairs, Wellington.

Tykkylainen, M. and C. Neil (1995), 'Communities: Evolving a Comparative Approach', *Community Development Journal*, **30** (1), 31–47.

Wallerstein, I. (1979), *The Capitalist World Economy*, Cambridge: Cambridge University Press.

Wenner, L. (1984), *Minerals, People, and Dollars: Social, Economic, and Technological Aspects of Mineral Resource Development*, Washington, DC: United States Department of Agriculture – Forest Service Northern Region.

Wilkinson, K. (1991), *The Community in Rural America*, Westport: Greenwood Press.

Wilkinson, K. (1986), 'In Search of Community in the Changing Countryside', *Rural Sociology*, **51** (1), 1–17.

Wilkinson, K., J. Thompson, R. Reynolds Jr and L. Ostresh (1982), 'Local Social Disruption and Western Energy Developments: A Critical Review', *Pacific Sociological Review*, **25** (3), 275–296.

10. Community Monitoring Community: Assessing Resource Management Performance

Christopher D. Irons

INTRODUCTION

Changes in social norms appearing in the form of competition policy, decentralisation of resource management decision making and concerns about maintaining resource viability in the face of changing terms of trade demand new tools for resource management. The view of resource management as the sole domain of the natural sciences is shifting towards a more integrative view wherein the societal influences on resource use practices are becoming increasingly significant. Societal influences include those with environmental, legislative, sociopolitical and economic dimensions. Information from this new perspective can be described as socioecological because it is concerned with interactions that influence the relationships among human and natural systems, the domain of social ecology.

Socioecological information can be derived from examining interactions from a position outside a system, in this case the system of resources management. In social ecology, the interactions between people and resources and the relationships between government agencies, primary producers and other stakeholders can be described in the context of the whole system. This view contrasts with research and evaluation methods that are applied from a standpoint within part of the system, usually the part occupied by government agencies and sometimes that of industry associations such as the National Farmers Union. If the overall level of awareness within a system is to be raised, or if some other form of intervention is to be successful, the assumptions held within all the parts of a system need to be made explicit. Only then is it possible to evaluate the significance of the behavioural change brought about by interventions with any clarity. In fact, desirable changes in behaviour are often impeded by impaired communication. This chapter addresses a means to overcome such impediments.

BIOPHYSICAL CONTEXT

For most rural Australians of European descent, the socioecological relationship patterns that prevail to this day started to fuse during prehistorical times on a faraway continent. Each season brought with it the relative certainty of a particular range of environmental conditions. Not only did these conditions largely determine the plant varieties that were grown prehistorically in Europe, establishing a range of assumptions about food and fibre production that were modified by one generation after another for thousands of years, but they also framed the development of society within expectations and institutions based on those assumptions (Diamond, 1997). Diamond argues that the development of technologies stems as much from the way natural circumstances influence culture as it does from a society's ability to interact successfully with its environment.

In *Listen, Our Land is Crying!* bio-palaeontologist Mary White (White, 1997) focuses our attention on the overall cause of the deteriorating relationship with the land and water systems in Australia, rather than directing it only at the symptoms it produces such as increasing dryland salinity and dying wetland and waterway systems. Few would disagree with the facts presented by White, yet there are many interpretations of their significance, and opinions vary widely about what should be done. Consequently, addressing the deteriorating relationship between managers and natural resources in Australia has been slow or ineffective because many of those who can hear the sounds of land and water resource degradation are not listening to, or are denying, what they really mean. There are good reasons for this.

For instance, some people make better listeners than others. When people cannot or will not listen to the human and natural systems that surround them, their relationships with each other and with the rest of the environment become strained and degraded. In view of this, I outline a process that is being developed to address the root cause of resource and environmental degradation – poor communication between stakeholders.

This approach to resource and environmental management is more concerned with the causes of degradation than with prescribing treatment for the symptoms. The process of behavioural change is influenced by a shift in societal values that occurs following raised awareness of previously unconsidered implications of an action or activity. Hence, understanding the current societal values of stakeholders (those who effect and are affected by decisions) in a particular management regime is a prerequisite for interventions aimed at changing them.

The natural sciences can tell us much about the relationship between ourselves and our natural resources and environment. In recent state of environment reporting, scientists have focused on the state of the environment and described the human pressures upon it (DEST, 1994). They have considered how its changing state puts pressure on the human part of the environment and how humans should respond.

Recent research (Irons, in press) shows that socioecological relationships are not fixed: their 'reality' differs markedly from one stakeholder grouping to another. These differences influence perceptions of the risks involved and thus lead to a variety of responses when changes occur in society and the rest of the environment. In this research, neither *theory* nor *reality* appears to be fixed; rather they appear to change over time. Adaptive management regimes can accommodate this dynamic and so they are arguably more effective in mitigating risk than those that do not. The process described in this chapter offers a tool or instrument for such adaptive approaches to managing people and other natural resources in a changing environment.

THE TECHNOLOGICAL 'FIX'

In contrast to Beck (1992) I would argue that faith in technological fixes has increased during past decades in post-industrial countries. Food and fibre production has gradually come to depend almost entirely on non-human energy sources, especially fossil fuels and their chemical derivatives, and less on human ability to adapt our needs to particular circumstances. Access to such power has blinded many of us to the ancient reality that human well-being depends on the health of the ecosystems around us. Our technical ability to manipulate those systems to meet the familiar markets we serve at home and overseas has obscured our inability to adapt ourselves to the local conditions presented by new lands such as Australia.

The maritime climate and deep post-glacial soils that supported early food and fibre technology in Europe led to a pattern of management regimes and expectations among the early settlers that have since required constant modification to suit Australia's continental climate and arid lands. Ever since local conditions threatened the survival of the first European settlement more than 200 years ago, the variability of Australia's climate and its unfamiliar ecosystems have continued to make the risk associated with most types of Western agriculture seem greater in Australia than among most of its market competitors. To grow a tonne of Australian wheat, for instance, requires up to five times more land surface area than does the same quantity of wheat grown in England. In an age of increasing energy dependence, the technology developed to manage the extra risk associated with such broadacre cropping has materialised in hardware solutions largely developed overseas, whereas the software, or institutional arrangements, needed to address local conditions has been slower to develop. A similar situation exists in most other types of agriculture.

Exogenous hardware development and implementation has outstripped the capacity of the local software needed to sustain changes in natural resource management in Australia. Introducing European stock, digging and drilling wells, and fencing the rangelands provide examples of hardware developments that have been implemented over the last 200 years. Yet, the rights associated with land tenure and water use, the 'software' of risk management, are still being determined.

This socioecological relationship rests on perceptions and behaviour that ultimately influence the condition of the resource base upon which many rural communities depend. Improving the relationship requires changes that are socially acceptable, economically viable and ecologically sound (Firey, 1990). Tools that incorporate these criteria within a decision support framework can be useful to catchment practitioners and resource managers. The Performance Assessment and Diagnostic Instrument (PADI) described in this paper is a software tool for developing technology that meets these criteria. PADI is a multi-layered self-assessment tool for use by all the stakeholders in any community that is seeking to repair the relationship between people and other natural resources.

PADI is designed to inform catchment practitioners, managers and strategists by identifying community expectations and the perceived effectiveness of policy. It is designed to improve communication through education and, thus, to enhance the working relationships among all stakeholders by increasing awareness of the multiple perspectives and priorities that affect the many objectives they seek to realise. When this information is incorporated within a Geographical Information System (GIS), it can inform strategic planning and support adaptive decision making processes such as APIM (Adaptive Policy, Institutions and Management) (Dovers, 1999). The rest of this chapter summarises the thinking behind PADI, describes some results from testing it and outlines its potential for further development.

PADI DESIGN AND DEVELOPMENT

PADI was developed and tested during an investigation within the CSIRO Dryland Salinity Program into the consequences of providing a suite of bio-physical indicators of catchment health. That study found that governments and communities across Australia have invested heavily in environmental management and planning using a 'social response' model, without addressing the need for integrative assessment tools to determine community expectations and the perceived effectiveness of new policy approaches (Irons and Walker, 1996). As such a tool was needed to investigate catchment health, PADI was developed to facilitate the flow of information about how human perceptions and behaviour influence resource management. This socioecological information usually flows among decision makers and other stakeholders when they communicate about biophysical issues of concern but it tends to be unquantified and subjective. The effect of commodity prices on remedial on-farm activity is one example of this. PADI provides a formal, repeatable and transferable method of quantifying and comparing the socioecological dimensions of natural resources management. Examples taken from the field test of PADI show the variety of information available to benefit decisions affecting the allocation of funds, the activities aimed at resource rehabilitation and the acceptability of new technologies, and provide an advance assessment of the likely success of policy interventions aimed at specific groups.

Design Objectives

The design objectives of PADI were to assess the community dynamics influencing catchment health, to diagnose any symptoms that might benefit from intervention, and to establish the criteria for positive change. Community dynamics are explained in terms of the interactions between three groups of stakeholders: (1) service providers (including resource managers); (2) primary producers; and (3) all the 'other' stakeholders that fall into neither of the first two groups. This model follows a major thread in Cultural Theory, a theory that has contributed to the practice of environmental risk analysis (Douglas and Wildavsky, 1982).

In the development and testing of PADI, 'service providers' included extension officers and farm consultants (41 per cent of the test sample), 'primary producers' included the farmers, professional fishers and other people involved in entrepreneurial activities (such as stock and real estate agents and bankers) (45 per cent). 'Other stakeholders' (14 per cent) consisted of respondents in neither of the first two categories, although some were members of farming families and included secondary school-age respondents and people with off-farm incomes. The opinions of the third group often tend to be ignored in natural resources management although the group represents the largest and most diverse section of society and thus raises questions of equity in sociopolitical and economic considerations.

Priorities and awareness of the issues influencing catchment health varies between one group and another. This can lead to misunderstanding and conflicts of interest that demand the objectivity of negotiation and mediation skills before new policies can be implemented successfully. Hence, a primary design objective was to provide information that would inform such interventions. This required a shift in the way we usually think about natural resources management as a matter of 'doing the right thing' to a more pragmatic paradigm that accommodates a range of expectations with multiple solutions.

Social Constructionism

The way of thinking used in the development of PADI is social constructionism (Gergen, 1994; Hannigan, 1995) This view holds that 'knowledge' is continually 'constructed' through interaction with others and the rest of the environment. Constructionists argue that values are contextual so that priorities vary according to perspectives on a situation. Consequently, a contructionist view permits multiple 'truths', rather than the single, universal, truth found in positivism. As any 'truth' is open to question in constructionism, it is particularly relevant when using techniques including negotiation and mediation between stakeholders who have different roles in resources management.

The emphasis on roles in constructionism has echoes in a recent research initiative examining the roles of women in agriculture. That initiative indicates a shift in policy focus from the issue, agriculture, to the roles of a group of stakeholders, in this case rural women, and how such roles influence natural resources management and social change in rural areas (Elix, Lambert et al., 1998). Similarly, PADI is concerned with the roles of stakeholders in the health of a catchment and how they influence decisions affecting resource and environmental management.

The illusion of commonality is due to underestimating how profound is the influence of roles on perceptions and of perceptions on behaviour. Reducing the variety of decision makers to a group with similar roles can maintain the illusion of common goals, with all the advantages that brings to agreeing on a solution and getting the job done. Alternatively, the illusion can be dispelled by not only accepting the existence of multiple views of the same goal, but by embracing the insights they provide into resolving complex problems.

Making the decisions required to achieve multiple objectives requires information about the societal values affected and their relative importance to those involved. This information provides an alternative to the goal-oriented solution of breaking down difficult tasks into smaller ones when dealing with complex situations. Rather than reduce a challenging objective to manageable but less meaningful proportions, the social constructionist method of deconstructing perceptions of a situation, analysing it and then reconstructing it changes the way a problem is perceived by increasing the knowledge available to solve it. The additional knowledge is due to increasing the diversity of perspectives from which an issue is viewed by involving a wider range of stakeholders in the process than is accommodated by other methods. This is made possible by a contextual orientation towards solutions rather than one of isolating the 'problem'.

Applying PADI to a solution as broad as catchment health, for instance, encompasses a wider range of values than is usual in resource management where activities are focused on one or more particular issues from the outset. In contrast, PADI provides the context within which issues can be prioritised by investigating the values of the community as a whole. This method is supported by the assumption held in many areas of strategic planning that diverse views lead to more favourable outcomes (Stirling, 1994). It is assumed that the more democratic a decision, the more sustainable it will be. As conflicting opinions are framed by perspectives built on persistently gratifying relationships among people and their environment, the more diverse the perspectives focused on a decision, the greater the chances of the outcome accommodating the widest possible range of societal values.

The greater the range of societal values accommodated by a solution, the greater the likelihood of behavioural change. Understanding the concerns of the community as a whole leads to an understanding of observed and reported behaviour. Behavioural responses are based upon perceptions about the way things are and the way they should be.

Prerequisites for Change

Behavioural change theory and praxis indicates three prerequisites for social and personal change: (1) knowledge (that change is necessary), (2) resources (knowing what to do, funding, materials and so on), and (3) approval of a significant other, such as an advisor, partner, peer group or institution (Kilpatrick, 1996; Seamon and Kenrick, 1994). Firey's (1960) observation that sustainable development depends on changes that are (1) socially acceptable, (2) economically viable and (3) ecologically sound gives a socioecological spin to these prerequisites of behavioural change.

Each of the three perspectives – personal, technical and organisational – predominating among the occupational groupings used in PADI is linked to these criteria (Table 10.1). These linkages suggest that interventions must meet all the criteria shown in Table 10.1 before behavioural change can be achieved and then maintained. In other words, lasting changes in societal values come about only when the awareness of all three occupational groups is raised. This is why lack of 'awareness', or ignorance due to the difficulty of quantifying the problem, is one of the most frequently cited impediments to adaptation.

Table 10.1   Criteria for Socioecological Change

Socioecological change	Behavioural change theory	Perspective
Social acceptability	Awareness	Personal
Economic viability	Resources	Technical
Ecological soundness	Approval/support	Organisational

In integrative resource management the difficulties of quantifying the problem (ignorance) are arguably greater than quantifying the solution (diversity) (Stirling, 1994). This leads to the conclusion that attention is better focused on the solution than the problem. When only one or two perspectives are employed in seeking solutions, such as the technical and organisational perspectives that predominate in natural resources management, success may be considerably curtailed because some solutions will be hidden from the community by the ignorance of those who remain unaware of the situation. Integrative thinking is required in order to employ all three perspectives to focus on the solutions and the process of behavioural change. For this reason, various tests for stakeholder capacity to employ multiple perspectives are incorporated within the design of PADI. Furthermore, the process of applying them can enhance integrative thinking.

Tools designed to quantify the problem of ignorance in resources management abound. They include multiple criteria evaluation (Nijkamp et al., 1990) and multiple perspective analysis (Bowonder, 1987; Linstone, 1984) but their adoption has been hampered by the difficulty of quantifying the unquantifiable. PADI is assembled around the idea that the problem of ignorance is, by definition, indeterminate. Yet the solution, diversity, is relatively easy to determine by reporting the opinions of the widest possible range of informed stakeholders.

The more familiar Adaptive Environmental Assessment and Management (AEAM) technique is an approach that identifies societal values to inform the management of single resources (Holling, 1978; Walters, 1986). Arguably, PADI is more effective in dealing with the complexity of management approaches needed to integrate all the relevant dimensions of catchment health in order to meet the criteria for socioecological change. Frequent exclusion of 'other stakeholders' views, the 'personal' perspective, in catchment management decision making in favour of the technical and organisational views of the more directly involved stakeholders is one of the persistent problems in NRM. PADI provides a truly integrated view of societal values relevant to resource and environmental management. The level of integration raises the questions of who will champion (and fund) the use of the instrument. The metaperspective that PADI provides can highlight areas where institutional innovation may prove beneficial, yet until there is a genuine awareness that changes to resource and environmental management regimes are essential, the value of the PADI process will be limited.

The PADI Process

The PADI process follows the logic that ignorance, usually stated as 'lack of awareness', about the external world is by definition an indeterminate problem and is, therefore, unquantifiable. Yet the solution, diversity of opinion, looks relatively easy to define (Stirling, 1994). Rather than concentrate on quantifying the unquantifiable among catchment health issues, practitioners that use PADI can benefit from access to a variety of solutions so that they can foster the ones that show most promise. One aspect of what has been termed P3ADI (Priority, Perception and Performance Assessment and Diagnostic Instrument for Resource and Environmental Management) is compatible with the adaptive policy and management interventions that are seen as being essentially experimental because they consistently test and improve understanding and capabilities along the way (Dovers, 1997, 1999; Gunderson et al., 1995; Holling, 1978; Lee, 1993). In this view, abandoning the need for common goals not only legitimises multiple solutions, but also leads to enhanced social organisation and technology.

PADI facilitates the flow of socioecological information and directs it in three ways. First, the instrument increases awareness of possible outcomes of decisions by ensuring a basic exploration of goals (de Bono, 1994) – the personal perspective. Second, it generates an integrated response to questions about the priority that the target community gives to the issues related to these goals – the technical perspective. Third, perceptions of the comparative capacity and effectiveness of individual stakeholders can be used to indicate where resources management is considered to be successful and to identify impediments to progress – the organisational perspective.

In addition to the increase in awareness among stakeholders produced by using the instrument itself, the results of the survey can be reported for comparing markets separated by space and/or time. Results can be accumulated across regions and within catchments and sub-catchments although the value of comparison declines as the granularity of the data increases. Consequently, an index of granularity, such as population density/productivity per unit area, may be required to make such comparisons useful.

PADI data is gathered for three purposes. The first provides a baseline from which to assess the rest of the results, the second a prioritised list of issues, and the third a diagnostic summary of resource management activity and actors. This approach can be described in terms of the vectors found in the OECD pressure, state, response model used in environmental planning (SEAC, 1996):

- a vision of the desired *state* of catchment health (the way things should be);
- prioritisation of the *pressures* that impede the realisation of this vision (the way things are);
- an analysis of individual and institutional *responses* to these pressures (what is being done and by whom).

Whereas the natural sciences are primarily concerned with the first and, to some extent, the second of these vectors, work on the *response* vector is located in the domain of the social sciences. The challenge of integrating all three vectors is met in PADI under the rubric of social ecology. However, for the purposes of clarity, the results are summarised here under the headings of *state, pressure* and *response*, following details of the test procedure.

Test Procedure

PADI was developed and tested during a 1995 investigation within the CSIRO Dryland Salinity Program into the consequences of providing a suite of biophysical indicators of catchment health. As part of the investigation, PADI interviews were conducted with 100 stakeholders in the health of the Lake Corangamite Basin, Victoria. The basin, located between Ballarat, Camperdown and Colac, is a naturally occurring terminal lake system (using evaporative rather than estuarine drainage) set in a volcanic landscape that includes the largest permanent inland saline lake in continental Australia, Lake Corangamite. Water quality, soil salinisation, pest plants and animals, salinity and drainage are the predominant resource management issues.

The PADI interview guide
Summary of questions:

State
- What are the three most important things to find in healthy catchment?

Pressure
- What is the most significant issue affecting catchment health?
- What needs to be done about it?

Response
- Who should be doing something?
- How well is it being addressed at present?
- Why is it being done (a) so well and/or (b) so badly?
- Who should meet the cost of addressing this issue?

Validation
- What/who influences your opinions on this issue?
- How are you addressing this issue?
- How do you tell when you and/or others are making any difference?
- Are you prepared to make a long-term commitment to monitoring changes affecting this issue?
- What indicator(s) would you monitor?

The test procedure involved developing a questionnaire in cooperation with stakeholders in the health of the Lake Corangamite Basin. The resulting interview guide, summarised above, remained flexible enough to incorporate feedback from subsequent interviewees but became stable after the 12 initial face-to-face interviews. The quality of the data gathered during the remaining 88 interviews is therefore almost uniformly consistent.

The questions used in the interviews expand the AEAM approach with three notable additions. First, the question that determines what a healthy catchment means to each interviewee provides an overall context within which respondents can prioritise specific issues. This establishes the first set of role/expectation relationships and permits examination of any difference in priorities among respondents. Second, the constructionist's critical approach to 'truth' facilitates the treatment of roles and expectations (issues) as variables, permitting a deeper analysis of differing perspectives. This permits a more detached view of the situation among stakeholders and, hence, facilitates wider acceptance of diverse perspectives and possible solutions. This, in turn, increases the likelihood of behavioural change.

The third addition to the AEAM approach introduces the rigour of quantification to many of the more subjective responses. A formula is used to calculate the perceived effectiveness, potential and capacity of various groups of stakeholders for comparison within and between catchments. These perceptions are related to the issues influencing catchment health, and what is being or should be done about them by the stakeholders in one or more of the three roles: Service Provider, Primary Producer and Other Stakeholder.

Summary of PADI Test Results

Some examples of the results of the enquiry in the Lake Corangamite Basin offer an insight into some of the potential benefits that can be derived from PADI, including enhanced:

- understanding of local societal values by contrasting views of stakeholders' perception of what it means for a catchment to be healthy;
- prioritisation and direction of interventions by identifying key issues;
- identification of criteria to be met for successful interventions;
- views of community perceptions of the effectiveness and capacity of stakeholders in influencing catchment health.

Results described below refer to the questions listed in the PADI interview guide.

State

Analysis of the 255 replies to the question, 'What are the three most important things to find in a healthy catchment?', showed that 42 per cent of replies referred to ecological health, 24 per cent to social well-being, 21 per cent to sustained livelihood and 11 per cent to economic viability. Responses from both Primary Producers and Service Providers indicated similar levels of emphasis on all four types of attribute, whereas Other Stakeholders' responsiveness suggested a higher priority for social well-being and economic viability.

Indications of integrative thinking were assessed by examining how many of the four types of attribute were mentioned by each respondent, awareness of at least three being prerequisites for socioecological change. Seventeen per cent of the answers contained reference to one type, 49 per cent to two and 34 per cent to three or more. The greatest number of responses from Primary Producers and Service Providers mentioned two types of attributes (about 60 per cent in each case) but a similar percentage of Other Stakeholders' responses mentioned three or more attributes. Gender appeared to have no influence on capacity for integrative thinking.

These results indicate that practitioners (service providers and primary producers) tended to be less aware of the social and economic dimensions of catchment health, perhaps reflecting the terms of reference under which they work. Roles also appeared to influence the capacity (or the need) for considering more than one attribute with 'Other Stakeholders' demonstrating the greatest tendency to adopt multiple perspectives. These results show only one third of the sample identified the full set of criteria for socioecological change and that the most common omission was awareness. However, lack of awareness, and that usually means 'not thinking the way I do', was said to be a major *pressure* on the health of the catchment. This suggests that the perceived *state* of catchment health varies according to stakeholder type.

Pressure
Replies to the question, 'What has the most influence on the health of the Corangamite Basin?' indicated that the most commonly perceived pressure was a lack of 'awareness' (18 per cent), followed by 'water quality' (14 per cent), 'land-use planning' and 'terms of trade' (both 13 per cent), 'economy and employment' (11 per cent), 'agricultural practices' (10 per cent), with 'soil fertility, salinity and weeds' and 'water quantity' at 6 per cent each, and 'demographic change' trailing at 5 per cent.

Primary Producers showed the most even distribution of responses across these pressures. Service Providers' responses indicated little concern about economic pressures, a similar level over social ones (including awareness) and rather more concern about ecological and operational pressures. In contrast, Other Stakeholders' responses indicated almost twice as much concern over social pressures (including awareness) than the other two groups, little concern over economic and ecological pressures but almost as much concern about operational pressures, such as agricultural practices, as Service Providers.

These results suggest that the emphasis of policy designed to improve catchment health should be spread more evenly across the pressures identified by the sample as a whole, rather than just those perceived as important by one group. This raises complex issues of perceptions about the effectiveness and capacity of stakeholders requiring an analysis of reported activity to show what is being done now to respond to these pressures.

Response
Analysis of respondents' actions as activists (unpaid), showed that most effort is directed at addressing 'awareness', followed by 'land-use planning', 'economy and employment', 'agricultural practices' and 'water quality' in order of decreasing response rates. Paid activity aimed at influencing catchment health was concentrated on addressing 'water quality', followed closely by 'land-use planning', then by 'awareness', followed by 'agricultural practices' with 'terms of trade' and 'soils, salinity and weeds' equal and mentioned half as many times as 'water quality'. The most effective means to improve catchment health for Primary Producers was said to be addressing 'terms of trade', whereas replies from Other Stakeholders and, to a lesser extent, Service Providers indicated that addressing 'awareness' was key. Service Providers showed little interest in addressing 'terms of trade'.

Contrasting priorities and values are even more apparent between Primary Producers' and Service Providers' responses. Their interest in activities to address 'water quality', their principal concern, is shared by few Primary Producers, whereas Service Providers show little interest in Primary Producers' primary objective to improve 'terms of trade'.

Institutional analysis of the stakeholders in catchment health identified by respondents showed that all three categories of stakeholder were perceived to share equal responsibility for catchment health. Their respective capacity to do so and their effectiveness, however, varied considerably. Community groups (categorised as Other Stakeholders), especially Landcare and similar groups, were perceived to be the most effective in addressing catchment health issues, although their capacity was said to be less than the Service Providers who were perceived to have the most unused potential. Responses indicated that Primary Producers' effectiveness in addressing catchment health concerns was perceived to be minimal by most respondents.

These results raise questions about current policy directions that seek to improve sustainable production without acknowledging the key role played by Other Stakeholders, in particular those involved with Landcare. The reasons given by respondents to support these opinions are too complex to discuss in this summary. Even so, some conclusions can be drawn from the information that has been presented.

CONCLUSIONS

The differences between the way things are perceived to be and the way they should be according to each of the three roles in this analysis explain why 'awareness' is considered a primary influence on catchment health. 'Lack of awareness' usually means 'not thinking the way I do'. The negative connotations of this view prevent other priorities being valued in the search for solutions to resources management problems. PADI offers a first step towards viewing essential differences in values from a more detached perspective than other analytical tools permit. Learning to accept diverse priorities permits the benefits of diversity to be realised in the overall enhancement of management performance.

The contrasting perspectives described in this chapter identify the bases for conflict but also indicate the impediments that need to be overcome for an intervention to succeed. The results of testing PADI suggest that interventions aimed at behavioural change among Primary Producers to address water quality, for instance, are likely to be less effective than initiatives leading to an improvement in the terms of trade. Linking the two may be more effective. In settings where 'Other Stakeholders' predominate among those paying a levy for catchment management services (as in the levy imposed on all households in the regional catchments in Victoria), the expectations of the wider community must be considered. In the PADI trial summarised above, community expectations appear to be more concerned with addressing planning issues and raising awareness than with either the technical solutions to water quality, or the organisational solutions to declining terms of trade. In such settings, perceptions of resources management performance may be improved through integrative solutions aimed at satisfying the desires of the full range of stakeholder types.

Although PADI is being developed by rural Australians, many of the theories employed in it are relevant to situations that exist beyond the shores of the Australian continent. Perhaps the most significant theory for integrating the various dimensions of resource and environmental management is the meta-theory of social constructionism. It offers a way of thought that opens up possibilities for understanding and appreciating the differences between all those involved so that the problem of ignorance can be solved by using the benefits of the diverse opinions available.

REFERENCES

Beck, U. (1992), *Risk Society: Towards a New Modernity*, M. Ritter (trans.), London: Sage Publications.
Bowonder, B. (1987), 'Integrating Perspectives in Environmental Management', *Environmental Management*, **11** (3), 305–315.
de Bono, E. (1994), *Water Logic*, London: Penguin.
DEST, Department of Environment, Sport and Territories (1994), *State of Environment Reporting Framework for Australia*, Canberra: DEST.
Diamond, J. (1997), *Guns, Germs and Steel: the Fates of Human Societies*, London: Jonathan Cape.
Douglas, M. and A. Wildavsky (1982), *Risk and Culture: An Essay on the Selection of Technological and Environmental Dangers*, Berkeley, CA: University of California Press.
Dovers, S. (1997), 'Institutionalising Sustainability: a Pragmatic View', paper presented at the Environmental Justice: Global Ethics for the 21st Century, University of Melbourne, Australia.
Dovers, S. (1999), 'Public Policy and Institutional R&D for Natural Resources Management: Issues and Directions for LWRRDC', in C. Mobbs and D. Dovers (eds), *Social, Economic, Legal, Policy and Institutional R&D for Natural Resource Management: Issues and Directions for LWRRDC*, Occasional Paper No. 01/99, Canberra: Land and Water Resources Research and Development Corporation, pp. 78–107.
Elix, J., J. Lambert et al. (1998), *Missed Opportunities: Harnessing the Potential for Women in Agriculture*, Canberra: Rural Industries Research and Development Corporation.

Firey, W. (1990), 'Some Contributions of Sociology to the Study of Natural Resources', in R. Lee et al. (eds), *Community and Forestry: Continuities in the Sociology of Natural Resources*, Boulder, CO: Westview Press, pp. 15–26.

Firey, W. (1960), *Man, Mind and Land: A Theory of Resource Use*, Glencoe, IL: The Free Press.

Gergen, K. (1994), *Realities and Relationships: Soundings in Social Construction*, Cambridge, MA: Harvard University Press.

Gunderson, L., C. Holling and S. Light (eds) (1995), *Barriers and Bridgeheads to the Renewal of Ecosystems and Institutions*, New York: Columbia University Press.

Hannigan, J. (1995), *Environmental Sociology: A Social Constructionist Perspective*, London: Routledge.

Holling, C. (1978), *Adaptive Environmental Assessment and Management*, New York: John Wiley and Sons.

Irons, C. (in press), *P3ADI: A Priority, Perception and Performance Assessment and Diagnostic Instrument for Resource and Environmental Management*, Working paper, Canberra: Centre for Resource and Environmental Studies.

Irons, C. and J. Walker (1996), *Meeting Community Needs for Monitoring Catchment Health*, Technical Memorandum 96.31, Canberra: Commonwealth Scientific and Industrial Research Organisation.

Kilpatrick, S. (1996), *Change, Training and Farm Profitability*, Discussion Paper 10, Canberra: National Farmers Federation.

Lee, K. (1993), *Compass and Gyroscope: Integrating Science and Politics for the Environment*, Washington, DC: Island Press.

Linstone, H. (1984), *Multiple Perspectives in Decision Making*, New York: Elsevier.

Nijkamp, P., P. Rietveld and H. Voogd (1990), *Multicriteria Evaluation in Physical Planning*, Amsterdam, New York, Oxford and Tokyo: North-Holland.

SEAC, State of the Environment Australia Committee (1996), *Australia: State of the Environment 1996*, Sydney: CSIRO Publishing for the Dept of Environment, Sport and Territories.

Seamon, J. and D. Kenrick (1994), *Psychology*, New Jersey: Prentice Hall.

Stirling, A. (1994), 'Diversity and Ignorance in Electricity Supply Investment', *Energy Policy*, **22** (3), 195–216.

Thurow, L. (1983), *Dangerous Currents: The State of Economics*, New York: Random Press.

Walters, C. (1986), *Adaptive Management of Renewable Resources*, New York: Macmillan.

White, M. (1997), *Listen, Our Land is Crying!*, Kenthurst, NSW: Kangaroo Press.

PART III

Sustaining Resources

11. Biodiversity: Evolving Paradigms for Rural Community Development

David M. Bates and Terry W. Tucker

INTRODUCTION

Worldwide, substantial numbers of the rural population in less-developed countries occupy upland regions and depend largely on subsistence-level agriculture in areas that are characterised by some combination of low and unreliable rainfall, rugged topography, poor soils, and degraded natural vegetation. Physically remote and economically distant from a nation's mainstream culture, upland households and communities face daunting challenges beyond those presented by the biophysical environment, with access severely limited to capital, goods, basic education, health care and other human services.

The upland realities define the setting and context of a Philippines-based programme known as Conservation Farming in the Tropical Uplands (CFTU). This programme brings together 16 diverse partner organisations[1] which share a common purpose in assuring the long-term socioeconomic and ecological viability of upland regions. Toward that end, CFTU seeks to develop and promote sustainable agricultural and conservation practices and facilitates collaborative working relationships among rural peoples, government agencies, non-governmental organisations, international research centres and academic institutions. CFTU's focus on upland regions recognises that in the Philippines and elsewhere in the tropics the social, economic and environmental health of these generally neglected areas is crucial to long-term national development. Thus, the uplands are viewed in the continuum of national well-being with intra- and interrelated issues extending from households to communities, municipalities, regions and beyond.

A basic premise of CFTU has been that increasing productivity and security in agricultural systems and their environments would lead to improved socioeconomic states and, in turn, conservation of native biota and enhanced ecological health. The premise is appealing, but its fulfilment is questionable. Experience suggests that preservation of biodiversity within community landscapes, however desirable from a western ecological perspective, is likely to be minimal and constrained by the immediate needs and views of rural people and those of the NGOs and governmental agencies that serve them. Realities of this sort have challenged CFTU to question assumptions made about sustainability, biodiversity and rural community development, and to develop workable paradigms that interface human concerns with biological imperatives.

In this chapter sustainability issues are cast in the context of biodiversity. They illustrate the evolving views and emerging paradigms for establishing community-based landscape strategies and goals that have resulted from individual research programmes in the Philippines, tempered by participatory interactions among and between CFTU members and the people and communities with which they interact.

SUSTAINABILITY AND BIODIVERSITY

The continued humanisation of the earth and the concomitant demands placed on nature's support systems give urgency to issues of sustainability[2] (World Commission on Environment and Development, 1987). In that regard, the themes that characterised CFTU are not unlike those of much of the development-focused world, for they are directly concerned with a sustainable future and the betterment of the lives of rural people. In providing a context for sustainability we largely focus here on concepts and perceptions of biodiversity in managed ecosystems, that is ecomanagement, in which the prefix 'eco' carries both ecological and socioeconomic meaning. Experiences indicate that rethinking commonly accepted paradigms concerning biodiversity can result in more realistic approaches to sustainable ecomanagement in what are largely subsistence communities.

While opinions differ widely concerning the pathways to sustainability (Myers and Simon, 1994, for example), thoughtful analyses recognise that achievement of sustainability is predicated on a clear understanding of the myriad of interrelated factors that influence it and positive actions flowing from that understanding. Holistic approaches to sustainability, however, are more easily expressed in the abstract than found in the realities of given development situations, which bring to the fore the wide range of impinging factors, representative of disparate stakeholder views. In more realistic modes, humans generally confront the enormity of sustainable development problems by defining them in narrower biological, agricultural, economic, and/or social terms – something further fragmented by disciplinary foci and cultural biases. Such component studies may be used metaphorically as predictors of the whole or simply cast into view with the hope that they will coalesce into something that is, at the least, quasi-holistic.

Failure to attain sustainability is not for a lack of relevant component knowledge. Although there is always more to learn in any given field of study, the literature is vast and can be drawn on to fit essentially any development situation or occasion. Agricultural systems, for example, may be viewed from an array of narrower component perspectives – water, soils, economic, social, among many others (Hatfield and Karlen, 1994); from development (Hayami and Ruttan, 1985) and systems viewpoints (Ruthenberg, 1980); or from compounded approaches, as in agroforestry (Buck et al., 1998). They may be placed in agroecological contexts (Conway, 1986, 1987; Innis, 1997), be seen as summations of traditional knowledge or ideology (Alcorn, 1989; Nazarea, 1995; Warren et al., 1989), or taken as expressions of the plight of the poor (Chambers, 1997). Similar range and variety are evident in ecological and biodiversity studies, ranging from those economic (Costanza et al., 1997) to those dealing with extent and preservation (Reaka-Kudla et al., 1997), useful resources (Balick et al., 1996), traditional management (Alcorn, 1984; Nazarea, 1999), extractive reserves (Nepstad and Schwartzman, 1992; van Valkenburg, 1997), and ownership (Brush, 1993).

If knowledge *per se* is not the impediment to development of sustainable rural ecosystems, what might the impediments be? Here the possibilities are many. They may be found in unsupportable population levels, lack of access to biophysical, monetary and human resources, contradictory or negative governmental policies, degraded landscapes, and survival priorities, among others. Singly, or in combination, such factors may actually preclude development or lead to regression from the current state. But, in addition to these generally recognised factors, our experiences confirm the practical and philosophical gaps that exist between the social and biological sciences. Such gaps separate other stakeholders in development, including the governmental bodies, NGOs, and finally the people to be served. As stakeholders pursue their individual agendas, the realities basic to the creation of minimally-functional community landscapes tend to be obscured, if not lost. Nowhere is this better illustrated than in the differing views of what constitutes biodiversity and its relevance to the sustainability of rural communities.

At the risk of overgeneralising, it is fair to say that the biological community holds biodiversity from whatever viewpoint – genetic, taxonomic, community, or functional – to be sacrosanct. Yet, biodiversity, except in the most protected situations, continues to decline (Heywood, 1995). The simplification and homogenisation of the world's flora, like that of other globalisation phenomena, proceeds apace. The point is, of course, that whatever the biological imperatives, biodiversity in the future will be less than it is today and ever more a function of human choice and management (Vitousek et al., 1997). Putting aside ethical and even many practical issues, it is likely that only the functional aspects of biodiversity, found in the sum total of the myriad of interactions constituting ecosystems, will eventually define human concerns for it. Such concerns will seek the threshold at which critical services of ecosystems can be preserved, an issue that transcends biological resources alone (Schaeffer and Cox, 1992).

Not unexpectedly, social science approaches to biodiversity find their first home in concerns for human needs and determinants of human behaviour. Conservation or enhancement of biodiversity may be seen as a means of promoting positive development as, for example, by preserving cultures and traditional ways of life or as sources of income (such as through the gathering of non-timber forest products, including medicinal substances, or selective timber harvesting). The functional aspects of biodiversity are not ignored, but may exist more as a backdrop against which human roles are played out. As such, they may be downplayed as a critical element of sustainability. Not surprisingly, political concerns tend to parallel these 'backdrop' points of view – after all, people do, at least in the short term, survive the loss of biodiversity and severe environmental degradation. Many of the socioeconomic and political concerns are expressed in references cited above and other thoughtful presentations, for example, Young (1992), Krattiger et al. (1994) and McNelly (1995).

Peoples of rural upland communities in the developing world are not unmindful of the arguments favouring preservation of biodiversity or of the direct effects that destruction of it has on their lives, especially evident in vastly altered hydrology, soil erosion and declining soil fertility, vegetation fragmentation, and the loss of subsistence and income-producing forest products. Yet, their responses are not dictated by academic or international concerns, but by the selective pressures that govern their choices and lives. By its very nature, human occupation of the land leads to alteration of the landscape and, with increased presence, to the loss of biodiversity. Simply put, humans seek to maximise their return on biotic resources by channelling biomass production to meet their own needs – the essential strategy of agriculture and ultimately of fitness, itself (Bates, 1998). People respond to this selective regime in predictable fashion, first by harvesting nature's bounty (free or essentially free goods), then by mining the land agriculturally, and finally by attempting to convert at least part of the land to some form of permanent vegetation, sometimes simply through abandonment. The sequence may occur rapidly or may be prolonged, depending on the availability of critical inputs. In worst-case scenarios the agricultural phase may be short-lived or even absent.

THE PHILIPPINES

Upland farmers in many parts of the Philippines find themselves in or entering the last phase of the land-use management cycle. Experiences in the municipality of Matalom, western Leyte, where the International Rice Research Institute, the Visayas State College of Agriculture and Cornell University historically collaborated and for which there are long-term field data and other documentation concerning upland farming systems, are generally instructive. Here, during the past fifty years or so, intensive farming has followed logging into the uplands and the original forested vegetation has now largely been replaced by a mosaic of land uses. In the upper reaches of the landscape, some pockets of forest persist, though threatened, in ravine bottoms, but the steeply sloped hillsides have been cut and are now abandoned to scrub intermixed with herbaceous weeds and grasses. Recurrent burning and the loss of seed trees and accompanying dispersal agents leave little hope for forest regeneration without massive human intervention – an unlikely event. Below this, upper zone farm communities seek to compensate for land degradation by adjusting the balance between use or outtake and the declining capacity of the resource base. Adjustments range from out-migration, especially of young people, to the adoption of improved in-field management of active cropland and their short-term fallows. Elsewhere pasture, largely under coconut, persists, as do secondary scrub/forest patches – the results of long-term fallows.

Farmer knowledge and motivation and capacity for experimentation, innovation and adoption in Matalom have been documented by Tucker (1998), while Godilano (1998) has used spatial analysis to provide a framework for community-based watershed analysis and management in the municipality. The results of these studies show a trend, especially on calcareous soils, toward greater integration of trees into the agricultural landscape and thus permanency of plantings, although this is strongly biased toward farmer-owned plots rather than those tenanted. Arguably, biodiversity is increased in agroforestry systems but the extent is limited and the quality questionable. The ubiquitous timber exotics gmelina (*Gmelina arborea*) and mahogany (*Swietenia macrophylla*) are present, although the self-sowing ipil-ipil (*Leucaena leucocephala*) is more common, and indigenous trees, such as baganga or bagalunga (*Melia dubia*), tugas or molave (*Vitex parviflora*), and anislag (*Securinega flexuosa*) are encourgaged. Among fruit trees and other perennials the coconut is preeminent, but is joined by an array of commonly encountered tropical fruits; for example, the mango (*Mangifera indica*). Of the 35 agroforestry and 36 perennial food and commercial species listed by Godilano, the vast majority are exotic or, if indigenous, are widespread in the Philippines.

The studies of Tucker and Godilano do not stand in isolation. Comparable observations have been made by Acebedo (1999) working with farm communities in the municipality of Bilar on the island of Bohol. Here, the situation is more complex for human activities and choices are constrained by the presence of the Rajah Sikatuna National Park and the Loboc Watershed Rehabilitation Project. Nonetheless, farmers seek to regain a measure of productive livelihood and subsistence by converting portions of degraded agricultural plots to perennial, remunerative vegetation. Complex associations of fruit and timber trees may be grown around households, while mahogany and gmelina dominate field-plantings. These are complemented by regenerative woodlots, which result from purposeful fallow or abandonment.

The factors that have favoured agroforestry in Matalom and Bilar are not esoteric concerns for biodiversity, but rather those of survival in stressed and controlled environments. Farmer responses are in keeping with selective values reflecting human choice, as noted above. The increased presence of trees in the homestead and community landscapes gives a misleading aura of diversity. No matter how complex the composition of these agroforestry systems may be, they will be less diverse than the native vegetation, whatever the measure of that diversity.

EVOLVING PARADIGMS

CFTU experiences in the Philippines bring together the preservationist mindset of biologists, the people- and community-focused concerns of social scientists, and the realities of rural upland life. Issues of sustainability are found in the conflicts between development and preservation of biodiversity, between discipline-based academic viewpoints and those of rural communities, and between the ideal and the attainable. The resolution of these conflicts is a precondition of effective community-based landscape management, which harmonises fundamental understanding of the social and biological realms (Berkes and Folke, 1998). Such harmonisation calls for rethinking the relationships between biodiversity and development in order to create paradigms that better reflect attainable realities in rural communities. These realities undoubtedly will conflict with the western ecological sensibilities and may well lower the state of local and even global ecosystem health, but they also may have the advantage of precluding irreversible degradation (Daily, 1995) by providing adequate levels of ecological services.

As guidelines for NGOs and others, including academics, working in community development we put forth a series of statements that invite participatory discussions about the nature of biodiversity, its role in the community ecosystem health, and the levels of it that are desirable and attainable. These statements are neither inclusive nor proposed as dicta. Rather they are points for discussion and reference, which can help stakeholders more clearly develop goals and strategies for their actions.

By its very nature, development leads to the loss of biodiversity, whether defined by species numbers or habitat complexity. Biodiversity declines until it finds an equilibrium state between human imperatives and exploitive capability. Equilibrium states fluctuate in relationship to the extent and levels of human activity, that is, settlement, intensive monocropping, agroforestry, fallow and abandonment, among others.

The minimal goal of community landscape planning is to maintain equilibrium states above the threshold of ecosystem functions and services through adjustments in human activity and behaviour. Actual and perceived household and community benefits are the driving forces of biodiversity conservation. Tenure status, coupled with small fragmented landholdings, constrains community landscape planning and effective increases in biodiversity. Protected areas, such as parks, reserves, and the like, may be islands of biodiversity and ecological services, but otherwise provide little of immediate or direct value to community livelihood. Ecoregional planning appeals to academics and officialdom, but implementation, which is local, may be disruptive to households and communities.

It is not for biological and social scientists to determine the lifestyles of peoples with whom they are engaged, but rather to give peoples the knowledge and means to make their own decisions.

CONCLUSIONS

Acceptance of lowered expectations for biodiversity suggests abdication of earthly stewardship; however, we do not imply that biodiversity lacks relevance to the sustainability of local ecosystems or that of worldwide biosphere health. In truth, we do not know what ecological conditions will ultimately sustain humanity or the degree to which biodiversity will guarantee it. We do know, however, that people occupy and degrade fragile environments, that the process is ongoing, and that it will continue into the foreseeable future. Rather than ignore these realities with idealised expectations for the preservation of biodiversity, we argue for the further identification and refinement of parameters within which conservation of biodiversity may realistically proceed. Bringing together biological and social imperatives, we suggest that rural communities practice what might be called 'best-bet' options for community environmental/diversity/landscape issues. These may have marginal impact on biodiversity and the improvement of ecosystem functions, but they may be what are attainable in our humanised world.

ACKNOWLEDGEMENTS

We thank our colleagues in CFTU partner organisations and the rural peoples of the Philippines for so generously sharing their hospitality, knowledge and insights with us, and the Cornell University International Institute for Food, Agriculture and Development (CIIFAD) for providing the means to make the programme possible.

NOTES

1. Member organisations of CFTU. *Development-focused NGOs*: Eduardo Aboitiz Development Studies Center; International Institute for Rural Reconstruction; Mg-Uugmad Foundation; Philippines Partnerships for the Development of Human Resources in Rural Areas; PROCESS Foundation; World Neighbors. *Government Agencies*: Bureau of Soil and Water Management of the Department of Agriculture; Department of Agriculture, Region 8; Department of Environment and Natural Resources, Region 8. *International Research Centres*: International Center for Research in Agroforestry; International Rice Research Institute. *Academic Institutions*: Bohol Agricultural College; Cornell University; University of the Philippines, Los Banos, Agroforestry Program; University of Waikato; Visayas State College of Agriculture.
2 Sustainability is an elusive concept, perhaps more an idealised state in given contexts than one attainable by rational human action. Yet, even as an ideal, it serves to focus thoughts on long-term issues of survival resulting from the human presence on earth.

REFERENCES

Acebedo, V. (1999), *Participatory Analysis of Plant Resource Management on Bohol, Philippines*, PhD dissertation, Ithaca: Cornell University.

Alcorn, J. (1984), 'Development Policy, Forests and Peasant Farms: Reflections on Huastec-Managed Forest's Contribution to Commercial Production and Resource Conservation', *Economic Botany*, **38**, 389–406.

Alcorn, J. (1989), 'Process as a Resource: The Traditional Agricultural Ideology of Bora and Huastec Resource Management and Its Implications for Research', *Advances in Economic Botany*, **7**, 63–77.

Balick, M., E. Elisabetsky and S. Laird (eds) (1996), *Medicinal Resources of the Tropical Forest*, New York: Columbia University Press.

Bates, D. (1998), 'Ethnobotanical Perspectives of Agroforestry', in L. Buck, J. Lassoie and E. Fernandes (eds), *Agroforestry in Sustainable Agricultural Systems*, Boca Raton: Lewis Publishers, pp. 339–359.

Berkes, F. and C. Folke (eds) (1998), *Linking Social and Ecological Systems: Management Practices and Social Mechanisms for Building Resilience*, Cambridge: Cambridge University Press.

Brush, S. (1993), 'Indigenous Knowledge of Biological Resources and Intellectual Property Rights: The Role of Anthropology', *American Anthropologist*, **95**, 653–686.

Buck, L., J. Lassoie and E. Fernandes (eds) (1998), *Agroforestry in Sustainable Agricultural Systems*, Boca Raton: Lewis Publishers.

Chambers, R. (1997), *Whose Reality Counts? Putting the First Last*, London: Intermediate Technology.

Conway, G. (1986), *Agroecosystem Analysis for Research and Development*, Bangkok: Winrock Institute for Agricultural Development.

Conway, G. (1987), 'The Properties of Agroecosystems', *Agricultural Systems*, **24**, 95–117.

Costanza, R., J. Cumberland, H. Daly, R. Goodland and R. Norgaard (1997), *An Introduction to Ecological Economics, International Society for Ecological Economics*, Boca Raton: St. Lucie Press.

Daily, G. (1995), 'Restoring Value to the World's Degraded Lands', *Science*, **269**, 350–354.

Godilano, E. (1998), *Spatial Analysis Framework for Community-Based Watershed Management in Tropical Uplands of the Philippines*, PhD dissertation, Ithaca: Cornell University.

Hatfield, J. and D. Karlen (eds) (1994), *Sustainable Agricultural Systems*, Boca Raton: Lewis Publishers.

Hayami, Y. and V. Ruttan (1985), *Agricultural Development. An International Perspective*, revised edition, Baltimore: The Johns Hopkins University Press.

Heywood, V. (ed.) (1995), *Global Biodiversity Assessment*, United Nations Environment Program, Cambridge: Cambridge University Press.

Innis, D. (1997), *Intercropping and the Scientific Basis of Traditional Agriculture*, London: Intermediate Technology Publications.

Krattiger, A., J. McNeely, W. Lesser, K. Miller, Y. St. Hill and R. Senanayake (eds) (1994), *Widening Perspectives on Biodiversity*, Geneva: IUCN, Gland and International Academy of the Environment.

McNelly, J. (ed.) (1995), *Biodiversity Conservation in the Asia and Pacific Region. Constraints and Opportunities*, Manila: Asian Development Bank.

Myers, N. and J. Simon (1994), *Scarcity or Abundance: A Debate on the Environment*, New York: Norton.

Nazarea, V. (1995), *Local Knowledge and Agricultural Decision Making in the Philippines: Class, Gender, and Resistance*, Ithaca: Cornell University Press.

Nazarea, V. (1999), *Ethnoecology: Situated Knowledge/Located Lives*, Tucson: University of Arizona Press.

Nepstad, D. and S. Schwartzman (eds) (1992), 'Non-Timber Products from Tropical Forests', *Advances in Economic Botany*, **9**, Bronx: New York Botanical Garden.

Reaka-Kudla, M., D. Wilson and E. Wilson (eds) (1997), *Biodiversity II: Understanding and Protecting Our Biological Resources*, Washington: Joseph Henry Press.

Ruthenberg, H. (1980), *Farming Systems in the Tropics*, 3rd edition, Oxford: Clarendon Press.

Schaeffer, D. and K. Cox (1992), 'Establishing Ecosystem Threshold Criteria', in R. Costanza, B. Norton and B. Haskell (eds), *Ecosystem Health. New Goals for Environmental Management*, Washington: Island Press, pp. 157–169.

Tucker, T. (1998), *Informal Farmer Experimentation in Resource-Poor Environments: A Study of Differential Propensity and Capacity*, PhD dissertation, Ithaca: Cornell University.

van Valkenburg, J. (1997), 'Non-Timber Forest Products of East Kalimantan – Potentials for Sustainable Forest Use', *Tropenbos,* Series 16, Leiden: Backhuys Publishers.

Vitousek, P., H. Mooney, J. Lubchenco and J. Melillo (1997), 'Human Domination of Earth's Ecosystem', *Science,* **277**, 494–499.

Warren, D., L. Slikkerveer and S. Titilola (eds) (1989), *Indigenous Knowledge Systems: Implications for Agriculture and International Development,* Washington: Technology and Social Change Program, Iowa State University, Ames and Academy for Educational Development.

World Commission on Environment and Development (1987), *Our Common Future,* Oxford: Oxford University Press.

Young, M. (1992), *Sustainable Investment and Resource Use. Equity, Environmental Integrity, and Economic Efficiency,* Man and the Biosphere Series, **9**, UNESCO, Carnforth and Paris: Parthenon Publishing Group.

12. The Brave New Order: Power, Visibility and the Everyday Landscapes of Australian Farmers

Ruth Beilin

Miranda:
O wonder!
How many godly creatures are there here!
How beauteous mankind is!
O brave new world
That has such people in't!
Prospero:
'Tis new to thee.
(Shakespeare: *The Tempest*, Act 5, Scene 1, lines 182–186)

INTRODUCTION

Miranda, is the daughter of Prospero. He is the former Duke of Milan and a powerful sorcerer. She has been raised on an island in a 'greenworld' away from other people. At the close of the play, she accompanies Prospero back to the real world, and for the first time sees other men. Hence the line, 'How many godly creatures are there here!' The situation is summed up in Prospero's response. He recognises these 'godly creatures' as the same ones who tried to depose him twelve years earlier, and who had him banished to the island. Nonetheless, despite his reservations, he allows that Miranda has every right to be optimistic, with: ''Tis new to thee.'

Aldous Huxley, of course, uses the Shakespearean quote: 'O brave new world' to herald a more explicit warning in his 1932 novel. Less patiently than Prospero, Huxley foresees a bleak future in the highly planned, globally networked and ordered Fordian world he describes. He depicts life for the more thinking (Alpha) person as mindless and soulless. The bureaucrats, however, who run this world from remote reading rooms in urban centres, are very satisfied. There are a few population groups who are not part of the novel's global system. They are 'politicos', confined on remote islands or 'tribals' contained in Savage Reservations. These groups and their landscapes have 'disappeared'. They are not known to the rest of the world order.

These two stories form a backdrop to this paper. They are symbolic of the ambivalence I feel at the contemporary landscape scene in rural Australia. My case material is drawn from the State of Victoria, but the concern underlying this analysis has national and international application. I suggest, as an example of this concern, that powerful bureaucrats, representing governments and markets, have a similar capacity to make landscapes disappear through a 'strike' of their administrative pens, as did the governments in these two stories.

Shakespeare, through his character Miranda, and Huxley in his novel, each recognised their time as one of enormous change. Global forces were impinging in the Elizabethan era, shaking the local ways of doing things in the island nation. England also perceived the advantage in embracing change, by penetrating distant landscapes for precious trade commodities. Huxley foresaw industrialisation and international capital superseding the relevance of nation-states and the consequent development of a world functional order. He challenges the reader to question whether change, associated particularly in western cultures with progress, is necessarily universally beneficial.

The sages suggest change is always with us and in the post-modern era, 'the prospect of change has become virtually a routine feature of everyday life' (Smart, 1992, p. 1). As global citizens and in local workplaces, we are advised in the language of the 1990s to 'position ourselves for change', even to anticipate it so as to be able to 'take advantage of anything it might offer us'. At a local level, however, we have become increasingly aware that the landscape in which we live and the global environment of which we are a part, show serious signs of wear. Landscape degradation – erosion, salinity, acidification – along with water quality, fire ecology, and climate change are all part of a more comprehensive understanding of local actions and global consequences. The landscape itself is 'changed'. Changing the way land and water are managed to incorporate ideas about longer-term sustainability and wise-use processes is a major challenge, particularly for those on the land.

LANDSCAPE AS A MIRROR OF CHANGE

'The essence of a landscape is in its flowing rhythms, uniting all the objects within . . . A landscape is not a series of enclosed or interpenetrating spaces but a flowing continuum' (Crowe, 1958, p. 25).

Crowe's landscape ties together two of the central themes of this paper, those of ecology and management. The 'continuum' might easily refer to the connectedness associated with ecosystems, while the recognition of enclosed and delineated spaces speaks to the creation of place and its importance in defining local landscapes. Jackson has argued, however, that for thousands of years the meaning of land 'scape' was not to be found in scenery, but in everyday farming systems (1986, p. 68). Farmers, through their work and land management, create everyday landscapes. The landscape is their biography (Beilin, 1998b; Samuels, 1979). Historically, farmer survival depended on the ability to respond with flexibility to change by changing land management practices. These changes might be in actual location and size of spaces they worked, in their ownership or in their right and access to common land. Common land enhanced the possibility of family and community survival, and as common land was only accessible through membership in a family or a community it is symbolic of the social interaction behind landscape management decisions. The backbone of the vernacular landscape rested in social relationships that facilitated access to the commons.

In Australia, more recently than other frontier western nations, the landscape was understood in terms of its potential agricultural and livestock wealth. It appeared 'natural' and wild, and was to be ordered and civilised so that its resources might be accessed for those who did not live locally, nor share a common dependence on this landscape. Civilising the landscape is a process of colonisation and colonisers have a historic tendency to perceive landscape spaces as empty of people. The landscapes of conventional agriculture in Australia are associated with technological innovation to maintain productive capacity for world trade.

The landscape is also constructed conceptually, through trade and agricultural policy decisions. The changes they demand manifest themselves, at a local level, in the usefulness of a road, the viability of a small market village, or in the habitation patterns across the hills. As populations decrease in rural areas, there are fewer people to remember landscape changes. Our collective memory, largely located now in urban enclosures, records the agrarian view as a static and picturesque object.

The appropriation of common land coincides with the disappearance of communities from the landscape, with colonisation processes aimed at maximising production. The view is transformed to reflect a different expectation of public and private land management.

Fence lines become synonymous with a civilised and occupied landscape. The settler fences affirmed the barriers between the new colonists and the rapidly dispossessed Aboriginal land managers. The fences prevented Aboriginal people burning to maintain grassland vegetation communities.

While individual and common property rights are socially constructed forms of ownership, the concept of common property depends on tacit cooperation of the players regarding land use (Steelman and Carmin, 1998). The commons disappeared and the landscape was 'taken up' with the orderliness of production systems. Colonisation is necessarily about power. It brings change to the landscape. The changes in Australia reflected distant landscape ideas and production needs (Beilin, 1998a). Contemporary international global agriculture is similarly powerful, penetrating the Australian rural landscape and changing its landscape patterns. Australian agricultural technology supported innovative farming. It long overcame the Australian conditions, but created a tension between the underlying character of the Australian landscape and production dictates. The appearance of blue-green algae in the water, salinity, and landslips are just a few examples visually alerting us to changes associated with landscape degradation. We have cause to question our nation's land management in a global production system.

CATCHMENT MANAGEMENT

Australian land management emphasises the rights of private landowners to individually manage their landscapes. In the State of Victoria, some 63 per cent of the land is in private hands. Conforming to liberal political traditions, the prevailing land-use ethic reinforces a moral obligation to preserve the public good with minimal interference in private property rights. Land-use regulations may limit individual property rights but reinforce a fundamentally people-first position (Shrader-Frechette, 1993a, p. 49). The faith in private property rights manifest by individual landowners, masks the reality of the global processes influencing land management for production and values.

Federal interest in sustainability has focused attention on the lack of biodiversity on private agricultural landscapes as well as upon the need to encourage a moral recognition of the local and the global importance of off-reserve conservation zones. Voluntary compliance programmes, rather than regulation, are perceived to be the way to promote sustainable land-use management. Similar to Australia, 60 per cent of the land in the US is privately owned, and there is a significant increase in voluntary, but in this case market-oriented, conservation programmes such as set aside of environmentally sensitive land or conservation easements between an owner and the state (Wiebe et al., 1997). Programmes like Australia's Landcare, Bushcare, Coastcare, Streamcare, and Waterwatch encourage local groups to enter partnerships with government and promote landscape management changes at a community level. Prior to the surge in these programmes, River

Management Authorities and soil conservation groups laid the foundations for land and water management within geographic areas (Ewing, 1995).

An international focus on catchments as potential units of integrated land and water management coincided in Australia, as others have noted elsewhere, with government efforts to downsize their ministries and agencies (Mitchell, 1997; Vanclay and Lawrence, 1995). This process of 'streamlining', creating partnerships with local governments and involving the private sector in the delivery of services implies a diminishing of central government intervention and regulatory responsibilities (Mitchell, 1997). As a consequence of the amalgamation of agencies and boards in the 'streamlining process', the UK experience in writing Catchment Management Plans (CMPs) resulted in plans confounded by inherited institutional processes and purpose (Gardiner, 1997). The new CMPs' operational plans tended to reflect the culture and politics of the planning manager rather than an understanding of their broader meaning or likely use, and generally did not involve communities in the planning process (Gardiner, 1997).

The Trend to Catchment Management

The international trend to catchment (or watershed) management suggests a global recognition of the values associated with this approach. Its origin is basically as a spatial form. Catchments are originally units of hydrological science. Over the last twenty years, however, these have been transformed to administrative land and water management units. Administration and management are, by association with hydrology as a science, made to appear scientific. There is seen to be a synergy between the objectives of resource management, administration control and a systems approach to managing the land. Language is important in conveying intention, and 'catchment' evokes the idea of a container, of things being caught. Sustainable development, ecosystems and communities are contained within the general sense of a 'catchment' as a geographic (rather than community-defined) area.

Consider the time of the enclosures in the United Kingdom. Vroom (1990) suggests enclosure of the English Open Field system with hedgerows took approximately 200 years. Others argue it was a more gradual and longer process from 1235 onward (Anon., 1992b, p. 132). Significantly, enclosing of land made it property for an elite group and encouraged the trading of land as a commodity. The newly landless offered their labour as a commodity. The United Kingdom progressively destroyed its hedgerow system after World War II, to amalgamate fields and encourage larger-scale production. However, in contemporary times the European Union (EU) is actively encouraging the reconstitution of hedgerows. Their arguments for doing so emphasise biodiversity. It is notable that the EU is determined to maintain European farming landscapes, to the extent that many regions are protected from development under conservation and heritage preservation regulations. These landscapes represent scenic types. In reality the EU imports most of its food from other nations through its global trade. It can afford to maintain quaint and historic modes of production, and even to reconstitute biodiversity, because its landscapes now represent the antithesis of change. Its hedgerows enclose the present as romantic images of regional lifestyles. The 'rooms' within these green walls house landscape portraits in a living museum. These are cultural enclosures, providing the nation with a good source of dollars from heritage tourism.

The treed hedgerows or shelterbelts in the Australian experience connect individual farms to the catchment. This provides new lines on the landscape, sympathetic to ecological principles, while linking properties together within the catchment. The catchment as a geographic region, combining with the social systems ideas of landscape ecology, extends the concept of landscape scale beyond private ownership, connecting individual farm landscapes. The symbolic and real power of private property as represented in farm fence lines is erased in the name of ecology, but the catchment's real organisational value to global trade is in the removal of local barriers to the global capital system. These fence lines are only symbolic barriers given the reality of market penetration, but their symbolic importance cannot be underrated in relation to private property rights.

The local rhetoric of catchment management is not explicitly about these global connections. Indeed, it promotes local knowledge, partnership and ownership of land and water issues among the residents of the catchment. The Catchment and Land Protection Act of 1994 in Victoria, Australia specifically states that the Act intends to set up a framework for the integrated management and protection of catchments, and to encourage community participation in the management of land and water resources.

CATCHMENT AND LAND PROTECTION ACTS

The Catchment and Land Protection Act (CALP) of 1994, and the Water Act of 1989, have provided the legislative base for incorporating catchment management into the institutional processes of the State (Sutherland and Doolan, 1997). Another change, an amendment to the Catchment Land Protection Act (1998) changed CALP Boards to Catchment Management Authorities and allowed these authorities to derive income from rating (taxing) local property. The reference to 'protection of the catchments' is undoubtedly in response to the Victorian State government's perception of an internal threat to ecological values. This focus distracts attention from the reality of global, and therefore external, landscape penetration. It also does not make explicit the permeability of the catchment battlements, as transnational corporations are already present within these landscapes. The catchment, then, is not a local defence force for an ecosystem. A more complex understanding of this landscape scene is required.

Catchment Management in Victoria

Consider how the catchment overlies previous landscape patterns. These older patterns were constructed by those living in these landscapes. They are both community-based and commodity-based patterns associated with *place*. Catchment management, at the very moment of professing to be *place-based*, erases difference, collapses scale and dissolves 'the local'. Places, actors and local knowledge lose their influence. Through the statutory powers given them, the Catchment Management Authorities in Victoria are effectively regional governments, appointed rather than elected, able to decide on the ecological and landscape management of their domains by controlling regional, state and federal funding. Local farmers have a compulsory tithe to these CMAs. Federal and state governments reinforce the CMAs by directing programme funding through their boards. (An example of this is National Heritage Trust funds for Landcare, Australia's community-based conservation programme.)

On the surface, within the landscape, the workings of the CMAs should be transparent. Examination of the socioeconomic issues involved in the CMA process reveals several concerns. First, there is farmer consultation in the setting of strategies that form the approved CMA plans. As with Gardiner's (1977) report on the CMPs in Scotland compared to England, the smaller number of people in a catchment resulted in more grassroots involvement and more community-based activities. But in observing how power works within the landscape, it is apparent the government-appointed CMA representatives are not necessarily representatives of the people. They can easily be, and often are, the same group of elite and powerful people who from generation to generation dominate communities (Krannich and Smith, 1998). Within the CMAs are representatives of powerful transnationals. They hold significant 'gifts' in hand for the regions they enter and local people, on the CMAs, are aware of this corporate power to change the landscape. 'Assumptions that the interests of individuals, communities and capital will necessarily converge are no longer tenable' in the so-called partnership model because the ability of farmers to participate is based on power relations within their local scene (Gray and Phillips, 1997, p. 98). A fair negotiation process cannot be assumed between unequal members and compromise may be elicited from weaker landscape proponents, where none should have been required.

A second cause for concern within the CMAs centres on the linking of ecology to the catchment system. There is a kind of romance about attaching ecological benefit to management plans, as in the creation of tree corridors along formerly bare fence lines. Government departments are keen to reintegrate fragmented landscapes (Hobbs and Saunders, 1993; Webb, 1994). Here concepts such as biodiversity can be played out as improved landscapes, including nature-like reserves abutting agriculturally intensive fields. This is the creation of the landscape management mosaic, touted by landscape ecologists (Forman and Godron, 1986). However, there is no guarantee that the catchment management system is able to protect all aspects of the landscapes it encompasses. I have described how market forces easily penetrate the landscape, but there is also a more sinister aspect, associated with *global fundamentalism*, that of 'total use' resource exploitation. Even if conservation is an equal player in the deliberations of the CMAs – equal with production and resource harvestable landscapes – this only implies the potential commodification of conserved species. Is it not a brave new world to talk of how science and industry might combine to exploit indigenous flora and fauna gene pools?

More basic and less sinister is the recognition that safeguarding important ecosystems in the Australian situation actually involves knowing what is in them. Enclosing the landscape in catchment units is not a guarantee of ecological sophistication in landscape management. Ecological management is the key to maintaining ecosystems (Samson and Knopf, 1996). However, there is international recognition that fundamental ecological concepts remain untested or unproven (Gardiner et al., 1994, p. 64). Much of Australia's floral and faunal associations remain a mystery. This may not be a negative, given their possible exploitation by outside forces if they are of commercial value. However, the reality is that they may disappear because they are unknown, and because of the possibility of an administrative land-use decision, antithetical to very local conservation values. If catchment management is being promoted as a way of ensuring biodiversity as a counter to production values, then this lack of a local vector to the administrative policy centre could easily be a recipe for ecosystem failure.

Finally, there is the moral reality that managing a catchment as a resource exposes its communities and its landscapes to the threat of greater global exploitation, in effect creating a 'free trade zone' with all the advantages and disadvantages that entails.

THE BRAVE NEW ORDER

Central to the issues surrounding catchment management in the constructed landscape is the place of private land in relation to that of land held in common. I have attempted to draw attention to the contrariness of practice over expectation, because, despite society upholding private agrarian land rights, it has undermined the ability of farmers to control this land – something certainly reflected in their unsustainable production systems. Land management decisions, shaping private landscapes, reflect homogeneous world market demands despite varying local terrains and growing conditions. Conversely, the commons, which really was not public but ensured exclusive community or family access to supplementary land, is buried as an inappropriate form of land stewardship. This is despite the similarities of its central precepts in the creation, for example, of contemporary riparian nature reserves and shelterbelts on private land.

Using the Victorian example, the current 'catchment' is defined as 'an area which through run-off or percolation, contributes to the water in a stream or stream system'; and 'land' includes 'soil, water, vegetation and fauna on land' (CALP Act No.52/1994, pp. 2–3). A first step to resisting the global resource exploitation of agrarian landscapes and the disappearance of local 'places' is to change this definition to incorporate people. These everyday-landscape managers may offer resistance to change because of their diversity of purpose and varying levels of integration with global forces. This allows a pause for people to become aware of the implications and participate in decision making. Resistance to change is not necessarily negative and it offers a chance to improve the democratic process from the catchment outwards. The involvement of people interacting in an effort to inform the process creates a public sphere and the foundation of civil society (Drysek, 1996, p. 47). This creates a 'commons of intention' and recognises a people's landscape.

The second step is to acknowledge the position of public good within the catchment mandate as being of premier importance. There is, of course, the public good associated with the hydrological function of the catchment; with the positioning of satellite receivers; and the conservation values of national parks. These examples provide interesting evidence of the private benefit that stems, and may seriously detract, from the public good. For example, private farmers or multinational plantation owners who dam rivers or divert water upstream, starving both other farmers and conservation areas downstream, may be viewed as having undertaken activities which are not in the public good. Similarly, global telecommunication systems have the capacity to locate and connect us, but in so doing there is the risk of their infiltrating our culture, and reshaping and repackaging local scenes for global commodification and consumption.

The importance in identifying the catchment as a parallel commons lies, however, in exploring its significant differences. The strength of the commons was in its social organisation (Anon., 1992a). Concepts of ownership were less important than ideas relating to stewardship, custodianship or guardianship of land and water resources. Current catchment management strategies take as their first assumption that all resources within the catchment, including human resources if they are to be considered, are capable of being exploited. Biodiversity plans are generally shaped with 'production first' values in mind. This necessarily implies a 'use' basis for policy making. The commons, by contrast, do not originate from the point of scarcity, but of communal access. Administrators have harnessed ecology and economics, both social sciences, to facilitate the transfer of centralist policies and to tie catchment units to the larger regional and national strategic purpose (Shrader-Frechette, 1993b). This means that at any one time there are a set of assumptions and variables in operation that profoundly affect the outcomes. Both ecology and economics are good for modelling, but they continually need to be 'ground-truthed'.

In the best imitation of colonial forces, we interpret ecology to affirm bureaucratic intentions to order the landscape. Ecology is used to justify rural landuse conservation planning policies (DuPuis, 1996). However, because the goals of ecosystem management largely focus on the best ecological outcomes, the significance of people in the landscape is minimized (Solecki, 1998).

Administratively, harnessing the fragments of the landscape into the catchment provides leverage for state control of resources. I argue here, in the Habermasian tradition, that the state itself reflects the forces of global capital and is acting as the market place. The global banner offers a connectivity that is lacking in local areas. The romantic ecological view promotes connectivity, sought through linking corridors of trees across farms and reserves, and reinforces the apparent 'rightness' of global connections. Yet, by enclosing the landscape in catchments, the catchments themselves become the new commodities.

CONCLUSION

Miranda in *The Tempest*, is said to represent the new order of things that have evolved from the destructive forces of the past. She is symbolic of the future. She cannot arrive at the new lands, however, without recognising and questioning the processes of change required to the existing order.

In Huxley's *Brave New World* (1932) the choices for John Savage, the Tribal with Alpha parents, are only two. He must accept the bizarre constructs of the controlled Fordian landscape, or return to the Savage Reservation where he was always an outsider because of his parentage. Years later, Huxley wrote that the ending was the bit he would change in this famous novel. He proposed to offer Savage a chance to live in exile on one of the refugee 'politicos' islands. He defined the difference in exile as being: 'In this community, economics would be decentralist . . . science and technology would be used as though like the Sabbath, they had been made for man, not as though man were to be adapted and enslaved to them' (see Foreword in 1946 edition).

The philosophy underlying catchment management needs to be teased out and publicly debated. It cannot be assumed that we are all imagining the same future worlds or that we share the same agendas. Ideological correctness, such as was expected of the Fordians, is also associated with the appropriation of ecology in the landscape. It is hard to question something thought to be so holistic where, by association, good things must flow. On the other hand, recognising the same production landscapes underneath the ecosystem labels challenges us to explore again a way of integrating landscape policies. Central to such an integration is the reassessment of the meaning of private and common property rights.

Ecology originated with Aldo Leopold's concept of a 'land ethic'. Part of this ethic is the idea 'that humans must adapt to natural systems' (DuPuis, 1996, p. 109). Adaptation rather than exploitation of resources is the part we have still to explore. Similarly, the hierarchical reality of the current CMAs counters intuitive and systems-based thinking because the intention is to promote predominantly production landscapes. Systems can be people-centred such as those represented as organisational management networks, based on collaboration and convergence spirals (Cairncross, in Westly, 1995; Westly, 1995). What is called for is the integration of policy processes so that on-ground implementation of biodiversity strategies reflect cooperative management processes between communal decision makers. Steelman and Carmin (1998) define the conditions for this cooperation as: trust and credibility, equity, self-determination and stewardship. Cooperative catchment management can incorporate these criteria in its process. In rejecting the *Brave New World* Huxley foresaw, I urge landscape planners and policy makers, visionaries and bureaucrats to consider the significance of the commons as a land management tool that devolves power to those at a local level for the management of a landscape on which their communities depend. Similarly, people as the biographers of these landscapes represent not social capital, which is necessarily expendable, but a *social commons*, a pool of knowledge and concern about, and within, their landscapes.

REFERENCES

Anon. (1992a), 'The Commons: Where the Community has Authority', *The Ecologist*, **22** (4), 123–130.

Anon. (1992b), 'Development as Enclosure', *The Ecologist*, **22** (4), 131–148.

Beilin, R. (1998a), *Looking for Landcare: The Landscape and the Family Farm*, PhD Thesis, Melbourne: RMIT University.

Beilin, R. (1998b), 'Inside Out: Exploring the Connection Between Women's Life Stories and Landscape', *Rural Society*, **8** (3), 165–181.

Crowe, S. (1958), *The Landscape of Power*, London: Architectural Press.

Drysek, J. (1996), *Democracy in Capitalist Times*, New York: Oxford University Press.

DuPuis, E. (1996), 'In the Name of Nature: Ecology, Marginality, and Rural Land Use Planning During the New Deal', in E. DuPuis and P. Vandergeest (eds), *Creating the Countryside: the Politics of Rural and Environmental Discourse*, Philadelphia: Temple University Press, pp. 99–134.

Ewing, S. (1995), *It's in Your Hands: An Assessment of the Australian Landcare Movement*, PhD thesis, University of Melbourne, Department of Geography and Environmental Studies.

Forman, R. and M. Godron (1986), *Landscape Ecology*, New York: Wiley.

Gardiner, J. (1997), 'ICM in the UK – An Overview of Progress', in 2nd National Workshop on Integrated Catchment Management, 'Advancing Integrated Resource Management: Processes and Policies', Canberra: River Basin Management Society, ANU, 29 Sept.–1 Oct.

Gardiner, J., K. Thomson and M. Newson (1994), 'Integrated Watershed/River Catchment Planning and Management: A Comparison of Selected Canadian and United Kingdom Experiences', in *Journal of Environmental Planning and Management*, **37** (1), 53–67.

Gray, I., T. Dunn and E. Phillips (1997), 'Power, Interests and the Extension of Sustainable Agriculture', *Sociologia Ruralis*, **37** (1), 97–113.

Hobbs, R. and D. Saunders (eds) (1993), *Reintegrating Fragmented Landscapes: Towards Sustainable Production and Nature Conservation*, New York: Springer-Verlag.

Huxley, A. (1932), *Brave New World*, Flamingo Modern Classic Edition 1994, London: Flamingo.

Jackson, J. (1986), 'The Vernacular Landscape', in E. Penning-Rowsell and D. Lowenthal (eds), *Landscape Meanings and Values*, London: Allen and Unwin, pp. 65–81.

Krannich, R. and M. Smith (1998), 'Local Perceptions of Public Lands Natural Resource Management in the Rural West: Toward Improved Understanding of the "Revolt in the West"', *Society and Natural Resources*, **11**, 677–695.

Mitchell, B. (1997), 'Melbourne + 9: Canadian Approaches and Progress Regarding Integrated Catchment Mangement', in 2nd National Workshop on Integrated Catchment Management, 'Advancing Integrated Resource Management: Processes and Policies'. River Basin Management Society, ANU, 29 Sept.–1 Oct.

Samson, F. and F. Knopf (1996), 'Putting "Ecosystems" into Natural Resource Management', *Journal of Soil and Water Conservation*, July–Aug., 288–292.

Samuels, M. (1979), 'The Biography of Landscape: Cause and Culpability', in D. Meinig (ed.), *The Interpretation of Ordinary Landscapes: Geographical Essays*, New York: Oxford University Press, pp. 51–88.

Shakespeare, W. *The Tempest*, Langbaum, R. (ed.), The Signet Classic Shakespeare Edition, 1964, New York: Signet.

Shrader-Frechette, K. (1993a), 'Four Land Ethics: An Overview', in L. Caldwell and K. Shrader-Frechette (eds), *Policy for Land: Law and Ethics*, Maryland: Rowman and Littlefield Publishers, pp. 43–62.

Shrader-Frechette, K. (1993b), 'Problems with Ecosystemic Criteria for Land Policy', in L. Caldwell and K. Shrader-Frechette (eds), *Policy for Land: Law and Ethics*, Maryland: Rowman and Littlefield Publishers, pp. 209–226.

Smart, B. (1992), *Modern Conditions, Postmodern Controversies*, London: Routledge.

Solecki, W. (1998), 'Local Attitudes on Regional Ecosystem Management: A Study of New Jersey Pinelands Residents', *Society and Natural Resources*, 11, 441–463.

Steelman, T. and J. Carmin (1998), 'Common Property, Collective Interests, and Community Opposition to Locally Unwanted Land Uses', in *Society and Natural Resources*, 11, 485–504.

Sutherland, P. and J. Doolan (1997), 'Victoria's Catchment Management Authorities Community Empowerment with Accountability', in 2nd National Workshop on Integrated Catchment Management, 'Advancing Integrated Resource Management: Processes and Policies', Canberra, ANU: River Basin Management Society, 29 Sept.–1 Oct.

Vanclay, F. and G. Lawrence (1995) *The Environmental Imperative: Eco-social Concerns for Australian Agriculture*, Rockhampton: CQU Press.

Vroom, M. (1990), 'Introduction and Theme', *Landscape and Urban Planning*, (18), 189–195.

Webb, N. (1994), 'The Habitat, the Biotope and the Landscape', in J. Dover (ed.), *Fragmentation in Agricultural Landscapes*, Proceedings of the 3rd Annual Conference of IALE, UK of the International Association for Landscape Ecology, 13–14 Sept. Bilsborrow, Preston: Myerscough College, pp. 21–29.

Westly, F. (1995), 'Governing Design: The Management of Social Systems and Ecosystems Management', in L. Gunderson, C. Holling and S. Light (eds), *Barriers and Bridges to the Renewal of Ecosystems and Institutions*, New York: Columbia University Press, pp. 391–427.

Wiebe, K., A. Tegene and B. Kuhn (1997), 'Finding Common Ground on Public and Private Land', *Journal of Soil and Water Conservation*, May–June, 162–165.

13. Competing Forestry Management Paradigms in Australian State Forests

Barbara J. Geno

INTRODUCTION

The conquering and settlement of the 'new' continent of Australia was an integral part of the project of modernity. The promises of modernity can be summarised as 'control over nature through science, material abundance through superior technology and effective government through rational social organisation' (Norgaard, 1994, p. 1). The problem of modernity has been that increasing reliance on science and technology to produce material abundance has brought with it the risk of environmental destruction (Schnaiberg and Gould, 1994). It has also become increasingly evident that science, as a social construction, is subject to interpretation and evidence of ecological crisis is contestable (Benton and Short, 1999, p. 148). The perception of these risks led to a growth in environmentalism in the past three decades (Buttel, 1999), culminating in a call for sustainable development (see Redclift and Woodgate, 1997). Environmental risks are mitigated by the further application of science and technology (Beck, 1992) and the use of environmental impact assessment and environmental management systems in a process of 'ecological modernization' to achieve (ecologically) sustainable development (Mol, 1995).

Modernisation also brought 'globalisation' which impacts on development as markets and political institutions transcend national boundaries (Buttel, 1999; Schnaiberg and Gould, 1994). The forces of globalisation affect political institutions of the modern nation-state through the widespread adoption of 'managerialism', where the [nation] state adopts policies in response to international market forces (Buttel, 1999) or attempts to run government bureaucracies profitably in order to support a welfare society (O'Connor, 1973). Managerialism emphasises the rational decision making characteristics of the modern project and reinforces the Weberian emphasis on a calculative rationality focused on money and accounting, and, as such, fuels a global capitalist economy (O'Connor, 1994; Schnaiberg and Gould, 1994).

Increasingly, it is thought that global environmental problems call for global solutions, and the need to 'overcome the incompatibility between the political rationality of state economic regulation and the requirements of environmental sustainability' (Hay, 1994, p. 221). Thus the perceived role of the nation-state has expanded from the traditional modernist goals of 'economic growth, monetary stability, national security, and so on' to an 'embedded autonomy' which embraces a state–society synergy (Buttel, 1999, p. 10). More and more global agreements are reached with regard to the management of environmental risks and natural resources (Sklair, 1994). As part of the quest for ecologically sustainable development to take the place of environmentally destructive modern development, mechanisms are sought which involve citizens in decision making regarding the use of natural resources (Gould and Schnaiberg, 1996). This participatory democracy precedes the rational society of Weber where the state is insulated from society (Evans, 1995, p. 41). Under Evans' concept of a state–society synergy, mechanisms for the management of natural resources work within a framework of mutual reinforcement with civil society (Evans 1995, p. 228). Yet, the forces of Weber's rationality are still evident in the modern nation-state, seemingly co-existing with these new developments.

In this chapter, a critical analysis conducted on the annual reports of six state forestry agencies in Australia revealed the potential for conflict between the modernisation of state agencies in adopting managerialism and the attempt to institute ecologically sustainable development. This conflict is most evident between the evolving corporate management practices and the ecologically sensitive management demanded by adoption of the Montreal Process (otherwise known as the Santiago Agreement, 1995) for the conduct of sustainable forestry by national and state government (Turner and Pribble, 1996). Two different forest management paradigms developed in parallel during the period examined in this case study of Australian state forest agencies. A sociological context is employed to give meaning to the implications of this parallel development.

EVOLUTION OF FORESTRY MANAGEMENT IN AUSTRALIA

For nearly a century, Australian forests were considered to be so vast as to require little attention with regard to conservation or management as a scarce natural resource. Early exploration of Australia was as much to identify usable agricultural land, harvestable quantities of animals, birds and fish, and usable timber resources as it was to provide a place to locate both convict and free settlers (Carron, 1985). Timber cutting started nearly a century before comprehensive timber inventory or widespread concern for conservation. The states varied in their recognition of a need for professional forest management; however, most states instituted Forestry Commissions led by professional foresters shortly before or just after the First World War (Carron, 1985). Statement of accounts from the State Forestry Commissions during most of this century report on the value of timber sold and the expenses of protecting the forests from fire and disease; the primary concern of forest management was the harvesting of economically valuable timber.

SUSTAINED YIELDS AND MULTIPLE-USE MANAGEMENT

As a consequence of the 'sustained yield' approach, professional foresters were employed as forest managers, which followed European experience in forestry management (Dellert, 1998; Vanclay, 1996b). The management of forests centred on the concept that annual cuts should be sustained at a level that was roughly equivalent to the annual growth in the forest (Corona and Scotti, 1998; Vanclay, 1996a). This type of management arose from a science based on forests with single dominant species that experience fairly uniform growth that can be readily measured (Mladenoff and Pastor, 1993, pp. 157–158). Management strategies are based on comprehensive measurements in the forest of potential sawlogs and annual growth increments in order to deliver consistent supplies of timber to the sawmillers and thus support a viable timber industry (Forestry Commission Tasmania, 1982). Sustained yield models are much more difficult to implement in diverse natural forests such as the rainforests found in Australia (Vanclay, 1996a).

While forest management was dominated by sustained yield models with the aim of supplying the industry until well into the 1980s, most state forestry commissions also recognised the principles of multiple use in both native forests and plantations (Carron, 1985). Under multiple use management systems, management planning and timber harvesting regulations sought to ensure that valued landscapes and important biological and cultural sites received state protection. By the 1990s, multiple use had become expansively defined by various states into such concepts as: 'provid[ing] the community and government with a range of forestry services including recreational opportunities, management of native forests for the conservation of flora and fauna, development of farm forestry, forest protection, technical supply and productive use of waste water' (Primary Industries South Australia, 1995); 'multiple-use management, which aims to balance the intrinsic values of the forest and the range of potential uses' (DPI Queensland, 1998) and 'mak[ing] sure that native forests are managed for all values recognised by Western Australians, while noting that the importance of any particular value will vary on the forest estate' (Department of Conservation and Land, 1994).

Pressure from conservationists which began in the late 1970s led to numerous changes and greater transparency in forest management practices. This demand for change arose from the concern about the environmental risks of modern development and the discourse of environmentalism began (Redclift and Woodgate, 1994). The focus on the preservation of all values of the forests emerged from a Commonwealth initiated process and the report from the Sustainable Development Working Group on Forest Use (Commonwealth of Australia, 1992, p. 1). It was becoming increasingly recognised that forests were not just a source of timber but that the ecology of forests is a critical natural resource upon which human systems depend (Love, 1997; Rose and Simmons, 1992; Swanson and Grant, 1997). At the industry level, the response was to shift from the use of native forest to plantation-grown timber to supply sawmills and to establish a representative reserve system of protected native forest, as well as to seek ecologically sustainable management of native forests which were outside the reserve system (Commonwealth of Australia, 1995).

MANAGERIALISM IN PUBLIC SECTOR FORESTRY

The forces of modernism were at work in the public sector during the same period with an increasing perception that public sector agencies should adopt corporate practices and organisational structures with accountability mechanisms similar to the private sector or 'managerialism' (Parker and Gould, 1999). Managerialism introduced management practices such as accrual accounting, strategic planning and other techniques consistent with modern economic rationality. It fostered continued economic growth with the consequence being the overall acceptance of a 'treadmill of production' (see Buttel, 1997, p. 46) by the public sector. The legal structure of the agencies charged with the management of forestry assets in many states were changed to stand-alone agencies or state-owned corporations. As part of the process, plantation and native forest management diverged with full corporatisation of plantations in most states and native forestry corporatised in Tasmania, New South Wales, and Queensland by the mid-1990s. The annual reports of the period reflect the increased attention to managerial 'best practice'.

Public sector reform and endorsement of managerialism have concentrated on 'efficiency, effectiveness, cost savings and streamlining' (Broadbent and Guthrie, 1992, p. 3), a form of economic rationalism. Guthrie (1993, p. 17) stated the five key principles of managerialism: clear consistent objectives, delegation of ministerial authority to lower levels of the organisation, evaluation through the development of performance indicators, rewards and sanctions for performance, and managers should be allowed to manage without political interference. All of these principles were observed in the annual reports starting in the late 1980s, though states vary in their elucidation and adoption of managerialism. Vision statements began to appear in 1987 to 1988, with human resource management principles and customer focus appearing later. Certain management 'fads' can also be observed sweeping the forestry agencies, such as 'customer focus' and annual reports sporting comprehensive vision and mission statements, all part of a 'new' managerialism which is solely market driven (Parker and Gould, 1999). Weber suggested that the state and private sector enterprise would be different institutions (Murphy, 1994), but the new managerialism proposes that public and private sector practices be identical and respond equally to global market forces.

Many of the changes to forestry agencies were achieved through changes in accounting practices, which Weber considered essential to capitalism (Murphy, 1994, p. 144). Financial accountability draws primarily on legal and economic 'rationalities' which are respectively defined as 'promoting order, assigning responsibility, regulating difference and containing conflict' and 'the economic calculus by which alternative ends and/or means are compared' (Degeling et al., 1996, p. 32). Economic rationalism, as a component of managerialism, has been particularly criticised as ignoring values other than those which can be expressed in dollar terms (Jacobs, 1994). It also leads to a situation with 'an even greater obsession with what is spent, and move from the long-term interests of policy delivery (never much in evidence given the political myopia of Ministers) to the meeting of short-term targets (equivalent to the short-termism of capital markets)' (Gray and Jenkins, 1993, p. 65). Thus, it can be seen that managerialism contributes to the growth machine and continued environmental destruction (Schnaiberg and Gould, 1994).

While the public reform movement to change accounting practices to accrual accounting systems has enabled the states to consider better accounting methods to value forestry assets, the focus of the improvements in accounting for the timber industry has led to the search for forestry valuations which enhance the 'bottom line' or show that the forestry operations are either profitable or efficient in their operations through invoking cost effectiveness. By recognising incremental annual forest growth as 'revenue', albeit unrealised, the forestry agencies are able to enhance their profitability on paper and legitimise their management practices. Public sector forests are a valuable publicly owned asset in the form of not only land and trees but also in terms of its ecological functions, or 'free services'.

Pallot (1992, p. 50) draws a distinction in public sector management between accounting performed to demonstrate stewardship of community-owned assets and accounting performed to demonstrate cost-efficient use of ordinary assets that are used in the day-to-day operations. Thus, the annual reports of government agencies should not be necessarily focused on private sector-type accountability. Yet, in examining the annual reports from the six states it is clear that a conventional private sector accountability has been adopted in reporting the financial affairs of the agencies. This is exacerbated when they are subsequently corporatised, as is the case in New South Wales and Tasmania. This actively works against the emergence of sustainable forestry where the forests are managed to preserve other forest values.

THE SUSTAINABLE FORESTRY MANAGEMENT PARADIGM

In Australia, forest cover has declined by 50 per cent since settlement (State of the Environment Advisory Council, 1996, p. 33) and this loss has been associated with land degradation and other negative effects (Mercer, 1995). A debate regarding the conservation of rainforests and old-growth forests began to press the Forestry Commissions in Australia as early as the late 1970s. By the 1990s, key threats to sustainability of land resources were recognised as including inadequate conservation of old-growth forests and other forest types (State of the Environment Advisory Council, 1996, p. 33). Tree removal and land clearing remain significant contributors to greenhouse emissions. The international agreements regarding greenhouse emissions and biodiversity conservation led to a perception of the need to conserve native forests. Sustainable forestry management practices were recommended as part of the National Greenhouse Strategy to provide long-term storage of sequestered carbon (Commonwealth of Australia, 1998, p. 76).

Environmental impact assessments as routine practice arose to address the problem of environmental risk as part of preventative environmental policy during the late 1970s (Simmons, 1989). Environmental impacts assessments are intended to outline the risks of any development project or set of land use practices. They have been used extensively in Australia since the 1970s in preparing forest management plans. The science of environmental impact statements can be contested as hazards are 'defined and evaluated not privately ... but through a matrix of "quasi-governmental power positions" incorporating debate among scientific experts, juridical interpretation in the courts and comment in the mass media' (Rutherford, 1999, p. 105). EIAs readily demonstrate the social constructionism of both the 'environment' and science (Hannigan, 1995; Mol, 1995). Environmental impact assessment and other scientific studies form the backbone of the technical rationality which is used to justify forestry practices under the ecological model. Implementing sustainable forestry requires the application of more and more science and technology to demonstrate long-term sustainability (Amaranthus, 1997).

The reliance on environmental impact reviews leads to conflict between the economic rationality of the managerialism of the agency managers and the scientific rationality of the ecologically trained foresters (Binkley, 1998). The annual reports examined frequently refer to the expenditure of large amounts of funds yearly in conducting these studies and the preparation of environmental impact assessment and forest management plans that are based on ecological studies. Agencies are politically motivated to escape from the need to file environmental impact statements as part of forest management plans. The agencies are also increasingly disillusioned by the knowledge that equally 'scientific' impact statements can come to widely differing conclusions regarding the allowable timber cut.

A 'NEW' RESOURCE MANAGEMENT PARADIGM FOR FORESTRY

The dominant resource management paradigm of this century held that the environment exists to produce goods and services and that amenities are merely coincident to commodity production (Brown and Harris, 1992). Traditional forest management practices are characterised by clear cutting, herbicides and slash burning with centralised decision making by 'experts'. A 'new resource management paradigm' arose recently which suggests that amenity outputs are of primary importance, that nature exists for its own sake, and environmental protection takes priority over production with concern for both current and future generations (Brown and Harris, 1992, p. 234). Forest management is less intensive and is focused on long-term conservation. Decision making in the new resource paradigm is consultative, participatory and decentralised. The extreme end-point of community ownership and economic involvement in the new resource management paradigm suggests that forestry be entrusted to community-based ecoforestry and community economic systems (Drengson, 1994). These changes in forestry management philosophy have been documented in North America (Xu and Bengston, 1997) and were observed in the analysis of the 15 years of Australian annual reports.

The annual reports of the forestry commissions and successor organisations reflect the anguish that the forestry professionals encounter in relinquishing centralised control and expert decision making. By the early 1990s a consultation process was in place in most states and was included as part of the National Forest Policy by stating that 'the Australian community will have a sound understanding of the values of forests and sustainable forest management, and will participate in decision making processes relating to forest use and management' (Commonwealth of Australia, 1992, p. 3). However, the democratisation of forest management in the new resource management paradigm has been subject to 'agency capture' through the re-emergence of scientific management and the privileging of expert knowledge through implementation of environmental management systems under the Montreal Process.

ENVIRONMENTAL MANAGEMENT SYSTEMS AND ISO 14001

Environmental management systems are a standardised set of processes and accompanying documentation which can be used for a variety of purposes. Many different models and different definitions have arisen in the management and accounting literature. Gray et al. (1993, p. 90) pointed out that environmental management system (EMS) are a combination of the organisation's environmental policies, environmental strategies and the ongoing environmental audits. Gray et al. (1993, p. 52) identified a number of stages in developing an EMS:

1. Assess impact through environmental review.
2. Develop policy with a policy statement and guidelines.
3. Set corporate objectives and targets with measurable objectives.
4. Identify responsibilities and divisional/departmental objectives/ targets.
5. Integrate management systems.

Procedures and controls interact with information and reporting to provide for environmental management in the organisation. The sequencing of the EMS has the advantage of recommending an environmental audit to determine the areas in which the organisation should set environmental policy as an *a priori* activity. The differing models for environmental management systems were refined by the International Standards Organization Committee into a set of guidelines. The ISO 14001 guidelines contain the following elements (Lamprecht, 1997, p. 76):

1. *Environmental policy.*
2. *Planning*, including environmental aspects, legal requirements, objectives and targets, environmental management programmes.

3. *Implementation and operation* containing sections on structure and responsibility, training, awareness and competence, communications, environmental management system documentation, document control, operational control, emergency preparedness and response.
4. *Checking and corrective action*, including monitoring and measurement, non-conformance and corrective and preventive action, environmental management audit and management review.

Environmental management systems under ISO 14001, like ISO 9000 quality systems, are process-oriented and inherently serve to document processes rather than focus on actual outcomes. The utility of the EMS for addressing environmental risk is found in the quality of the proposed measures and monitoring. It is possible to have an EMS which faithfully captures unsustainable environmental management.

STANDARDISATION OF FOREST MANAGEMENT

The worldwide conflict over forest resources between forest managers and environmentalists led to considerable controversy regarding the precise management practices that are consistent with a sustainably managed forest. The UNCED Conference in Rio de Janeiro in 1992 reinforced the necessity to develop methods of distinguishing timber products which come from sustainably managed forests from products that do not, with numerous groups working on the development of universal standards. A confusing array of sustainable management systems, many of which include certification of the timber as sustainable, now exists. Goals, criteria and indicators are usual components of the management systems for certification (Lamport, 1995; van Bueren and Blom, 1997).

The Montreal Process, adopted by Australia, provides for 'criteria and indicators for the conservation and sustainable management of temperate and boreal forests' (van Bueren and Blom, 1997, pp. 52–54). The focus of the Montreal process is to translate broad principles of forestry management such as 'conservation of biological diversity' and 'maintenance of productive capacity of forest ecosystem' into measurable indicators for forest unit management practices such as 'the number of forest dependent species' and 'annual removal of wood products compared to the volume determined to be sustainable' (van Bueren and Blom, 1997, p. 52). Environmental management systems, such as the ISO 14001, can be used to provide for input and process indicators to measure sustainability (van Bueren and Blom, 1997, p. 28). The National Association of Forest Industries (NAFI) in Australia endorsed the use of the ISO 14001 environmental management systems to standardise sustainable forestry management (NAFI, 1998). Queensland and New South Wales have also adopted the strategy of using environmental management systems.

Lamport (1995) notes that the use of ISO 14001 guidelines does not establish absolute requirements for environmental performance. This is because EMSs are process-oriented and provide for a management system, but do not prescribe management practices that are sustainable. DPI Forestry (n.d.) suggested that the use of ISO 14001 quality systems for environmental management of forests can 'optimise and maintain long term productivity, minimise on and off-site adverse impacts, improve environmental operations through the adoption of commercial best practice, enhance public acceptance of products and DPI Forestry activities and facilitate environmental certification of timber products by industry'. State Forests of NSW (1998, p. 12) announced that 'the system defines clear roles and responsibilities and written procedures for State Forests staff and contractors in everyday forest management'.

AGENCY CAPTURE OF ENVIRONMENTAL MANAGEMENT

When all of the prose of the annual reports is considered, it is evident that the states vary in the extent to which they have embraced the principles of sustainable forestry management. Queensland and NSW are the most committed to the use of environmental management systems under ISO 14001. The reasons for this were not immediately evident in the case analysis. However, conversations with individuals in the Department of Natural Resources, who audit Queensland forest management, with DPI Forestry and with the head of State Forests NSW forest management section revealed that EMS is an ongoing management plan which uses codes of practice to determine day-to-day operations and is replacing the environmental impact statement previously required by law. Traditionally, environmental impact statements are prepared by ecologists and other scientists. The environmental management system, in contrast, employs a management philosophy and is drawn up by a professional manager trained in ISO guidelines. Standardization through codes of practice is viewed as 'cost-effective' (Turner and Pribble, 1996). This represents a return to the scientific management and rationality of modernity and rejects the democratisation of the new resource management paradigm by excluding public participation in the development of codes of practice.

CONCLUSIONS

It can be argued that the implementation of ISO 14001 quality management systems under the Montreal Process in Australian native forests represents agency capture of the new resource paradigm, and of sustainable forestry by managerialism. It can also be argued that, through the choice of the use of environmental management systems and standardised codes of practice, the state agencies in charge of forestry are primarily concerned with profitability of the operations while being seen to be implementing sustainable forestry. It should be readily apparent that cost-effectiveness and commercial concerns are reflected in both the management philosophies and the statements made concerning forest management. It is also evident in this case study that neither multiple-use management nor sustained yield as management practices were dislodged by the inclusion of principles intended to meet criteria set under the Montreal Process.

While the process of implementing ISO 14001 environmental management guidelines in forestry management in Australia is incomplete at present, examination of the two states which are furthest down that track would indicate that the scientific rationality represented by experts conducting environmental impacts assessment has been replaced by the managerial rationality of those planning continuous improvement and quality systems and environmental codes of practice (see, for example, McCormack, 1996). Whether the environmental management systems required by the Montreal Process are more effective in attaining sustainable forestry remains to be seen. The message for the professional foresters who are being displaced by professional managers in the state system is to seek to open the discourse of sustainable forestry to public participation and to resist the corporatisation of Australia's forests. The corporatisation process clearly fuels a capitalist process that acts as a counterforce to ecologically sustainable development. These developments point to the potential for a state-led backlash to the emerging state–society synergies which promise solutions to the ecological crisis.

REFERENCES

Amaranthus, M. (1997), *Forest Sustainability: An Approach to Definition and Assessment*, General Technical Report PNW-GTR-416, Portland: USDA Forest Service, Pacific Northwest Research Station.

Beck, U. (1992), *Risk Society: Towards a New Modernity*, M. Ritter (trans), London: Sage Publications.

Benton, L. and J. Short (1999), *Environmental Discourse and Practice*, Oxford: Blackwell.

Binkley, C. (1998), 'Sustainable Forestry, the Forestry Profession and Forestry Education: Some Lessons from North America', *Journal of Sustainable Forestry*, 7 (1/2), 111–126.

Broadbent, J. and J. Guthrie (1992), 'Changes in the Public Sector: A Review of Recent "Alternative Accounting Research"', *Accounting, Auditing and Accountability Journal*, 5 (2), 3–31.

Brown, G. and C. Harris (1992), 'The U.S. Forest Service: Toward the New Resource Management Paradigm?', *Society and Natural Resources*, 5, 321–345.

Buttel, F. (1997), 'Social Institutions and Environmental Change', in M. Redclift and G. Woodgate (eds), *The International Handbook of Environmental Sociology*, Cheltenham: Edward Elgar, pp. 40–54.

Buttel, F. (1999), 'Environmental Sociology and the Sociology of Natural Resources: Strategies for Synthesis and Cross-Fertilization', paper presented at the International Symposium on Society and Resource Management, 7–10 July, Brisbane: University of Queensland.

Carron, L. (1985), *A History of Forestry in Australia*, Canberra: Australian National University Press.

Commonwealth of Australia (1992), *National Forest Policy Statement: A New Focus for Australia's Forests*, Canberra: Australian Government Printer.

Commonwealth of Australia (1995), *Wood and Paper Industry Strategy*, Canberra: Australian Government Printer.

Commonwealth of Australia (1998), *A Framework of Regional (Sub-national) Level Criteria and Indicators of Sustainable Forest Management*, Canberra: Forests Division, Department of Primary Industries.

Corona, P. and R. Scotti (1998), 'Forest Growth and Field Modelling: Questioning Support for Sustainable Forest Management', *Journal of Sustainable Forestry*, 7 (3/4), 131–143.

Degeling, P., J. Anderson and J. Guthrie (1996), 'Accounting for Public Accounts Committees', *Accounting, Auditing and Accountability Journal*, 9 (2), 30–49.

Dellert, L. (1998), 'Sustained Yield: Why has it Failed to Achieve Sustainability?', in C. Tollefson (ed.), *The Wealth of Forests*, Vancouver: University of British Columbia Press, pp. 255–277.

Department of Conservation and Land (1994), *Annual Report 1993/94*, Department of Conservation and Land Western Australia, Bentley Delivery Center.

DPI Queensland (1998), *An Overview of the Queensland Forest Industry*, Brisbane: DPI Forestry.

Drengson, A. (1994), 'A Model for Ecoforestry Community Economic Systems', *International Journal of Ecoforestry*, 10 (3), 110–112

Evans, P. (1995), *Embedded Autonomy: States and Industrial Transformation*, Princeton: Princeton University Press.

Forestry Commission Tasmania (1982), *Report for Year 1980–81*, Hobart: I. C. Carter, Acting Government Printer.

Gould, K. and A. Schnaiberg (1996), *Local Environmental Struggles: Citizen Activism in the Treadmill of Production*, Cambridge: University of Cambridge.

Gray, A. and B. Jenkins (1993), Codes of Accountability in the New Public Sector, *Accounting, Auditing and Accountability Journal*, 6 (3), 52–65.

Gray, R. with J. Bebbington and D. Walters (1993), *Accounting for the Environment*, London: Paul Chapman.

Guthrie, J. (1993), 'Australian Public Sector Accounting: Transformations and Managerialism', *Accounting Research Journal*, 6 (3), 15–25.

Hannigan, J. (1995), *Environmental Sociology*, New York: Routledge.

Hay, C. (1994), 'Environmental Security and State Legitimacy', in M. O'Connor (ed.), *Is Capitalism Sustainable?*, New York: The Guilford Press, pp. 217–231.

Jacobs, M. (1994), 'The Limits to Neoclassicism: Towards an Institutional Environmental Economics', in M. Redclift and G. Woodgate (eds), *Social Theory and the Global Environment*, London: Routledge, pp. 67–112.

Lamprecht, J. (1997), *ISO 14000: Issues and Implementation Guidelines for Responsible Environmental Management*, New York: AMACOM.

Lamport, L. (1995), 'The Cast of Certifiers: Who are They?', *International Journal of Ecoforestry*, **11** (4), 118–127.

Love, R. (1997), 'The Sound of Crashing Timber: Moving to an Ecological Sociology', *Society and Natural Resources*, **10**, 211–222.

McCormack, R. (1996), 'A Review of Forest Practice Codes in Australia', in D. Dystra and R. Heinrich (eds), *Forest Codes of Practice: Contributing to Environmentally Sound Operations*, Rome: FAO, pp. 105–115.

Mercer, D. (1995), A *Question of Balance: Natural Resources Conflict Issues in Australia*, Annandale, NSW: Federation Press.

Mladenoff, D. and J. Pastor (1993), 'Sustainable Forest Ecosystems in the Northern Hardwood and Conifer Forest Region: Concepts and Management', in G. Aplet, N. Johnson, J. Olson, and V. Sample (eds), *Defining Sustainable Forestry*, Washington, DC: Island Press, pp. 145–180.

Mol, A. (1995), *The Refinement of Production: Ecological Modernization Theory and the Chemical Industry*, Utrecht: Van Arkel.

Murphy, R. (1994), *Rationality and Nature*, Boulder, CO: Westview Press.

NAFI (National Association of Forest Industries) (1998), *Guaranteeing Sustainable Forest Management through New Environmental Management Systems*, On-line accessed 14 October 1998, <http:www.nafi.com.au/faq/management/ environment.html>

Norgaard, R. (1994), *Development Betrayed: The End of Progress and A Coevolutionary Revisioning of the Future*, London: Routledge.

O'Connor, J. (1973), *The Fiscal Crisis of the State*, New York: St. Martin's Press.

O'Connor, M. (1994), 'On the Misadventures of Capitalist Nature', in M. O'Connor (ed.), *Is Capitalism Sustainable?*, New York: The Guilford Press, pp. 125–137.

Pallot, J. (1992), 'Elements of a Theoretical Framework for Public Sector Accounting', *Accounting, Auditing and Accountability Journal*, **5** (1), 38–59.

Parker, L. and G. Gould (1999), 'Changing Public Sector Accountability: Critiquing New Directions', *Accounting Forum*, **23** (2), 109–136.

Primary Industries South Australia (1995), *Annual Report 1994/95*, Adelaide: Primary Industries South Australia.

Redclift, M. and G. Woodgate (1994), 'Sociology and the Environment: Discordant Discourse?', in M. Redclift and G. Woodgate (eds), *Social Theory and the Global Environment*, London: Routledge, pp. 51–66.

Redclift, M. and G. Woodgate (1997), 'Sustainability and Social Construction', in M. Redclift and G. Woodgate (eds), *The International Handbook of Environmental Sociology*, Cheltenham: Edward Elgar, pp. 55–70.

Rose, R. and P. Simmons (1992), 'Forestry and Conservation: An Examination of Policy Alternatives', in *Proceedings of the EPAC Seminar on the Pricing of Natural Resources*, Canberra: ABARE, pp. 175–181.

Rutherford, E. (1999), 'Ecological Modernization and Environmental Risk', in E. Darier, *Discourses on the Environment*, Oxford: Blackwell, pp. 95–118.

Schnaiberg, A. and K. Gould (1994), *Environment and Society: The Enduring Conflict*, New York: St. Martin's Press.

Simmons, U. (1989), 'Ecological Modernization of Industrial Society: Three Strategic Elements', *International Social Science Journal*, 121 (3), 347–361.

Sklair, L. (1994), 'Global Sociology and Environmental Change', in M. Redclift and G. Woodgate (eds), *Social Theory and the Global Environment*, London: Routledge, pp. 207–227.

State Forests of NSW (1998), *State Forests of New South Wales Annual Report 1997–1998*, Pennant Hills: SFNSW.

State of the Environment Advisory Council (1996), *State of the Environment Australia: Executive Summary*, Canberra: Department of the Environment, Sport and Territories.

Swanson, F., J. Jones and G. Grant (1997), 'The Physical Environment as a Basis for Managing Ecosystems', in K. Kohm and J. Franklin (eds), *Creating a Forestry for the 21st Century: The Science of Ecosystem Management*, Washington, DC: Island Press, pp. 229–238.

Turner, J. and J. Pribble (1996), *Evaluation of Santiago Declaration (Montreal Process) Indicators of Sustainability for Australian Commercial Forests*, Pennant Hills: State Forests NSW.

van Bueren, E. and E. Blom (1997), *Hierarchical Framework for the Formulation of Sustainable Forest Management Standards: Principles, Criteria and Indicators*, Leiden, The Netherlands, Tropenbos Foundation.

Vanclay, J. (1996a), 'Assessing the Sustainability of Timber Harvests from Natural Forests: Limitations of Indices Based on Successive Harvests', *Journal of Sustainable Forestry*, 3 (4), 47–58.

Vanclay, J. (1996b), 'Lessons from the Queensland Rainforests: Steps Towards Sustainability', *Journal of Sustainable Forestry*, 3 (2/3), 1–25.

Xu, Z. and D. Bengston (1997), 'Trends in National Forest Values among Forestry Professionals, Environmentalists and the News Media, 1982–1993', *Society and Natural Resources*, 10, 43–59.

14. Governance, 'Local' Knowledge and the Adoption of Sustainable Farming Practices

Vaughan Higgins, Stewart Lockie and Geoffrey Lawrence

INTRODUCTION

This chapter is concerned with the attempts of state agencies and their representatives to promote more productive and sustainable relationships between farmers and 'natural' environments. We argue that while it is important to recognise the direct attempts to regulate agricultural environments and farm management practices, there is much to be gained from an analysis of the more subtle ways in which agencies attempt to influence how people think about the environment and understand their place within it, as well as their responses to what they 'know' about that environment. This chapter focuses upon the relationships between power, knowledge, and the symbolic and material construction of agricultural environments. In doing so it draws heavily on Foucault's analysis of governmental rationalities and the ways in which these are used to coordinate 'action at a distance' amongst otherwise disparate actors. Thus, for example, Miller and Rose (1990) argue that modern government occurs not just via direct 'political' forms of intervention or force, but through mechanisms which allow calculations and strategies at one place to be linked to action at another. In relation to Australian agriculture, this theoretical approach has been most extensively used, to date, in the analysis of changes to state policy and activity associated with the National Landcare Programme (see Lockie, 1999; Martin and Woodhill, 1995).

Our purpose here is neither to offer a detailed analysis of Landcare, nor to imply that state agencies have enacted some sort of sleight of hand in successfully misrepresenting the ways in which they influence community groups and farmers. Rather, it is to further develop our understanding of the rationalities and techniques through which governments and their agencies exert some form of 'action at a distance' in Australian agricultural environments, and the ways in which 'local' knowledges are implicated in these attempts to govern. In this chapter, we have deliberately sought to move away from predominantly environmentally-focused areas of state activity, such as Landcare, to an analysis of an area that has had its genesis in attempts to promote a productivist agenda for agriculture, but which recently has sought to engage with questions of environmental sustainability. The cotton industry, and attempts to influence it, provide an interesting case study. There is controversy surrounding the cotton industry's image both as environmentally destructive, due to its input-use intensity and off-site impacts, and as the economic saviour of many agricultural communities, due to the large amounts of economic activity that subsequently develop around cotton-growing areas. We do not consider the entire Australian cotton industry here, but a specific case in Central Queensland in which 'local' knowledges attempted to shape the priorities of relevant state agencies. Through use of the case study, we seek to analyse how 'local' and 'expert' knowledges act on each other in the process of constituting and adopting 'sustainable' resource management strategies. In doing this, we treat 'sustainability' not as a pre-constituted object of governance, but as a contingent effect of specific ordering strategies (see Law, 1994).

Finally, it is important to note that this represents not an isolated example of indirect attempts to shape Australian agriculture. Large-scale examples include: the National Land and Water Resources Audit, which through the provision of information has attempted to provide a more 'rational' basis for decision making at all levels; and, in the State of Queensland, the Water Allocation Management and Planning (WAMP) process which attempts to provide adequate water for the maintenance of ecological processes at the same time as providing for the transferability of water entitlements. The latter has been enacted in the belief that market signals will direct water towards its most economically viable use. Not only, then, are governments attempting to exert 'action at a distance', but they are attempting to do so utilising specific rationalities and technologies of governance that construct actors in 'economically rational' terms. However, as this chapter argues, such strategies require a consideration of 'local' farmer knowledges in order to understand the process of governance. Before developing this analysis, in the context of the case study presented here, we will elaborate upon the theoretical approach relevant to our research.

POWER, RESISTANCE AND THE GOVERNING OF ENVIRONMENTAL KNOWLEDGES

The last decade or so has seen some substantial shifts in Australian agricultural policy. These have entailed, first, a number of strategies popularly associated with 'economic rationalism' and 'deregulation' which have dismantled collective mechanisms to deal with risk – such as statutory marketing boards – and placed increasing pressure on farmers to develop the capacity to calculate and manage these risks for themselves. The second has been the increasing attention to issues related to agricultural land and water degradation, with a particular focus on programmes designed to foster self-help, cooperation and long-term strategic planning at all levels ranging from individual farms through localised neighbourhoods to river catchments and beyond. While it is tempting to interpret these developments as evidence that governments are abandoning farmers to the vagaries of wildly fluctuating global marketplaces and to the global-sourcing and pricing strategies of transnational agribusiness corporations, it is just as beneficial to discern in these shifts a number of novel ways in which governments are attempting to influence farmer interpretation of, and response to, a changing agricultural environment (Lockie, 1999). In this chapter we focus on the relationship between knowledge and power that is fundamental to these strategies. As Foucault (1980) reminds us, knowledge is the will to power and 'truth'. It is important, therefore, that we examine how knowledges are deployed by actors to make particular practices both 'knowable' and 'truthful'.

The relationship between control over the production of knowledge and control over the ensuing trajectory of agricultural development is well recognised within the agrarian sociology literature. Utilising the theoretical framework of Marxist political economy, this literature demonstrates that the research agenda pursued by state agri-research agencies in no small way supports the interests of corporate agribusiness by reinforcing the dependence of family farmers on technological and chemical inputs while promoting the overproduction of undifferentiated bulk commodities (Bonanno et al., 1994; Burch et al., 1996; Buttel and Newby, 1980; Lawrence, 1987; Strange, 1988). It is also argued that ensuing increases in land, and input-use, intensity have been responsible for pollution, degradation, species decline and other unsustainable outcomes (see Berry, 1977; Lawrence et al., 1992; Magdoff et al., 1998; Redclift, 1987; Vanclay and Lawrence, 1995). In recognition of these outcomes authors such as Kloppenburg (1991) have called for the replacement of reductionist agricultural science by an alternative 'farmer-led' approach in which local knowledges are privileged over those of technical 'experts'. While the latter are viewed as perpetuating structures of domination and control, the 'indigenous' knowledges of farmers are viewed as providing the platform for the emergence of ecologically-sound and socially-just farming systems (Kloppenburg, 1991; Kloppenburg and Burrows, 1996). Kloppenburg's suggestion that local knowledges can be the basis for the transformation of Cartesian science has been criticised for making a somewhat naïve and romanticised distinction between 'indigenous' and 'scientific' knowledge which ignores the extent to which farmers and scientists interact in the process of creating agricultural knowledges (Molnar et al., 1992). This is not to say that these processes are somehow untainted by relations of power. Our approach here is neither to presuppose the domination of corporate interests in the production of agricultural knowledges, nor to advocate how such domination might be resisted, but to focus on the mutual conditioning engaged in by actors involved in processes of knowledge creation and dissemination.

The alignment of farming practices, by state and agribusiness agencies, with broader political objectives and programmes is not then a simple matter of 'experts' exercising control over farmers. Rather, it involves more broad and 'indirect' mechanisms in which agencies seek to shape the environment within which farmers make their decisions, as well as the 'appropriate' responses that should be made to that environment (Lockie, 1999; Murdoch and Ward, 1997). Knowledge plays a crucial role in linking the strategies of 'authorities' to the actions of individuals as the 'expert' knowledges of agents, such as doctors, managers, planners, economists and social workers, transform the concerns of government into the technical and 'non-political' language of 'truth'. Armed with the language of 'rationality' and 'truth', these 'expert' knowledges seek to influence the concerns of individuals by offering to teach them the techniques by which they might live in a healthier way, work more efficiently (Rose and Miller, 1992) or, in the case of farming, manage their properties more prudently (Higgins, 2000). In this way, individual preferences and choices are aligned with governmental objectives through the enhancing of self-regulatory capacities, rather than by means of coercion. The 'non-political' activities and calculations of experts allow governments to address 'private' matters while maintaining the formal freedoms of subjects.

Science, and Action at a Distance

Drawing on the work of French sociologists, Michel Callon and Bruno Latour, Murdoch and Clark (1994) and Clark and Murdoch (1997) argue that 'scientific' knowledge appears to have the greatest ability to act 'at a distance'. Scientific knowledge, however, far from being non-political, is itself an effect of power. For Murdoch and Clark (1994, p. 127), scientific knowledge is effective at acting 'at a distance' due to its capacity to reduce numerous and heterogeneous elements into a single explanans or 'universal law' – or what Callon and Latour (1981) refer to as 'black boxing'. It does this not by studying local manifestations of universal phenomena, but through taking 'local' phenomena and 'reconstituting them as universal, standardised scientific products' (Clark and Murdoch, 1997). In other words, the success of science-based disciplines depends on the reshaping of 'local' knowledges and practices so that they conform to the rules and norms of scientific networks. The extension of such knowledge is not, however, guaranteed. It is reliant on the ability of science to enrol and align local actors into a network that favours the strategies of scientists (see Callon, 1986). Once each person in that network 'can translate the values of others on their own terms, such that they provide norms and standards for their own ambitions, judgments and conduct', rule 'at a distance' becomes possible (Rose and Miller, 1992, p. 184). While this process has the potential to marginalise 'local' knowledge, Clark and Murdoch (1997) note that such knowledge can also be used to mediate or contest the terms of such enrolment. This raises the issue of how 'local' knowledge is related to resistance and power.

The dependence of governmental strategies on their ability to reshape 'local' knowledges suggests two further possibilities. One is that these strategies will themselves be shaped to conform with local 'ways of knowing'; another is that local 'ways of knowing' will in turn act at a distance on agencies and rationalities of government, particularly in terms of their influence on the delimitation of objects of governance. As Long and Villareal (1994, p. 47) note in relation to agriculture, knowledges and technologies are constantly being reworked 'to fit with the production strategies, resource imperatives and social desires of the farmer or farm family'. This suggests that resistance is more complex than simply overt opposition to a 'powerful' actor, or group of actors. According to Foucault, power and resistance need to be seen as relational concepts: 'there are no relations of power without resistances; the latter are all the more real and effective because they are formed right at the point where relations of power are exercised' (Foucault, 1980, p. 142). A relational view of power implies that resistance, rather than being an external obstacle to rule, enables the operation of governmental programmes by making such strategies 'knowable' to those whom it seeks to govern. That is, programmes are 'translated' (Callon, 1986, 1991) according to 'local' knowledges and practices. Resistance, understood in this sense, does not act as an external source of programme failure, but is essential to the success of programmes (O'Malley, 1996). However, it is important to emphasise that such power is never absolute, and the process of 'translation' involves the original objectives of governmental programmes being reshaped according to the particular goals of the target group. Equally, the incorporation of local 'ways of knowing' does not guarantee the success of a programme, as the strategies of scientists or policy makers may incorporate practices that are seen as contradictory or otherwise irrelevant (O'Malley, 1996). Attempts to align 'local' knowledges and governmental objectives may result in concessions by representatives of all groups, thus serving to mutually define and shape the legitimate objects of governance in the process of acting upon them.

ACTION LEARNING IN THE COTTON INDUSTRY

As mentioned in the introduction, the Australian cotton industry's input-use intensity has given it a wider public image of environmental irresponsibility *at the same time* as it is viewed by governments and inland communities as an economic saviour. We do not deal with the entire Australian industry here, but with one attempt at intervention in this industry designed to improve both the environmental and economic performance of a small group of cotton growers. It is important to note that this attempt at intervention did not represent a centralised government attempt to implement state policy and programmes in relation to the cotton industry, but a more localised attempt by state agency representatives to promote their interpretation of a neo-liberal 'way of governing' (see Rose, 1993) and to enrol other members of both the cotton industry and state agencies into this process. In order to conceptualise theoretically the process of interaction between 'local' and 'expert' knowledges we draw upon both Foucaultian-inspired literature on 'governmentality' and, a 'sociology of translation' developed originally by Callon (1986) and expanded upon by Clark and Murdoch (1997) and others.

Drawing upon managerial and rural development discourses, the 'Local Best Practices' (LBP) project sought to develop a participatory self-help approach utilising small-group settings as 'non threatening' environments in which producers would be able to share knowledge, identify problems and then seek, via field trials and benchmarking, practical solutions to those problems (Queensland Department of Primary Industries, 1996). In this respect, the LBP approach represents a good example of an attempt to govern farm practice through the enhancement of growers' self-regulatory capacities. An important feature of the LBP process was its assumption that the information held by 'experts' had validity when it was requested by the farmer group. The process allowed for technical/expert knowledge to be requested by the producers at various times in the action learning cycle when they believed that their own knowledge required supplementation. That producers had control over the procurement of expert knowledge was viewed as reversing the conventional 'transfer of technology' approach to extension in which experts identify the problems to be solved and seek to convince producers to adopt particular strategies to achieve the expert-defined outcomes (Vanclay and Lawrence, 1995). However, while the LBP approach may not have been 'expert-driven', it still allowed state agency 'experts' to establish their definition of actors and problems as an indispensable 'obligatory point of passage' (Callon, 1986) in the network of relationships they were attempting to build with growers. Such definitions focused on growers as 'economically rational' risk managers and the problems of the cotton industry as essentially economic in nature. These definitions were materially stabilised through the Cotton Industry Research and Development Corporation's 'Best Practices' manual.

A 'Local Best Practices' group was formed in the Weemah irrigated cotton-growing area of Emerald, in Central Queensland, in 1996. For three years the group was assisted by a project team established to evaluate the LBP process as a potential 'alternative' to existing approaches (see Lawrence et al., 1999). The group, comprising eight male growers, met at times generally coinciding with periods of reduced on-farm labour commitment. The group progressed through several problem-solving cycles and was able to identify opportunities for improved 'sustainable' practices. During discussions, the existing 'best practice' of furrow irrigation was viewed by producers as having a number of problems and limitations. Among these were water wastage, soil erosion, fertiliser loss and lifestyle disadvantages associated with the constant moving of irrigation pipes. Drip irrigation was identified by growers as a potential alternative to help alleviate at least some of the problems that had been identified. The growers subsequently sought assistance to 'field trial' drip irrigation.

The Growers and the Experts

It was here that the 'experts' sought to use their definitions of 'best practice' as an 'obligatory point of passage' to circumscribe the requests of growers. The growers' requests for advice from specialists in the field of drip irrigation and for the field testing of this new option in Emerald, were largely ignored. When – on a group-organised trip to the Australian 'centre' of cotton growing (Northern NSW) aimed at providing first-hand knowledge of drip irrigation – the Emerald growers met cotton researchers and other specialists, they were greatly disappointed with the response they received. While some of the northern NSW growers provided helpful information, the specialists did not appear to believe that the Emerald district had the potential for drip irrigation. Officials at the Cotton Research and Development Corporation seemed reluctant to provide support for research in the Emerald district (which they tended to view as marginal or inconsequential to the Australian cotton industry). The 'experts' were here attempting to assert themselves as the key actors in the network (Callon, 1986) by defining the group of growers according to a geographic area and by constructing a set of alliances and interests based on the 'expert's' knowledge of that area. This process, however, was contested by the growers.

Upon return to Emerald from NSW the growers asked if the local Queensland state departments might assist them in field trials. They were unable to elicit a positive response. The group therefore decided to undertake its own trial, with six sites providing a comparison between drip and furrow irrigation. This attempted to redefine the 'obligatory point of passage' according to the dissatisfaction of growers with furrow irrigation, and 'counter-enrol' the 'experts' (Callon and Law, 1982). Early results indicated that both water-use efficiency, and cotton yield, increased with drip irrigation – something that inspired the group to ask for large-scale trials. This request was again ignored by state-employed 'experts' (Lawrence et al., 1999) and at present the group has no real means of assessing the economic and environmental benefits of drip irrigation versus the costs which must be borne by growers if they are to invest in it. What the growers do understand is that, in reducing water application and in allowing better monitoring and control of fertilisers, drip irrigation may be a more environmentally-sustainable form of cotton production in the Emerald area (Meyers, 1997).

The option of moving to a drip irrigation system must be seen in the context of present cotton production in Emerald. As indicated earlier it is a quite profitable system, but one requiring the continuous applications of potent chemical inputs of pesticides and fertilisers, with yield and profit dependent on a guaranteed water supply and technological 'solutions' to production problems. Indeed, the cotton industry promotes the benefits of adopting a technological-based approach to farm management (see Lawrence et al., 1999; Lockie, 1998). What the growers were requesting from agencies in no way challenged the technical trajectory. In fact, it would have supported it by allowing – via drip irrigation – a much more predictable and accurate means of adding agri-chemicals to the environment. Together with this, in cutting back on water requirements the overall costs of production would possibly have been reduced. This supports the proposition by Molnar et al. (1992) that 'local' farmer knowledges cannot be considered independently from those of scientists. In suggesting a 'new' approach, the growers were not only drawing on their own meanings of what constituted 'sustainable' land management, but were also utilising those scientific knowledges which they saw as being of long-term economic benefit.

Sustainability improvements were thus constructed as flow-on benefits from the financial advantages growers believed to be associated with more healthy and productive agricultural landscapes.

The issue here is that, despite the seemingly obvious coherence between the 'new' suggestions of the growers and the current methods developed by the experts, the growers still found their views marginalised. Essentially, the growers were unable to act 'at a distance', and enrol the scientists, as their ideas regarding drip irrigation did not accord with the interpretations of 'best practice' by the 'experts'. The 'experts' argued that the Cotton Research and Development Corporation had already compiled and distributed its own 'Best Practice' manual for the industry. However, what the growers argued the manual lacked was a process, or means, by which they could 'benchmark' current practices. The manual was delivered to Emerald growers as a fait accompli, as a technical support document devised by scientists for those involved in large-scale cotton production in Australia. It had little regional specificity and failed, on many counts, to provide the Local Best Practices group with anything that could be usefully applied to address the problems they had raised in their group sessions (Lockie, 1998). Nevertheless, any concessions to grower's ideas might have served to politicise the concept of 'best practice' undermining both the scientific authority of the 'experts' and the 'value-neutrality' of the manual.

The growers had sought to influence the activities of industry researchers, and local agency staff, and to trial a new approach for the Emerald region. In doing so they were informally proposing that their own 'best practices' approach was at least as important as any manual of the same name that had been prepared by the industry. Their approach failed to be transformed into practice due to the meanings attached to the discourse of 'best practice' by the industry. The Emerald growers failed to enrol the technico-scientific 'experts' who were unable to 'translate' the growers' concerns into a standardised scientific discourse. This resulted in a problematisation of roles and a breakdown of the network. It was the 'experts' who resisted enrolment into the grower's network by employing their well-rehearsed arguments that: (1) the industry already had a 'best practices' manual which should be followed; (2) trickle irrigation was expensive and probably not suited to Emerald soils; and (3) there were no funds available to trial the approach the growers sought. These arguments sought to divert attention from the growers' interpretations of 'best practice' to the industry's success in dealing with environmental safety and profitability – as set out in the manual. It also attempted to constitute the 'best practices' manual as a key 'obligatory point of passage' in first, defining the identities of growers and, second, constituting problems as 'scientific' in nature, and therefore worthy of attention. This failure to counter-enrol the 'experts' meant that the growers had nowhere to turn. Indeed, the lack of large-scale trials has largely prevented the LBP group from progressing with the drip irrigation option.

CONCLUSION

Cooperative programmes that make explicit use of the capacities of community members to govern themselves in one form or another have become increasingly favoured strategies by governments and state agencies. Such intervention, however, depends in crucial ways on how 'local' actors 'translate' the objectives of government. Often, the effect of programmes is very different to their objectives due to the 'translation' processes that occur. Certainly, the 'local' knowledges of the Central Queensland cotton growers involved in the Weemah Local Best Practices group confirm the complexity of aligning the calculations of state agencies with the actions of 'community' members. Here, attempts by the group to define and influence research programmes were delegitimised at the point that their understandings of industry best practice could not be translated into the existing 'knowledge' and priorities of researchers.

The cotton study shows that the adoption of 'new' farming practices does not necessarily conform to a simple 'top-down' or 'bottom-up' process. Rather, particular rationalities and technologies of governance structure what knowledges are seen as legitimate or illegitimate, and thus what practices are deemed 'sustainable'. For example, the Weemah LBP group did not dispute the role of science in applying instrumentally rational techniques to the improvement of farming practice, only the research priorities of particular agri-science agencies. This, as we have seen, was a highly contingent process as actors sought to form obligatory points of passage, enrol and counter-enrol actors, and stabilise power relations through particular materials. Thus, it would be simplistic to suggest that farming practices were becoming dominated by some unified and unsustainable economically 'rationalist' ideology driven by global capitalist development. Equally, the broader political rationalities within which farmers make their decisions mean that their 'local' knowledges and practices are not entirely untainted by relations of power. While farm practices and agricultural environments are certainly increasingly constructed via state agencies as knowable and manipulable according to techniques of science and business management, they have their effects discursively and materially at a local level and are a matter for empirical investigation. It is here that 'sustainable knowledges' are constituted and the strategies of state agencies translated. An approach that combines concepts from both the governmentality and actor-network literature clearly has merits. It is one which reminds us of the micro-power relations among a multiplicity of actors, and one which also leads us away from the reductionist conclusion that the state is 'appropriating' sustainability so as to legitimise further capitalist expansion. Rather than assessing 'sustainability' from some normative standpoint, the important tasks for social scientists are to study how 'sustainable' practices are constructed through social networks, and to assess these in relation to the governmental rationalities that underpin them.

REFERENCES

Berry, W. (1977), *The Unsettling of America: Culture and Agriculture*, New York: Avon Books.

Bonanno, A., L. Busch, W. Friedland, L. Gouveia and E. Mingione (eds) (1994), *From Columbus to ConAgra: The Globalization of Agriculture and Food*, Kansas: University of Kansas Press.

Burch, D., R. Rickson and G. Lawrence (eds) (1996), *Globalization and Agri-food Restructuring: Perspectives from the Australasia Region*, Aldershot: Avebury.

Buttel, F. and H. Newby (eds) (1980), *The Rural Sociology of the Advanced Societies*, Montclair: Allenheld.

Callon, M. (1986), 'Some Elements of a Sociology of Translation: Domestication of the Scallops and the Fishermen of St Brieuc Bay', in J. Law (ed.), *Power, Action and Belief: A New Sociology of Knowledge?*, London: Routledge and Kegan Paul, pp. 196–233.

Callon, M. (1991), 'Techno-economic Networks and Irreversibility', in J. Law (ed.), *A Sociology of Monsters: Essays on Power, Technology and Domination*, London: Routledge, pp. 132–161.

Callon, M. and B. Latour (1981), 'Unscrewing the Big Leviathan: How Actors Macro-structure Reality and How Sociologists Help Them to Do So', in K. Knorr-Cetina and A. Cicourel (eds), *Advances in Social Theory and Methodology: Toward an Integration of Micro- and Macro-sociologies*, Boston: Routledge and Kegan Paul, pp. 277–303.

Callon, M. and J. Law (1982), 'On Interests and their Transformation: Enrolment and Counter-enrolment', *Social Studies of Science*, **12**, 615–625.

Clark, J. and J. Murdoch (1997), 'Local Knowledge and the Precarious Extension of Scientific Networks: A Reflection on Three Case Studies', *Sociologia Ruralis*, **37** (1), 38–60.

Foucault, M. (1980), 'Two Lectures', in C. Gordon (ed.), *Power/Knowledge: Selected Interviews and Other Writings 1972–77*, Brighton: Harvester Press, pp. 78–108.

Higgins, V. (2001), 'Self-Reliance, Governance and Environmental Management: The Rural Adjustment Scheme', in S. Lockie and W. Pritchard (eds), *Consuming Foods, Sustaining Environments*, Australian Academic Press: Brisbane (forthcoming).

Kloppenburg, J. (1991), 'Social Theory and the De/reconstruction of Agricultural Science: Local Knowledge for an Alternative Agriculture', *Rural Sociology*, **56** (4), 519–548.

Kloppenburg, J. and B. Burrows (1996), 'Biotechnology to the Rescue? Twelve Reasons Why Biotechnology is Incompatible with Sustainable Agriculture', *The Ecologist*, **26** (2) (March/April), 61–67.

Law, J. (1994), *Organising Modernity*, Oxford: Blackwell.

Lawrence, G. (1987), *Capitalism in the Countryside: The Rural Crisis in Australia*, Pluto: Sydney.

Lawrence, G., M. Meyers, S. Lockie and R. Clark (1999), 'An Action Learning Approach to Grower-focused Change: Research Among Cotton Producers in Queensland', in D. Burch, J. Goss and G. Lawrence (eds), *Restructuring Global and Regional Agricultures: Transformations in Australasian Agri-food Economies and Spaces*, Aldershot: Ashgate, pp. 289–306.

Lawrence, G., F. Vanclay and B. Furze (eds) (1992) *Agriculture, Environment and Society: Contemporary Issues for Australia*, Melbourne: Macmillan.

Lockie, S. (1998), 'Environmental and Social Risks, and the Construction of "Best Practice" in Australian Agriculture', *Agriculture and Human Values*, **15**, 243–252.

Lockie, S. (1999), 'The State, Rural Environments and Globalisation: "Action at a Distance" via the Australian Landcare Program', *Environment and Planning A*, **31** (4), 597–611.

Long, N. and M. Villareal (1994), 'The Interweaving of Knowledge and Power in Development Interfaces', in I. Scoones and J. Thompson (eds), *Beyond Farmer First: Rural People's Knowledge, Agricultural Research and Extension Practice*, London: Intermediate Technology Publications, pp. 41–52.

Magdoff, F., F. Buttel and J. Foster (eds) (1998), 'Hungry for Profit: Agriculture, Food, and Ecology', *Special Edition of Monthly Review*, **50** (3).

Martin, P. and J. Woodhill (1995), 'Landcare in the Balance: Roles of Government and Policy Directions for Degrading Rural Environments', *Australian Journal of Environmental Management*, **2** (3), 173–183.

Meyers, M. (1997), 'Evaluating the "Local Best Practices" Method of Participatory Problem Solving', unpublished paper, Gatton: Rural Extension Centre, University of Queensland.

Miller, P. and N. Rose (1990), 'Governing Economic Life', *Economy and Society*, **19** (1), 1–31.

Molnar, J., P. Duffy, K. Cummins and E. Van Santen (1992), 'Agricultural Science and Agricultural Counterculture: Paradigms in Search of a Future', *Rural Sociology*, **57** (1), 83–91.

Murdoch, J. and J. Clark (1994), 'Sustainable Knowledge', *Geoforum*, **25** (2), 115–132.

Murdoch, J. and N. Ward (1997), 'Governmentality and Territoriality: The Statistical Manufacture of Britain's "National Farm"', *Political Geography*, **16** (4), 307–324.

O'Malley, P. (1996), 'Indigenous Governance', *Economy and Society*, **25** (3), 310–326.

Queensland Department of Primary Industries (1996), *Sustainable Beef Production Systems Project: Beyond Awareness to Continuous Improvement*, Rockhampton: Queensland Department of Primary Industries.

Redclift, M. (1987), *Sustainable Development: Exploring the Contradictions*, London: Methuen.

Rose, N. (1993), 'Government, Authority and Expertise in Advanced Liberalism', *Economy and Society*, **22** (3), 283–299.

Rose, N. and P. Miller (1992), 'Political Power Beyond the State: Problematics of Government', *British Journal of Sociology*, **43** (2), 173–205.

Strange, M. (1988), *Family Farming: a New Economic Vision*, Lincoln: University of Nebraska Press.

Vanclay, F. and G. Lawrence (1995), *The Environmental Imperative: Eco-social Concerns for Australian Agriculture*, Rockhampton: CQU Press.

PART IV

Institutions and Regulation

15. Old Practices Building New Institutions: A Commons Approach to the Rural Crisis

Phil Coop and David J. Brunckhorst

INTRODUCTION

The failure of natural resource management systems in recent years has been greater in magnitude than those observed historically. Current resource management has clearly failed to safeguard the dynamic capacity of ecosystems or to manage ecological and social systems for resilience and sustainability. There is considerable evidence of poor management of ecosystems with many conventional prescriptions of resource management now known to be unsustainable.

Ecosystems and human activity are inextricably linked, with social and ecological components closely entwined and any delineation between them artificial and arbitrary (Brunckhorst, 1998). If we are attempting to address broader-scale, long-term sustainability, it is clear that narrowly focused land-use approaches that manage for one particular production purpose perform poorly in maintaining ecological and social function across the landscape systems in which they occur (Brown and MacLeod, 1996; Holling and Meffe, 1996). Sustaining ecological processes and services requires resilience across multiple scales of complex systems that are influenced by human activity.

Human institutions that have built-in adaptiveness and resilience are capable of responding to, and managing, processes in a fashion that contributes to ecosystem resilience. Many common-property institutions have proven track records that extend over long periods and generally consist of self-governing associations of local users managing common property resources (CPR) or 'commons' (Berkes and Folke, 1998; Bromley, 1992; Ostrom, 1990).

Resilience refers to the buffering capacity of a system to absorb perturbations and return to its original state. Resilience therefore is a measure of the magnitude of disturbance (and its periodicity) that can be absorbed before a system changes its structure and functional behaviour (Holling, 1986; Holling et al., 1995; Walker, 1995). Often the greater the flexibility or adaptive ability of social systems, institutions and organisations, the greater their resilience. Loss of resilience in ecological systems undermines their capacity to continue to deliver life-support and other essential ecological benefits to humanity under a wide range of environmental conditions. Lack of resilience contributes to the failure to provide the environmental services associated with the assimilation of undesirable externalities that provides ecological buffering of human activity and resource use.

Instances of reduced resilience leading to breakdown or collapse of a natural resource base are often termed 'tragedies' after Hardin's article on the 'Tragedy of the Commons', published in *Science* in 1968. This is probably the most widely quoted, cited and reprinted article ever published on the social and behavioural dynamics of environmental problems. In his article, Hardin describes a situation in which behaviour that makes rational sense from an individual viewpoint, when repeated by enough individuals, ultimately proves disastrous to society. Specifically, the consumption of a natural resource by each of many individuals who have unrestricted access to the resource inevitably leads to the resource's destruction – a disaster for all. It used to be popularly believed that users of common resources were always trapped in an inexorable 'tragedy of the commons' (Hardin, 1968).

Many studies, especially since the mid-1980s, have shown Hardin's generalisation does not hold. If the resource is freely open to access by any user, a tragedy of the commons may eventually follow. Such failure would result, however, not from any inherent failure of common property, but from an institutional failure to control access to the resource, and to make and enforce internal decisions for collective use. The tragedy of the commons as described by Hardin is a misunderstanding of an open access system and a social (common property) commons. Thus, while an open commons provides unrestricted access that will eventually lead to the tragedy, a different sort of commons management can ensure a different outcome. For example, medieval commons endured sustainably for hundreds of years. They were not 'open access', but rather social common property resource (CPR) systems. There was an accompanying system of participatory democracy to regulate access to finite resources – essentially, a system of resource governance by community-based participatory democracy which ensured overexploitation did not take place.

UNDERSTANDING THE COMMONS

Hanna et al. (1995) have summarised the four main types of common-property institutions and their associated rights and duties (see Table 15.1). Hardin's 'tragedy' refers to open access to resources and does not refer to any kind of property rights, either private or collective. As discussed in this chapter, current experience of both state ownership and privatisation of property rights and resources have also failed to produce sustainable social–ecological systems.

The term 'commons' originally referred to jointly owned pastures on which herdsmen grazed their cattle (Bromley, 1992; Hardin, 1968; Hine and Gifford, 1996; Levine, 1986). The commons were an important structure for the early agrarian communities. They consisted of common property (not 'open' commons) managed by a self-governing association of local users. Many of these common property systems successfully endured for hundreds of years. A few have survived for over one thousand years. The term is used more broadly today referring to any desirable, divisible entity to which multiple harvesters (that is, individuals or groups who are able to use or remove some of it) have access (Gifford and Hine, 1997).

Table 15.1   Common-Property Institutions – Ownership, Rights and Duties

Institution	Ownership	Owner Rights	Owner Duties
Private property	Individual	Socially acceptable uses; exclusive control of access	Avoid socially unacceptable uses
Common property	Collective	Exclusion of non-owners; local regulation of users	Maintenance; constrain rates of use
Government ('state') property	Citizens	Decide on rules	Maintain social objectives
Open access (non-property)	None	Capture	None

Source: After Hanna et al. (1995).

The actual origins of these Common Property Resource (CPR) management commons are buried in antiquity. Dahlman (1980) suggested the European commons may have evolved through the development of the early Germanic tribes who originally laid out the open field system. According to Levine (1986) agricultural villages with shared pasturages first appeared in England in the Middle Ages (1100s) and became universal in the 1400s. These villages were often located on land owned by lords and were usually inhabited by 200 to 500 tenants. Each tenant was assigned a private, non-shared, plot of land on which to raise crops, but areas for grazing livestock were held and used in common by all village residents. The residents of small agricultural villages knew each other well, understood that their survival hinged on cooperation, felt responsible for each other, and had strong social bonds (Levine, 1986). The residents understood the capacity limits of their communal pasturages and developed their own mutually agreed-upon and mutually enforced systems to regulate use, without the need for an external authority (such as centralised government) to determine and impose these regulations (Gardner and Stern, 1996).

Thirsk (1964) identified four key attributes defining the core dimensions of age-old common field agriculture. First, the holdings of individual cultivators comprising many separate parcels scattered among unenclosed common fields termed 'strips in the arable'. Secondly, after the harvest, and usually during fallow years, these common fields reverted from private farmland to communal pasture ground, as all villagers exercised their customary right to graze their animals on the herbage temporarily available on the arable lands, termed 'common of shack'. Thirdly, the land that was unsuitable for cropping was utilised for common grazing and was termed 'common waste'. Finally, regulation and supervision of the entire system was provided by an 'assembly of cultivators' or 'communal regulation' (Dahlman, 1980).

Importantly, there seems to be a conscious effort to maintain the function of 'scattering'. Scattering describes the geographic allocation of arable land to the members of the common. As the term implies, these relatively small plots of land were scattered throughout the common. Scattering may have been imposed on the villagers so as to make the collective decision making institutions viable and effective. Scattering, as it was maintained in the reorganisation of a village, served to ensure a cohesive social fabric (Dahlman, 1980, p. 144). More recently it has been recognised that scattering was integral in providing productivity and ecosystem resilience for these institutions (Berkes and Folke, 1998).

Perhaps the element in the commons organisation of production that is alien to modern eyes is the peculiar fact that the same piece of land would revert from private property to collective, and back again, in a well-defined and controlled cycle (Dahlman, 1980). More recently, authors have shown that these institutions existed for hundreds, perhaps thousands, of years during which time social stability, productive capacity and ecological integrity were maintained (McKean, 1982). The land had been successfully managed by community collectives, 'not a tragedy of the commons but rather a triumph' (Cox, 1985, p. 60).

Ironically, scattering as a resource management tool became the basis of the 'inefficiency arguments' to support the enclosure movements, which led to privatisation. It was the forced enclosure movements of the fifteenth and sixteenth centuries that turned the commons into private property, and with it the claim of 'bringing efficiency and increased productivity to agriculture', but which ultimately resulted in widespread degradation (Bromley, 1992). Privatisation was hailed as the answer for more efficient and increased rural production and Hardin (1968) interpreted it as a solution to the tragedy of open access.

It was during the late 1700s to late 1800s that the centuries-old community-managed commons were broken apart. This was primarily due to land reform (the so-called 'enclosure movements') which was designed to increase the holdings of a few landowners and which effectively drove tenants from the communal land. The development of agricultural techniques that favoured large-scale farming , together with the effects of the Industrial Revolution also forced the closure of these commons (Cox, 1985).

Typical of these early commentaries was the statement by Seebohn (1912, p. 31) on the commons, 'Now [1912], judged from a modern point of view, it will readily be understood that the open field system, and especially its peculiarity of straggling or scattered ownership, regarded from an agricultural point of view, was absurdly uneconomical'. It was reinforced, at a later time, by Gray (1959, p. 37) who wrote, of the Agricultural Revolution, that:

> agricultural progress in England would ultimately depend on the disappearance of the open-field system. A form of tillage so inconvenient, so inflexible, so negligent of the productivity of the soil, could not endure after technical improvement in ploughing had made possible its abandonment and after its social advantages had come to be disregarded.

These negative views of commons as the 'dumb peasant model' became reinforced and they continued to be fenced off for private use. Unfortunately, the significant contribution made by these commons in sustainable resource allocation and management, and through their direct involvement in developing and testing new techniques, technologies and selective breeding methods, remains unrecognised even today (Dahlman, 1980).

History has demonstrated that the enclosure of the commons and subsequent privatisation of land or resources has generally failed to provide ecosystem health. Privatisation internalises the cost of overexploitation to the individual. Yet, it is impossible, or difficult, to privatise many ecological services (such as nutrient assimilation) or common resources (for example, air). In addition, privatisation does not reduce overexploitation, as an individual can sell up and then purchase, and deplete, another area. This is what privatisation and a market economy, by its nature, encourages; exploit to the fullest, then invest elsewhere.

A system of purely state-based regulation and administrative law does not appear to work either. States rarely dedicate themselves to long-term environmental stability and safety. The cycle of modern politics and government exacerbates this short-term view of resource development.

Today, only a solitary, consciously-preserved English common field township survives, at Laxton in Nottinghamshire. In contrast, in Peru and Bolivia common field farming continues to be practised over an extensive geographical area (Bromley, 1992).

COMMON PROPERTY RESOURCE MANAGEMENT AND INSTITUTIONS

Common property (common pool) resources are defined as a class of resources for which exclusion is difficult and joint use involves subtractibility (Berkes, 1989). These institutions have to deal with the two fundamental problems that arise from the basic characteristics of all such resources: how to control access to the resource (the exclusion problem), and how to institute rules among users to solve the potential divergence between individual and collective rationality (the subtractibility problem). Under most regimes, community-based rules and customs dictate rights of access, and institutions co-evolve to enforce them.

There is historical evidence that agricultural villages with common pasturages existed in many other places besides England and Europe, including Africa, Asia, India, and Central and South America. Nomadic pastoralists in Africa support themselves by grazing livestock in common pasturages. In the great majority of these cases thoughtful restrictions on access and intensity of use has averted the tragedy of the commons process by these community-based cooperative groups (Berkes and Folke, 1998; Gardner and Stern, 1996).

Interesting examples can still be found today in Switzerland, Spain and Japan. The mountain commons in both Switzerland and Japan have been sustained over centuries while being used intensively. On 1 February, 1483 the Swiss village of Törbel formalised in writing a charter governing the management of the summer alpine meadows which were grazed as a common resource (some evidence of this commons dates back to 1224, see Netting, 1976). The traditional Commons Lands (Iraichi) in Japan came into being between the thirteenth and sixteenth centuries, though the tradition of the commons may have begun more than a thousand years earlier (McKean, 1992). As late as the 1950s there were many expanses of common land in Japan still being managed collectively without ecological destruction despite the infusion of industrial wealth into rural Japan. Japanese villages obviously altered the landscape of the commons from its natural state, but they also clearly operated their commons according to the principle of sustainable yield so as not to degrade the natural resource base.

In Spain, 84 irrigators served by the Banecher River and Faitanar canals in Valencia, gathered to sign their formal articles of association in May 1435. However, many of the rules regarding distribution of water within the common property institution, carried into medieval and modern practice, were probably developed some 1000 years prior to the recapture of Valencia from the Muslims in 1238 (Ostrom, 1990). Keeping order and maintaining large-scale irrigation works in the difficult terrain of Spain has been a similar achievement. That record has not been matched by most of the irrigation systems constructed around the world in the past 50 years.

Netting (1976) dismisses the notion that communal ownership was simply an anachronistic holdover from the past. He demonstrates that for at least five centuries Swiss villagers have been intimately familiar with the advantages and disadvantages of both private and communal tenure systems and have carefully matched particular types of land tenure to particular types of land use. Although many villages have sold, leased, or divided their common lands in recent times, McKean (1982) attests that she has not found an example of a commons that suffered ecological destruction while it was still a commons.

An important characteristic of enduring, self-governing, commons is that they all face uncertain and complex environments. In contrast to the uncertainty of these environments the populations at these locations have remained stable over long periods of time. Members have shared a past and have anticipated sharing a common future (Ostrom, 1990). Communal tenure 'promotes both general access to and optimum production from certain types of resources while enjoining on the entire community the conservation measures necessary to protect these resources from destruction' (Netting, 1976, p. 145).

The fact that these social–ecological systems are found so widely, and have a track record often over a long period, suggests that they are highly adaptive and resilient and therefore capable of responding to, and managing, processes and functions in a fashion that contributes to ecosystem resilience. It would appear from the above discussion that a combination of attributes has provided an enduring sustainable system, both socially and ecologically.

CHARACTERISTICS OF ENDURING SOCIAL–ECOLOGICAL INSTITUTIONS

Contemporary studies on enduring commons and their communal governance institutions are beginning to provide some valuable principles for natural resource management. The likelihood of users designing successful common property institutions will be enhanced if the group is relatively small and stable; if it is relatively homogeneous, with the members using similar technologies and having similar values and discount rates; if there is reciprocity and trust; and if the transaction costs for making and enforcing rules is low (Berkes and Folke, 1998; Ostrom, 1990).

Jodha (1998) has identified three elements that individually or jointly strengthen social–ecological system links and contribute to natural resource-friendly traditional management systems. These are: first, a total dependence-driven stake in protection of natural resources; second, close proximity and a functional knowledge-driven approach to resource use; and, third, local control-determined sanctions and facilities governing resource use.

Gardner and Stern (1996) have discussed the important elements of successful CPRs. These are all designed to encourage social behaviour: regulations and incentives; programmes of education which seek to alter attitudes; informal (nongovernmental) monitoring and regulatory processes that operate in small social groups and communities, and finally, the use of moral and ethical appeals.

Common Property Resource institutions have been successful in maintaining ecological capital as well as social fabric and rural communities. The elements contributing to this success, described by the above authors, would appear to confirm Ostrom's (1990) eight characteristics of enduring, self-governing common property institutions. These are:

1. *Clearly defined boundaries.* Individuals or households who have rights to withdraw resource units from the CPR (appropriators) must be clearly defined, as must the boundaries of the CPR itself.
2. *Congruence between appropriation and provision rules and local conditions.* Appropriation rules restricting time, place, technology and/or quantity of resource units are related to local conditions and to provision rules requiring labour, material and/or money.
3. *Collective choice arrangements.* Most individuals affected by the operational rules can participate in modifying the operational rules.
4. *Monitoring.* Monitors, who actively audit CPR conditions and appropriator behaviour, are accountable to the appropriators or are the appropriators.
5. *Graduated sanctions.* Appropriators of common property resources who violate operational rules are likely to have graduated sanctions imposed (depending on the seriousness and context of the offence) by other appropriators, by officials accountable to these appropriators, or by both.
6. *Conflict resolution mechanisms.* Appropriators and their officials have rapid access to low-cost local arenas to resolve conflicts among appropriators or between appropriators and officials.
7. *Recognition of rights to organise.* The rights of appropriators to devise their own institutions (collective action) are not challenged by external governmental authorities.
8. *Nested enterprises.* Appropriation, provision, monitoring, enforcement, conflict resolution and governance activities are organised in multiple layers of nested enterprises.

Most recently, Folke et al. (1998) summarised principles drawn from case studies of linked social–ecological systems for building resilience and sustainability:

1. Using management practices based on local ecological knowledge.
2. Designing management systems that 'flow with nature'.
3. Developing local ecological knowledge for understanding cycles of natural and unpredictable events.
4. Enhancing social mechanisms for building resilience.

5. Promoting conditions for self-organisation and institutional learning.
6. Rediscovering adaptive management.
7. Developing values consistent with resilient and sustainable social–ecological systems.

In summary, there is increasing evidence that local level institutions learn and develop the capability to respond to environmental feedbacks faster than do centralised agencies. Linked social–ecological systems, such as the CPR institutions described above, have developed the flexibility to respond to changes and to adapt to them in an active way. Such adaptations were key to survival. Learning from local social–ecological systems and combining insights gained in adaptive management in western science may counteract many of the prevailing crises of conventional resource management.

CONTEMPORARY APPLICATIONS FOR INSTITUTIONAL REFORM OF THE RURAL SECTOR

The Ailing Rural Sector

Rural communities in western, federated, nations are currently facing a high level of income uncertainty. Their survival is dependent upon their ability to sustain their families by balancing social demands and the biophysical capacity of their landscapes with the requirements to meet debt repayments, to conform to increasingly stringent regulatory demands, and to produce within fickle and corrupted global markets.

To deal with these issues, the options available to landholders are generally limited to efforts to increase production from the same, or a larger, piece of land (Lawrence, 1987). One of the first things to occur is a reduced commitment to the ecosystem. The increased demands on the system lead to a loss of ecosystem function and resilience as the natural capital base is undermined, ultimately resulting in resource degradation. A decline in the productive resource base occurs through the loss of functional biodiversity, soil structure, organic material and moisture content, resulting in the gradual loss of resilience. This initially manifests itself by extending the recovery period from events such as drought (that is, lost resilience). In a relatively short time, production systems, even some traditionally considered to be 'secure and productively stable' start collapsing. Farms (especially those with substantial debt commitment) become non-viable. Eventually, broader-scale economic and social breakdown occurs across rural communities (Brunckhorst et al., 1997)

Elements of a Contemporary Common

The lessons synthesised from resilient, age-old, social–ecological institutions are useful in our own time in that they generate opportunities for people to participate in collective decision making. Although it is not fully understood why the commons is such a successful vehicle in integrating social and ecological components for enduring sustainability, there is a clear need for on-ground demonstration projects in order to examine these institutions in contemporary times (McKean, 1997). The brief review of CPR systems provided above highlights some lessons and principles that are valuable and applicable in the development of sustainable solutions for our ailing agro-ecological systems today. While these regimes might be employed in a variety of ways from a property level through Landcare groups to government agencies, it is most likely the synergy of all elements in establishing and managing contemporary CPRs has the tremendous potential to lead us towards a sustainable future.

An important aspect of a contemporary CPR model is the ability to allocate the available resources more efficiently, but within their functional capacity. This necessitates assessing natural capital across an ecological landscape that equates also with the collective of landholders who are willing to share, nurture, conserve, restore and harvest across the entire area. Areas better suited to certain activities, such as cultivation, will allow farming such as cropping and haymaking to be performed, while the remaining land may be used for diversified farming, grazing, conservation or restoration. This removes the pressure for individual landholders to conduct these activities independently and on unsuitable locations, cropping only the most suitable areas in the sub-catchment. Collectively, these farming enterprises are more efficient and include the potential for more suitable grazing and crop rotations. Members of the collective need to understand the distinction between resource utilisation and land tenure. Landholders may consolidate their herds and graze them across all properties involved in the CPR. This would allow the utilisation of grazing techniques such as rotational grazing regimes over a much wider area, offering benefits including improved pasture and weed management, drought management, as well as addressing issues associated with internal parasite resistance without the fencing costs normally associated with the adoption of these regimes. This allocation of the productive resource within the ecological landscape resembles the methods adopted by early commons with their strips in the arable, common of shack, and common-waste. This highlights the need for early recognition of the importance of the distinction between farming and grazing land at a broader scale, the capacity of the resource, as well as the necessity for broad-scale (resource and ecological) recovery.

The establishment of a common piece of land appears to be an important part of a contemporary CPR (Brunckhorst et al., 1997). It is something that would be the property of no one member of the CPR, but the responsibility of all. This piece of centrally-located land would serve several functions for development of the CPR collective. Initially, the members of the CPR might benefit through the upscaling of the productive resource simply through the benefits obtained by additional land. It would provide buffering against drought, relieve current productive pressures, and would be seen as a zone of focus throughout the CPR by providing connectivity for members of the CPR. The common land would also serve a more important role in that it would provide an area for experimentation, group decision making and collective management (Brunckhorst et al., 1997). Institutional learning can ensue as members become more confident in their ability to manage on a collective basis. The lessons of these activities would then be applied across all landholder members' areas, even though in this modern CPR individual property title is retained. This institutional learning, as it evolves, provides the framework for building collective responsibility; for monitoring of activities and the environmental condition of the sub-catchment; and for self regulation and adjustment (flexible adaptive management). In turn, through a sharing and management of infrastructure as well as natural resources, other capacities and resources such as time, labour, equipment and money are freed up for allocation in other activities or for farm diversification.

CAPACITY BUILDING WITHIN A CONTEMPORARY COMMON PROPERTY RESOURCE SYSTEM

The acceptance by landholders to participate in this type of institution is likely to be determined in the first instance by the ability to improve economies of scale and to improve financial viability through cost restructuring. The initial collective planning phase is substantial, however. Issues relating to enterprise consolidation and operation, the establishment of the managing body (including determining the rules, voting rights and formula for the distribution of CPR proceeds), and the identification of key infrastructure and equipment, must all be considered.

The establishment of a contemporary common will require the flexibility to accommodate issues relating to existing corporate structures and also to provide security of tenure – while managing the resources associated with the land as common property. This illustrates a novel yet important aspect of the CPR – that of distinguishing between the property rights associated with land tenure and the utilisation of the resources associated with the land. The CPR institution enables efficient management of the resources while not affecting the tenure associated with the land. Another benefit of the CPR structure is the efficient utilisation of the labour resource. Grazing and farming enterprises have an uneven seasonal labour requirement. The ability to call on labour when it is required from within the common is valuable as it provides an opportunity to redeploy these resources to investigate alternative on-farm and more importantly off-farm diversifications.

Labour is also available to undertake projects at a more suitable sub-catchment scale such as ecological restoration of the riparian areas.

The CPR provides the structural vehicle for buffering the long-term risk associated with existing and new primary production ventures. An important aspect in relieving the productive pressure from these resources is the development and integration of off-farm income sources. The CPR can provide an excellent vehicle for managing the risk associated with the start up and operational phases of these off-farm investments.

Is there any evidence of this beginning to occur? Adoption and adaptation of an enduring CPR planning and management approach is one of the challenges undertaken by Ecologically Restorative Industries Pty Ltd (ERI) on the New England Tablelands of NSW. The experimental model has provided the opportunity for the formation of a CPR collective incorporating a group of graziers, who, together, own (freehold tenure) and have a long-term interest in the sub-catchment. They have collectively agreed to work together and learn together how to operate a CPR system. Together with capacity-building support from an accountant, solicitor and staff of the UNESCO Institute for Bioregional Resource Management (University of New England), the landholders are assessing a variety of options. The first has to do with the necessary structures for operational as well as insurance and other requirements (Co-operative, Unit Trust, Incorporated Association or Company): it would appear that several will need to be linked. The second relates to formulae for sharing of resources including land, labour, infrastructure and profits – relative to the contributions of members. The third concerns the relative make-up of the combined herd and opportunities for ecological restoration of the sub-catchment, coupled with new diversifications that can be pursued using the additional labour and professional capacities that will be generated. ERI is actively involved in the development of the CPR as an experimental model; that is, as a potential vehicle demonstrating institutional transformation together with new forms of resource management creating enduring ecological and social systems.

CONCLUSION

Rural communities are facing an uncertain future. These communities are reliant on the long-term resilience of their productive resources and are attempting to utilise these resources to resolve short-term pressures. The result has been resource exploitation, not sustainability. There is an urgent need to redesign institutions of society for an ecologically sustainable future. Resource and ecosystem management is necessary but it requires fundamentally different approaches, not mere tinkering with current models and practices. Common property institutions have demonstrated the capacity of these collaborative systems to survive dynamic flexibility – delivering social and environmental stability for centuries.

The preliminary and experimental development of a modern CPR institution demonstrates that contemporary commons can provide a vehicle through which issues associated with rural decline may be addressed. This is principally achieved through collective decision making, efficient resource allocation, capacity building and risk reduction. This mechanism is enhanced with the ability to buffer the risk associated with collectively managing the productive resource. The significance of CPR for multiple resource assessment and management relates to its potential for providing an enduring solution to rural environmental and community decline.

REFERENCES

Berkes, F. (ed.) (1989), *Common Property Resources. Ecology and Community-Based Sustainable Development*, London: Belhaven.

Berkes, F and C. Folke (1998), 'Linking Social and Ecological Systems for Resilience and Sustainability', in F. Berkes and C. Folke (eds), *Linking Social and Ecological Systems: Management Practices and Social Mechanisms for Building Resilience*, New York: Cambridge University Press.

Bromley, D. (1992), *Making the Commons Work: Theory, Practice, and Policy*, San Francisco: Institute for Contemporary Studies.

Brown, J. and N. MacLeod (1996), 'Integrating Ecology into Natural Resource Management Policy', *Environmental Management*, **20** (3), 289–296.

Brunckhorst, D. (1998), 'Creating Institutions to Ensure Sustainable Use of Resources', *Habitat International*, **22** (4), 347–354.

Brunckhorst, D., P. Bridgewater and P. Parker (1997), 'The UNESCO Biosphere Reserve Program Comes of Age: Learning by Doing, Landscape Models for Sustainable Conservation and Resource Use', in P. Hale and D. Lamb (eds), *Conservation Outside Reserves*, St. Lucia: University of Queensland Press, pp. 176–182.

Cox, S. (1985), 'No Tragedy on the Commons', *Environmental Ethics*, **7**, 49–61.

Dahlman, C. (1980), *The Open Field System and Beyond: A Property Rights Analysis of an Economic Institution*, Cambridge: Cambridge University Press.

Folke, C., F. Berkes and J. Colding (1998), 'Ecological Practices and Social Mechanisms for Building Resilience and Sustainability', in F. Berkes and C. Folke (eds), *Linking Social and Ecological Systems; Management Practices and Social Mechanisms for Building Resilience*, New York: Cambridge University Press.

Gardner, G. and P. Stern (1996), *Environmental Problems and Human Behaviour*, USA: Allyn and Bacon.

Gifford, R. and D. Hine (1997), 'Toward Cooperation in Commons Dilemmas', *Canadian Journal of Behavioural Science*, **29** (3), 168–178.

Gray, H. (1959), 'English Field Systems', in C. Dahlman (1980), *The Open Field System and Beyond*, New York: Cambridge University Press.

Hanna, S., C. Folke and K.-G. Mäler (1995), *Rights to Nature*, Washington: Island Press.

Hardin, G. (1968), 'The Tragedy of the Commons', *Science*, **162**, 1243–1248.

Hine, D. and R. Gifford (1996), 'Individual Restraint and Group Efficiency in Common Dilemmas: The Effects of Two Types of Environmental Uncertainty', *Journal of Applied Social Psychology*, **26** (11), 993–1009.

Holling, C. (1986), 'The Resilience of Terrestrial Ecosystems: Local Surprise and Global Change', in W. Clark and R. Munn (eds), *Sustainable Development of the Biosphere*, Cambridge: Cambridge University Press, pp. 292–317.

Holling, C. and M. Meffe (1996), 'Command and Control and the Pathology of Natural Resource Management', *Conservation Biology*, **10** (2), 328–337.

Holling, C., D. Schindler, B. Walker and J. Roughgarden (1995), 'Biodiversity in the Functioning of Ecosystems: An Ecological Synthesis', in C. Perrings, K.-G. Mäler, C. Folke, C. Hollong and B. Jansson (eds), *Biodiversity Loss: Economic and Ecological Issues*, Cambridge: Cambridge University Press, pp. 44–83.

Jodha, N. (1998), 'Reviving the Social System – Ecosystem Links in the Himalayas', in F. Berkes and C. Folke (ed.), *Linking Social and Ecological Systems; Management Practices and Social Mechanisms for Building Resilience*, New York: Cambridge University Press, pp. 285–310.

Lawrence, G. (1987) *Capitalism and the Countryside: the Rural Crisis in Australia*, Sydney: Pluto.

Levine, B. (1986), 'The Tragedy of the Commons and the Comedy of Community: The Commons in History', *Journal of Community Psychology*, **14**, 81–99.

McKean, M. (1982), 'The Japanese Experience with Scarcity: Management of the Traditional Common Lands', *Environmental Review*, **6**, 63–88.

McKean, M. (1992) 'Management of Traditional Common Lands (Iriaichi) in Japan', in D. Bromley (ed.), *Making the Commons Work: Theory, Practice and Policy*, San Francisco: Institute for Contemporary Studies, pp. 63–98.

McKean, M. (1997), 'Common Property Regimes: Moving from Inside to Outside', *Proceedings of the Workshop on Future Directions for Common Property Theory and Research*, (cited 21 July 1998) <http://www.indiana.edu/~iascp/webdoc.html>

Netting, R. (1976), 'What Alpine Peasants Have in Common: Observations on Communal Tenure in a Swiss Village', *Human Ecology*, **4**, 135–146.

Ostrom, E. (1990), *Governing the Commons; The Evolution of Institutions for Collective Action*, New York: Cambridge University Press.

Seebohm, F. ([1912] 1980), 'The English Village Community', in C. Dahlman, *The Open Field System and Beyond*, New York: Cambridge University Press.

Thirsk, J. (1964) 'The Common Fields', *Past and Present*, **29**, 3–9.

Walker B. (1995), 'Conserving Biological Diversity through Ecosystem Resilience', *Conservation Biology*, **9** (4), 747–752.

16. Complexity, Society and Resource Management: The Complex Adaptive Systems Approach

Kate Brinkley, Melanie Fisher and Sonya Gray

INTRODUCTION

Complex adaptive systems concepts are a useful aid to thinking about natural resource management, public policy and the problems related to the sustainable use of common property or common pool resources. Using a complex adaptive systems approach provides a framework for integrating economic, environmental and social factors, for considering the interactions between these factors, and for exploring why public policies may have undesired and unexpected consequences.

While impressive advances have been made in the area of complex adaptive systems theory and computer-based modelling, considerable development is still required. New mathematical models and a better understanding of the 'rules' governing individual/policy/resource inter-actions are needed for the creation of more sophisticated and accurate computer models. To date, the advances in complexity science, mathematics and computing provide hope that complex adaptive systems modelling could one day provide sophisticated decision-support systems for policy makers that would greatly improve their understanding of the potential consequences of various natural resource management policy options.

SOCIAL SCIENCES AS POLICY INPUTS: PART OF A COMPLEX SYSTEM

Economics aside, the social sciences tend not to have the prominence in the natural resource policy process afforded the natural sciences. While consideration may be given to equity and social impacts, the interactions between individuals or groups and the natural resources they depend on are often not well understood or considered in the policy development context. However, natural resource management public policy is fundamentally about, or involves, people. It is essentially aimed at changing knowledge, attitudes and/or behaviour at the individual, group or industry level.

Developing effective resource management policies requires an understanding of the links between the social or behavioural, biophysical and economic drivers and motivators of behaviour. Social aspects (including cultural and political schemas, attitudes, perceptions, beliefs and values), economic factors and environmental ethics are all interdependent issues that form part of an integrated, complex system. The stated objective of many government natural resource policies is to achieve sustainable development – however defined and measured. This requires a systematic, holistic and long-term approach to the management of resources. Instead of focusing on a single discipline or issue, policy has to consider the balance between the largely biophysical needs of the natural system, with the largely social and economic needs of the human system (Bradbury, 1998).

A systems approach is therefore useful for developing effective sustainable resource management policies. However, this is a difficult task given the size and complexity of sustainable resource issues. Consequently, the tendency of decision makers to use a reductionist or incremental approach in dealing with sustainable resource management issues is understandable. Systems are too complex to study as a whole, so the whole is usually broken down into simple and easily understood subcomponents with a focus on the immediate and the urgent, and an emphasis on introducing incremental change to existing arrangements. Unfortunately, this approach reduces the likelihood of understanding the interactions between the parts of systems. Yet, such interactions contain information vital for comprehending the organisation and actions of the system as a whole. This is a significant issue, as these interactions can significantly influence the success or failure of policies aimed at overcoming the 'tragedy of the commons' problems often associated with natural resource management.

THE COMPLEXITY SCIENCE PARADIGM: THE COMPLEX ADAPTIVE SYSTEM

Complex systems theory forms the key field of study within the area of complexity science. It is of interest to the social sciences because human groups and societies form complex systems, and our interactions with and responses to ecosystems are also elements of complex systems. Complex systems are composed of networks of mutually interacting component parts or 'agents'. Each of these agents has its own internal states, rules or strategies that determine its behaviour in the environment and its relation to other agents. All agents are potentially capable of being autonomous – they can impact on other agents, sustain day-to-day patterns or break with routine when new challenges require new responses.

The most important feature of such systems is that the interaction of the components, each with its own simple strategies, seems to produce apparently complex behaviours when they function as a system.

Complex systems can be divided into two types: Complex *Non-Adaptive* Systems and Complex *Adaptive* Systems. Adaptive systems (such as biological organisms, species and ecosystems) selectively change over time, while non-adaptive systems (such as atoms and galaxies) do not have this ability (see Jacobson, n.d).

The interactions between humans and natural resources can be thought of as occurring within a complex adaptive system – for example, irrigation farmers and riverine systems, fishing communities and freshwater and marine ecosystems, logging communities and forest ecosystems. Key features of complex adaptive systems are adaptation or evolution, self-organisation and emergence.

Adaptation/Evolution

Complex adaptive systems exhibit evolutionary or adaptive processes by changing when subjected to pressures in their environment. Groups of agents may begin to learn, experience and anticipate the future when they self-organise. As such, they can adapt and change within, and as part of, a changing environment to improve their chances for survival. If a system is unable to adjust and adapt to its environment's dynamics, it collapses and becomes extinct (Rosenau, 1997). The classic example is biological evolution – species either change in ways which enable survival in a changing environment, or decline, or become extinct.

In the natural resource management context, examples might include changes in fishing patterns as individual fisheries become unviable, or the failure to respond to declining fish stocks in a given fishery leading to the economic collapse of a fishery and, potentially, the social collapse of that fishing community. Another example might be the move to crops requiring reduced or no irrigation as groundwater irrigation supplies begin to dry up, or a move to higher value crops as irrigation water prices increase. Those farmers unable to adapt to either reduced water supplies or increased water prices are likely to eventually exit the industry in that area and may be replaced by others who are able to make a living under those conditions.

Self-Organisation

When agents that are part of a system interact in a manner that is mutually accommodating and self-consistent they undergo a process of 'self-organisation'. Agents that are sufficiently related to each other to have recurrent behaviours, and that are able to interact on a regular basis, are capable of spontaneously generating higher levels of structural organisation. For example, dominance patterns in pack animals are the result of individuals within the group interacting with other individuals in set ways that in turn provide an organisational hierarchy governing aspects of the operation of the group. In a backyard chicken coop, each chicken understands which of the others it is dominant or submissive to – something that governs its interactions and responses. The higher levels of the chicken hierarchy get to eat first, are entitled to chase the lower orders away from a shady spot or desirable food scrap, and lead the others into the hen-house for the night. The patterned behaviour of the agents is able to form into an orderly whole, which then begins to acquire new attributes (see 'emergence' below).

In human terms, self-organisation can be seen in our membership of various types of organisations – from families, friendship groups, sporting, industry and community groups, to societies and nations.

Emergence

As agents undergo self-organisation, their collective behaviour begins to acquire new attributes and to demonstrate characteristics that are not exhibited by individual agents. The system that is generated is not merely the sum of the individual actions of its members, but a unique entity created by their joint interactions. The classic example is that of a flock of birds that will wheel and pitch through the sky in such perfect unison that they seem to form a single entity. The flock's synchronised movement, however, emerges not from any centralised or external control mechanism, but through the interactions of the individual birds continually positioning themselves in relation to their immediate neighbours (see Jacobson, n.d.).

Emergence is often illustrated using the phrase 'the sum of the whole is greater than the parts'. For example, individual decisions to buy household goods leads to further decisions by other individuals to produce, distribute and sell goods. The 'whole' in this case is Adam Smith's invisible hand operating in market-oriented economies to move the market towards the optimal production, distribution and pricing of the right type of goods to meet the needs of the myriad of individual consumers. This is not the result of centralised planning but occurs as the result of individual agents making individual decisions (the sum of the parts).

Common Property Resources and the Complex Adaptive System Paradigm

Human activity has expanded to affect virtually every ecosystem on the planet. This not only makes ecosystems more complicated (or more difficult to manage), it also means that environmental management decisions need to be based on much more than ecological knowledge (Green and Klomp, 1998).

Common property or common pool resources are those to which private property rights have not or cannot be allocated. Some of these resources are public good resources in that they cannot be owned or used by one individual to the exclusion of all others. Sadly, this can mean that the incentive for the individuals who use these resources is to overexploit them without concern for the longer-term survival of the resource. If no one person owns a fishery or the water in a river system, it is in each individual's interest to take as many fish or as much water as possible before someone else does. Each becomes engaged in a race to exploit. Even if the resource is clearly in danger of irreparable damage, individuals may not forgo their share of the resource when they know that others are unlikely to do the same – the supposed cause of Hardin's (1968) 'tragedy of the commons' (but see Chapter 15 for an alternative view).

Of course, this is not to say that, where property rights are clearly defined and the functioning of the resource well understood, the resource is well managed. Economic theory predicts that under this scenario, the resource would be exploited to the 'optimal level of degradation'. However, optimal degradation could include starving farmers eating their seed stock or mining their soil to exhaustion in the full knowledge that there will be no crop next season and that starvation will again be a problem. Therefore, despite the current interest in solving natural resource management problems through introducing property rights, even in affluent countries, this may not be enough to lead to sustainable resource management.

Examples of depleted common property resources can be seen worldwide – from collapsed fisheries, deforestation, and overuse of irrigation and groundwater stores, to increasing desertification, irrigation and dryland salinity and air and water pollution. While there are examples of successful voluntary management systems of common property resources, these are few and far between. Consequently, the idea that environmental failures appear to be ubiquitous in unregulated common property resource systems has been seen as justification of government regulation of access to common property goods (Gerritson, 1997).

The continued repetition of common property management failures, as shown by the contemporary problems of pollution and the formative history of almost every fishery in the world (Gerritson, 1997) indicates that government intervention has had very limited success. Choosing the policy instruments and implementation approaches most suited to ensuring the sustainable use of common property resources is a difficult but extremely important task. Critical questions for governments seeking to influence the use of common property resources are which policy instruments to use (coercion and control methods, approaches that mimic market operations, or a mix of the two?) and how to implement and enforce these measures.

HUMANS: COMPLEX ADAPTIVE SYSTEMS IN A POLICY ENVIRONMENT

Ideally, natural resource management policy developers would consider that the human systems they aim to influence form part of complex adaptive systems. The interactions of individual humans that lead to processes of self-organisation, emergence and adaptation create problems when trying to control or modify behaviour.

The non-linear functioning of complex adaptive systems may result in the disproportionate impact of certain events. Small, seemingly minor, events can give rise to large outcomes, especially when these minor events are considered as part of a collective whole. For example, concern that a government might be about to introduce restrictions on access to irrigation water could lead to individuals rushing to protest to their local political representative. While individually this might not amount to much, it could – in aggregate – place significant pressure on a government. It has the potential to influence either or both the final decision or the earlier consultation process.

Conditions prevailing at any moment in time can initiate processes of change that are substantial and dramatic (Rosenau, 1997). Even the slightest change in initial conditions can lead to very different outcomes. In human systems this means that emergent processes pass through a number of often-irreversible choice points that lead down diverse paths and on to diverse outcomes.

The anticipation of others' actions, the uncertainty of future resource availability and people's capability to meet their perceived needs usually result in the overexploitation of common property resources, even those under government control. Coercion or incentive mechanisms, whether associated with enforcement policies or policies which mimic market conditions, can never achieve perfect results.

The adaptive ability of complex systems may be the most problematic area for policy development. It has been argued that humans are 'smart agents' in an economic sense – rational, self-interested, maximisers/optimisers who focus on fixed (non-evolving) goals (Epstein and Axtell, 1996). However, this is rarely the case in practice. Instead of maximising or optimising, people use adaptive strategies to best achieve their individual goals within environmental constraints. Effective sustainable resource management policy is clearly not as simple as identifying the biophysical and economic conditions and decreeing the appropriate policy response.

People's individual needs, values, desires and beliefs form the foundations on which they base their decisions about how to respond to – or, indeed, whether or not to comply with – common property resource management regimes or policies. In theory, government management systems aim to form rational mechanisms that optimise all values and uses of a natural resource, both in the present and in the future. However, people's responses and adaptations to systems of government management are not based on complete rationality.

People's most basic needs may override future resource availability considerations. For example, people at risk of starving are less likely to take only their share of a common property resource, as the short-term imperative to feed themselves and their families outweighs longer-term resource condition considerations. People's perceived needs and beliefs are partly based on their limited rationality, which is due to the persistence of uncertainty created by the large number of resource users that exist in a finite resource-based world of uncertain and shared property rights. In theory, people might be expected to take more than their share if they believe a resource will disappear quickly. This begins to introduce large complexity issues as people begin to consciously react to others and anticipate what they believe others will do. 'Free-riders' (people who take advantage of those who have been termed 'naive cooperators') believe it is in their interest to 'cheat', as they consider that others cannot be trusted to adhere to the rules.

The adaptive behaviours which people undertake to achieve their needs and satisfy their beliefs and values make it impossible to have complete control over large populations. The resulting emergent characteristics and non-linear impacts which arise from the interaction of many humans, each following their internal rules, explains why common property resources managed by government policies may not avoid market failure even where policy directions seek to develop market-like conditions. The presence of rule-breaking (free-rider behaviour) or rule-bending actions that arise from adaptive behaviours causes stochastic effects. The result may be a breakdown or crash of the resource or other undesired and unexpected policy outcomes.

DISCUSSION: COMPLEXITY THEORY AS A SOCIAL SCIENCES AND POLICY TOOL

Modelling and Simulation

To date, comparatively little complexity science research has been undertaken in the social sciences (Mitleton-Kelly, 1998). Most work that has resulted in descriptions of complex adaptive systems has relied on observations of systems composed of non-human agents. However, the theories and insights from complexity science have proven to have tremendous appeal and utility to the social sciences. While research in this area is limited, the modelling frameworks and simulation methods that have been developed are starting to be used to study humans and social systems. In addition to the *Sugarscape* model which will discussed below, Gimblett et al. (1996) have used agent-based models to simulate different human recreation types and their trail usage in national parks. This has assisted field managers in making more informed decisions for managing recreation use in wilderness settings. Chris Barrett developed a simulation of Alburquerque (TRANSIMS) to test the air quality impacts of proposed changes to road traffic arrangements. David Lane and Brian Arthur developed a model of consumer choice relating to a two-product market (Apple Macintosh computers versus IBM PCs) under conditions of information contagion (Casti, 1997). The most interesting work from the perspective of potential application to sustainable resource management issues is that of Epstein and Axtell (1996). Their modelling work focused on developing simple models of human societies. These artificial societies were created by developing an environment subject to change (which they named *Sugarscape*) and populating it with agents who interact with each other and their environment on the basis of sets of rules. These rules can be varied or added to in order to examine issues like human carrying capacity, tribal formation and conflict, mass migration, the formation of social networks, wealth distribution, inheritance, trade, the operation of firms, warfare, and so on. These models are able to study large numbers of actors with changing patterns of interactions, both with each other, and the environment in which they were placed. They also provide the potential to undertake complex scenario modelling which could aid our thinking about how best to manage natural resources.

Sugarscape could, for example, provide a useful . starting-point methodology for policy development in natural resource management. Non-experts can run the modelling software on PCs and other desktop computers. This enables them to feed in various rules and environmental conditions and to observe the possible outcomes and consequences. Even though these models of the human world are simplistic they are still an aid to thinking about human interactions with natural resources and responses to different policy environments and instruments. By way of example, *Sugarscape* has been used to look at responses to the production of pollution as a by-product of consumption. *Sugarscape* uses sugar as the main resource that agents consume and accumulate. The sugar forms a continually renewable resource. However, the introduction of pollution (which is created by the production and consumption of sugar) meant that common property resource problems similar to those observed in the real world arose in the artificial world of *Sugarscape*. When pollution reached high enough levels it diminished the welfare of all agents. Epstein and Axtell (1996) note that this has implications for the 'tragedy of the commons' concept. In the simulation, both the pollution and consumption rates of agents are fixed, so the only way to reduce pollution is to reduce consumption. Agents are allowed to harvest more than they can consume, so even halving the extra production would cause the pollution rates to fall. While this means that this behavioural rule makes each agent worse off (by lowering their sugar income), the authors note that all agents would have been better off in the long run if they reduced unnecessary consumption.

The *Sugarscape* simulation also has implications for common property resource management through a conceptualisation of power framework. The management of common property resources through the allocation of property rights is fraught with difficulty. The primary problem is that it requires decisions on the distribution of wealth (Christy, 1999). Providing rights to some users can exclude others. The reallocation of resources from the many to the few (the ironically-termed 'tragedy of the commoners') concentrates power and alienates many from traditional sources of food and income (Brown and Spink, 1997). Epstein and Axtell (1996) found a similar process arose when they allowed agents to 'inherit' wealth. While all agents are given an initial endowment of sugar, they can accumulate wealth by gathering more sugar than they need to metabolise. This simple rule resulted in the production of skewed wealth distributions for a wide range of agent types and environmental specifications. When offspring agents were allowed to inherit the wealth of their deceased parents, wealth inequalities were found to grow even further. Axtell (1999) utilised a similar modelling process to develop a simulation of how firms emerge and evolve. This research also has important implications for the study of common property resources, as it demonstrated the evolution of free-riding behaviour within the simulation and illustrated that the presence of free-riders produces stochastic effects.

These examples indicate the potential for complexity modelling to contribute to our understanding of the relationships and interactions between individuals, groups and natural resources by enabling hypotheses to be generated and tested and different resource management approaches to be trialled using a scenario modelling approach.

Public Policy Design and Development

There has generally been little theoretical discussion of policy development within the complexity science framework. However, some authors have discussed policy development and complexity concepts in a general manner (Albin and Gottinger, 1983; Gell-Mann, 1994; Rosenau, 1997). Rosenau (1997) and Holland (1995) have noted the usefulness of complexity theory as it applies to policy development and monitoring.

> It provides a cast of mind that can clarify, that can alert observers to otherwise unrecognised problems, and that can serve as a brake on undue enthusiasm for particular courses of action. Stated more generally, it is a mental set, a cast of mind that does not specify particular outcomes or solutions but that offers guidelines and lever points that analysts and policy makers alike can employ to more clearly assess the specific problems they seek to comprehend or resolve. (Rosenau, 1997, p. 1)

> We could with substantial effort, model (tragedy of the commons) situations . . . A flight simulator version would be particularly helpful, letting the politician or economist observe the short-term and long-term outcomes of policies they consider feasible. Still, that is not really enough. We need some way of searching beyond familiar policies, which may offer little or may be caught in a legislative deadlock. The space of possible policies is large, and there may be some that exploit lever points, if we can just uncover them. (Holland, 1995, p. 163)

Although the intention of policy is to bring about more desirable outcomes, it can in practice block or constrain emergent patterns of behaviour, producing unexpected and undesired results. Consequently, policies need to be designed with a framework and infrastructure that facilitates and supports the new organisations, relationships, connectivities and ways of working that arise and emerge when policy moves society away from established patterns of work and behaviour (Mitleton-Kelly, 1998). Put more simply, policy approaches need to allow for some flexibility in societal behaviours. Policies should be formulated to be variable and unstable with regard to details (Lewin, 1992). This means that flexible policy making requires that decisions are 'developed from below' as opposed to imposed from 'above' (Meppem and Gill, n.d.). Gell-Mann (1994) argues that bottom-up initiatives, as opposed to top-down ones, are particularly suitable for managing common property resources.

Policy design that takes people's issues, needs and desires into consideration means that policies are more likely to be complied with. People's willingness to comply is usually grounded in a perception that it 'makes sense' to comply. Industry members and individuals will not follow policy rules if those rules seem to violate their practical needs and their commonsense considerations (Smith, 1990). However, it still must be allowed that policies will be queried and tested, especially when immediate situations, futures and benefits are considered by people (Parker and Stacey, 1995).

The idea of flexible and inductive policy making, and the knowledge that much uncertainty and vagueness exists, makes it clear that ultimate answers or best solutions to natural resource management policy problems are unlikely to exist (Dimitrov, n.d.). Albin and Gottinger (1983) suggest three methods to control common property resources:

- introduce property rights for all participants;
- use disincentive schemes to lower the design complexity of the system, so that certain private decisions would be compatible with the socially optimal decision; or
- enforce limited access or other regulatory devices (via the price system or not) that would effectively limit competition in order to husband common property resources.

The final choice of method for controllability (that is, avoidance of the tragedy of the commons) requires that control complexity (specifically that which keeps the entire system or at least parts of it under complete control) and design complexities (complexity that is associated with transformation processes in which full use is made of the systems potential) be matched. The relationship between the two types of complexity governs the stability of a complex adaptive system; when the two coincide, stable states and output space result. By modelling common property resources as dynamic and competitive complex adaptive systems, breakdown potentials between design and control complexity can be identified.

This systems approach for identifying breakdown potentials can be related to natural resource management policy options via the following questions: under what conditions can stability of an economic and social system be achieved through controls which take into account non-renewable, substitutable resources and increasing environmental limitations?; and, which external/internal control mechanisms are potentially most effective where the objective is to achieve stable configurations in either a global or local system dynamics?

The most effective conditions are those that have the infrastructure to allow some flexibility in societal interactions with natural resources, but have the ability to correctly match the design and control complexities of a system. The potentially most effective control mechanisms are those which induce social outcomes from the bottom up. In their discussion on complexity and the policy-making environment Epstein and Axtell, (1996) found that the *Sugarscape* model serves to illustrate that there may be highly indirect and counterintuitive ways to induce social outcomes. Combinations of small, local reforms – 'packages' exploiting precisely the non-linear interconnectedness of things – may result in desirable outcomes in the large. Non-linear systems might actually be easier to control than linear ones. It might only take a small push to engender a big change in the system. Small, low-cost policy changes could therefore have a large impact on overall social welfare.

The Australian experience with the Landcare movement illustrates the effectiveness of such bottom up, flexible policy approaches. The government-supported Landcare programme provides funding to farmers and others interested in forming collective action groups to address land and water degradation problems. Problems are identified, priorities decided and solutions implemented by members of these voluntary groups. The Landcare movement has been very successful in raising awareness of the existence of, and the need to address, degradation issues and in encouraging the formation of Landcare and other groups for this purpose. Work may be undertaken to address both public good and private benefit issues and there is a strong emphasis on local solutions for local problems, grass-roots ownership, empowerment and voluntarism (Cary and Webb, in preparation).

CONCLUSIONS

Public policy for the sustainable management of common property resources should be explained and developed within the framework of a complex system that considers not only economic and environmental factors, but also social and behavioural factors. Complexity science concepts can form a useful tool as part of social sciences inputs into the design of effective resource management policies. In particular, complex adaptive systems theory forms a useful conceptual framework within which to explore why present common property resource policies may be ineffective and how more effective policies might be designed for the future.

The computer-based models currently available to simulate complex adaptive systems present a useful method for studying human/policy/natural resource interactions. These models may assist in designing effective policies by illustrating how aggregate human behaviours that arise from simple behavioural rules produce unexpected results, and by identifying potential responses to a range of policy scenarios.

However, complexity science theory is in the early stages of its development, particularly in relation to simulating human-dominated systems. This is both an issue of mathematical theory and the identification of the key rules of human and social behaviour relevant to natural resource use.

However, there are strict limits to which complexity science theory must be confined. By its nature, it cannot – and is unlikely ever to – provide a method for predicting the outcome of particular events and specifying the exact shape and nature of developments in the future. For all the strides that complexity theorists have made, they are still a long way from a science that can be relied upon for precision in charting the future course of human affairs (Rosenau, 1997).

Complexity science tells us that there are limits to how much we can comprehend of the complexity that pervades world affairs. Policymakers have to become comfortable with acting under conditions of uncertainty (Rosenau, 1997). Therefore policies need to be flexible and adaptive; allowing for variations in human behaviour, while developing infrastructures and institutional arrangements which gradually move society's actions into areas that are consistent with desired policy outcomes. Complex adaptive systems models and the general theory of complexity science tell us that we can never control a human system completely – it is too complex and uncertain. However, in the future, complex adaptive systems modelling might eventually provide a technology for trialing different policy approaches in the safe confines of an artificial world peopled by imaginary agents who do not suffer when their industry is wiped out or when their resources are destroyed by an ill-advised policy response.

REFERENCES

Albin, P. and H. Gottinger (1983), 'Structure and Complexity in Economic and Social Systems', *Mathematical Social Sciences*, 5, 253–268.

Axtell, R. (1999), *The Emergence of Firms in a Population of Agents: Local Increasing Returns, Unstable Nash Equilibria, and Power Law Distributions*, Washington, DC: Brookings Institution.

Bradbury, R. (1998), 'Will the New Science of Complexity Subvert Oceans Policy?' Conference on Oceans, Governance and Maritime Strategy, Canberra 18–19 May 1998.

Brown, V. and M. Spink (1997), *Caring for the Commons: Socio-cultural Considerations in Oceans Policy Development and Implementation*, Socio-cultural Considerations Issues Paper 4, A Report Commissioned by Environment Australia.

Cary, J. and T. Webb (in preparation), *The Social Benefits of the Landcare Movement*.

Casti, J. (1997), *Would-Be Worlds: How Simulation is Changing the Frontiers of Science*, New York: John Wiley and Sons.

Christy, F. (1999), 'Common Property Rights: An Alternative to ITQs', paper presented to the FishRights 1999 Conference, 15–17 November 1999, Freemantle, Western Australia.

Dimitrov, V. (n.d.) *Use of Fuzzy Logic When Dealing with Social Complexity*, Hawkesbury: School of Social Ecology, University of Western Sydney, <http://www.csu.edu.au/ci/vol4/dimitrov1/dimitrov.html>

Epstein, J. and R. Axtell (1996), *Growing Artificial Societies: Social Science from the Bottom-Up*, Washington, DC: and Cambridge, Massachusetts: Brookings Institution/MIT Press.

Gell-Mann, M. (1994), *The Quark and the Jaguar: Adventures in the Simple and Complex*, New York: W.H. Freeman and Co.

Gerritson, R. (1997), *Collective Action Problems in the Regulation of Australia's Common Property Natural Resources Discussion Paper No. 7* (October 1997) Public Policy Program, Australian National University.

Gimblett, R., B. Durnota and B. Itami (1996), *Some Practical Issues in Designing and Calibrating Artificial Human Recreator Agents in GIS-Based Simulated Worlds*, <http://www.csu.edu.au/ci/vol3/bdurnota/bdurnota.html>

Green, D. and N. Klomp (1998), 'Environmental Informatics – A New Paradigm for Coping with Complexity in Nature', in R. Standish (ed.), *Proceedings of Complex Systems 98*, Sydney: University of NSW.

Hardin, G. (1968), 'The Tragedy of the Commons', *Science*, **162**, 1243–1248.

Holland, J. (1995), *Hidden Order: How Adaptation Builds Complexity*, Massachusetts: Helix Books.

Jacobson, M. (nd), *Complexity and Complex Systems: A Brief Overview*,. Cognition, Technology and Complex Systems Group, University of Georgia, <http://lpsl.coe.uga.edu/Jacobson/CTCS/Resources/complexity.html>

Lewin, R. (1992), *Complexity: Life at the Edge of Chaos*, New York: Macmillan.

Meppem, T. and R. Gill (n.d.), *Planning for Sustainability as a Learning Concept*, Armidale, Australia: New England Ecological Economics Group, Centre for Water Policy, University of New England, <http://une.edu.au/cwpr/NEEEG/Learn.html>

Mitleton-Kelly, E. (1998), *Organisations as Complex Evolving Systems*, OACES Conference Paper, Warwick 4–5 December 1998, <http://www.lsc.ac.uk/LSE/COMPLEX/OACESconf.htm>

Parker, D. and R. Stacey (1995), *Chaos, Management and Economics: The Implications of Non-Linear Thinking*, Monograph No. 31, St. Leonards: Centre for Independent Studies.

Rosenau, J. (1997), 'Many Damn Things Simultaneously: Complexity Theory and World Affairs', in D. Alberts and T. Czerwinski (eds), *Complexity, Global Politics and National Security*, Washington, DC: National Defence University.

Smith, M. (1990), 'Chaos in Fisheries Management', *MAST*, **3** (2), 1–13.

17. The Impact of Post-Structuralism in Theories Informing Public Sector Natural Resource Management Practice

Bruce Moon

INTRODUCTION

In elementary form, managing natural resources can be viewed as a means–end process. That is, with a desired outcome, the resource manager will determine the issues needing attention and define the appropriate theoretical basis as a reference frame. However, unlike those dealing with economic growth or chemical waste, natural resource managers cannot draw from a disciplinary-specific set of 'natural resource management' theories. Rather, resource managers draw from theories in other disciplines to deal with the resource matter. For example, a forester may draw from economic theories for resource value, but resort to chemistry or biology for theories on yield issues. In public sector natural resource management, the task is generally multifarious. Ideally, the task manager is multi-disciplined. But as theory is constantly evolving, the natural resource manager will be expected to 'catch up'. The premise of this chapter is that theoretical changes have occurred that affect the way public sector natural resource managers must deal with distributional issues.

The chapter is constructed in three parts. The first part overviews the transition in social science theorising from positivism to post-structuralism. This provides the basis to argue that the previously assumed theoretical solidity no longer exists – if it ever did. The second and third parts appraise two different aspects of theorising that affect the public sector natural resource manager: government administration and governance.

The substance of the second part is that a paradigm shift has occurred in the way government administration is theorised. While the difference between structure and process remains, three different theories are appraised – decision, power, and alliance theory – to explain that the theoretical perception of process has altered considerably. The previous adherence to structural determinism as a pattern to explain administrative process has been replaced by reference to cultural images which characterise the situational context in which administrative action is undertaken.

The third part extends the post-structural endeavour in public administration by exploring the newly emerged theory of governance. Governance is a means to conceptualise the process governments are now forced to adopt in order to achieve natural resource (and other) management solutions. In the current ideological climate, western governments all too often have neither the all-encompassing power nor the necessary resources to effect their will. The 'solution' is to enter into arrangements with non-government and/or other government organisations. The impact of this transition is that the role of culture and ideology are brought into the theoretical context.

Throughout the chapter it is argued that the public sector natural resource manager is now operating in a different environment to that traditionally embodied in theory. Moreover, the types of solutions for the natural resource manager rely less on what may be deemed the most logical outcome, and more on the breadth of agreement amongst other actors in positions of support and/or implementation.

THEORETICAL CHANGE: FROM POSITIVISM TO POST-STRUCTURALISM

A central tenet within the modernist philosophical discourse has been that knowledge is not only substantially ascertainable, but that it can also be systematically structured and hierarchically ordered (Parsons, 1951; Popper, 1972). Premised on metaphysical assumptions, philosophers and (later) scientists sought to explain the physical and social world according to a systematic structure. For knowledge about the physical world, this conviction has been amply justified. However, the systematisation of social knowledge has proved to be problematic. This is most obvious in the Comtean-inspired positivist tradition, where metaphor patterns social theory: Durkheim's social systems are styled on Darwin's biological structure (Münch, 1988, p. 22), Parsons' social order rests on 'rules' fashioned from physics (Burger, 1977, p. 333), and Saussure's model of social communication draws on linear mathematics (Fiske, 1990, pp. 41–47).

The appeal of structural determinism in positivism is not restricted to social theory. As an example, Taylor's ideas for business organisation were fashioned from engineering principles and employees were viewed as mechanical agents (George, 1972, p. 90). Even today, some managerial practice theorists continue to adulate this structural determinism (March, 1994; Simon, 1976).

The rise of post-structuralism reacts against the structural determinism in positivism. Popular post-structuralist exponents include Baudrillard (1978), Foucault (1980, 1982), Rorty (1982), and Derrida (1978, 1981). Outhwaite (1999, p. 9) observes that the impact of post-structuralism has not been to negate scientific research, but to deconstruct the credibility of a positivist social science based on: 'three simplistic conceptions: of the detached subject of knowledge, of the reduced and delimited object of knowledge, and of the knowledge process, or more precisely, the referential semantics of the production of knowledge'.

The relevance of post-structuralism is that the way natural resource managers perceive the role and function of government is largely still structured by the positivist tradition. Against the positivist presumption that order and purpose should structure theoretical endeavour, the post-structuralist 'turn' in social science has resulted in the theories of government administration and governance becoming more focused on issues that are situationally relevant. Theories of government administration and governance are central to the way natural resource managers approach their task.

THEORISING GOVERNMENT ADMINISTRATION

Traditionally, texts on government portray it as both an object and a process. As an 'object', government is presented as a relatively autonomous entity embodied with legal powers to effect a political and administrative will (Emy, 1974; Ham and Hill, 1984; Stewart and Ward, 1992). The will of government is to govern society (minimise conflict and maximise productivity) and to allocate resources (share wealth). Conventionally, the power of government is assumed to be sufficient to (re)fashion social relations (King, 1986, pp. 31–58).

As a 'process', government is both an institution (the set of rules) and an organisation (the actors). Positivists portray the mechanism of government as a linear input–output function. That is, if the actors properly follow the rules the overall task will be fulfilled.

The positivist theoretical presumption is that government has power to effect its will, and ideally that power will be structured into responsible tasks such that a societal order and purpose will be fulfilled (Weber, 1968) with sanctions and regulations used to reinforce intent (Foucault, 1979). This linear and vertical model assumes 'government' to be somehow omnipotent.

More recently, the process of government has been recognised as so immense that the whole task cannot be viewed with any degree of detail in one theoretical portrayal. Instead, various limited perspectives are used to identify some particular set of machinations. A paradigm shift is occurring in government administration theories as a consequence of post-structuralist endeavour, partly as a result of theorists reconsidering the way the operative variables of social interaction ought be perceived. Developments in decision, power and alliance theories are illustrative.

Decision Theory

Government administration is typically perceived as a collective undertaking, with decision makers assumed to be dependent on policy guidance and feedback. This contrasts with decision theory, with the latter largely addressing only autonomous actions. Here, developments in decision theory are appraised, and then related to collective group action.

Decision theory formally emerged in the late nineteenth century – embedded within theories dealing with organisational management (George, 1972). It appears that the economists' 'rational choice' model underpinned this early approach. The process of 'rational choice' assumes an actor lists all the opportunities for action, identifies consequences flowing from each opportunity, and selects that action that has the preferred set of consequences. As an organisational decision process, 'rational choice' assumes the employers' values are embodied. Thus, the decision maker is merely a knowledge processor.

Recently, decision theory has moved from the 'rational choice' standard, with alternatives emerging from the disciplines of psychology, sociology and political studies. Most approaches can each be categorised into one of two groups – prescriptive and descriptive. Prescriptive models tend to suggest how a decision ought be made, while the descriptive forms identify the characteristics purportedly influencing the social actor.

The assorted prescriptive models retain the 'rational choice' structure (March, 1994). An inherent difficulty with 'rational choice' is that the term 'rational' is a normative expression based on belief (Moon, 1998) and so decision logicality inevitably rests on agreement with the adopted guiding values.

Descriptive models hold that decisions reflect social pressures. That is, the decision reflects the outcome of persuasion which – to some degree or another – is organised politically. The materialisation of each or any of the social pressures into a decision largely rests on the perceived degree of persuasiveness and/or power.

Figure 17.1 combines the two categories into a diagram, with the attributes of structural influence (Public Opinion, Law, and so on) and institutional attributes (for example, Policies and Strategies) as indicative of social pressures (the descriptive mode), and employs the 'decision conduit' as the site where a decision is made (the prescriptive mode). Neither mode infers any process by which the 'descriptive' influences are effected/received, nor any mechanism for the decision action in the 'decision conduit'.

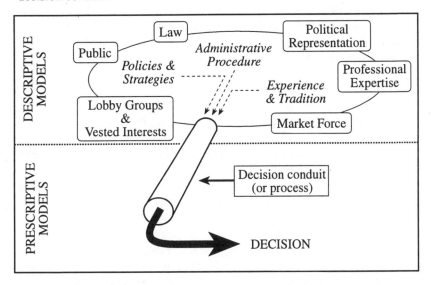

Figure 17.1   *Attributes Assumed in the Decision Context*

While much is understood about decision influences, the inability to gain firm empirical evidence on the exact decision action means that little can be demonstrated about how the decision maker actually makes decisions (Nisbett and Wilson, 1977). While prescriptive accounts are 'best practice' models, they can only be guides for decision making.

Psychologists have recently theorised that the critical factor in the process of making decisions is not the balancing of opportunities for action – as in the 'rational choice' based approach. Rather, it is an exercising of discretion over the relative merit of the various influencing attributes (Hogarth, 1980; Linstone, 1984; Taggart et al., 1985). The various influencing attributes are typically ordered according to norms and values signified by associative relationships (Bettenhausen and Murnighan, 1985; Feldman, 1984; Janis, 1982; Swap, 1984). Thus, a decision attribute may not be appraised according to the relative logic, rationality, or some other cognitively orderable criteria, but by a perception of relative 'goodness' in the guiding value/s.

Mitchell and Beach (1990) explored discretion and decision making as a cultural act, asserting that the decision maker draws upon normatively-bound images. These 'images' are informed by visions, goals and strategies adopted from those influencing the decision maker.

The natural resource manager has the choice between a deterministic approach where logic and discretion are constrained by prescribed values (prescriptive), or a 'best-fit' approach where the relative 'goodness' reflects culturally defined influences (descriptive). Recent developments in the understanding of power and how group decisions are produced add support to the descriptive approach being the operative standard.

Reconceptualising 'Power'

Power is often conceptualised as causal; a capacity to make another do something that they would not do otherwise. Power is usually viewed as both a means (instrumental power) and an end (structural power). Thus, a 'rational choice' decision maker has both instrumental and structural power; this view of decision making power is strong in the natural resource management literature (Butteriss and Sinden, 1994; Calantone, 1997; Selman, 1997).

The countless texts on the subject of power each provide different perspectives on the application, legitimacy, morality, usefulness, and/or process of power relations. An early (and positivist) exponent on the relationship between organisational structure and power was Weber (1968). For Weber, power is an authoritative structure by which organisational officers could utilise a capacity to act – or prescribe people to act – but always on the assumption that the expressed action would result in social betterment.

Exploring instrumental power, Lukes (1974) posited that it can be viewed in three dimensions. His view is that power is a discretionary function to award benefit and thus effects a mobilisation of bias. In the first dimension the discretion results in conflict, in the second dimension the decision maker avoids conflict, while in the third dimension the decision maker spreads the (potential) conflict across parties/groups to dissipate reaction.

Clegg (1989) extends Lukes' view by arguing that power patterns reflect the larger cultural arrangements in society. Power is both a means to effect control over all who are subjected to the power (structure), and/or a means to focus on the interests of the influencing group/s (agency). Clegg (1989, p. xv) asserts that there are three methods by which power is generally manifested, and these can be conceptualised as dispositional, facilitative, and agency:

Dispositional power is structural and is equated with a set of capacities to act under various laws, rules, privileges and responsibilities;

Facilitative power is a discretionary function in goal achievement, for example, the capacity to set a target, or to deliver an intention;

Agency power is a tool to organise resource distribution. Here, power can either be used to fulfil culturally expected norms, or as a means to gain cultural advantage.

Clegg is using the word 'Agency' to describe two different ideas. On one hand, 'Agency' describes a view that power is typically enacted in ways to give support to the existing social structure (reinforcing the *status quo*). On the other hand, 'Agency' describes how manifested power can destabilise social relations (undermining the *status quo*). In the structure/agency perspective of power, Clegg (1989) is reflecting the dialectical nature of the concept; power is exercised in 'situated action' (1990, p. 8). Though he admits that the notion of 'Agency' has been 'deliberately stretched to accommodate a number of different forms' (1989, p. 17), the dialectical consideration is a comparison between:

(a) the traditional view that power is a formalised right to give cause to social structure (originating in Hobbes' (1968) *Leviathan*) or a superior way to organise the use of resources (Weber, 1986), and;

(b) the alternative idea that power is used to advance particular ideological interests or beliefs (Foucault, 1979; Marx, 1973) or used as a metaphorical structure for the advancement of hegemony generally (Benton, 1981; Gramsci, 1971).

To distinguish between the two approaches to 'Agency' power, the first approach is termed *Instrumental* and the second *Dialectical*. Clegg (1989, p. 17) makes the point that 'Agency' power is 'something which is achieved by virtue of organization' and the organisation 'is essential to the achievement of effective agency' power. Nevertheless, *Instrumental* power must exist to enable the *Dialectical* aspect of 'Agency'. And, the same link exists between the 'Dispositional' and 'Facilitative' elements of structural power. It seems more fruitful to conceptualise the 'Structural' and 'Agency' perspectives of power as each having two paired elements, as illustrated in Figure 17.2.

The difference in the Agency mode of power in the *Instrumental* and *Dialectical* forms rests with intent. When the Agency mode of power is used to advantage the permanent interests of a few, it becomes *Dialectical*. Typically, the *Dialectical* form of power is portrayed as an improper or immoral usage, often as a tool to achieve segregation, differentiation, hierarchicalisation, marginalisation, and/or exclusion (Best and Kellner, 1991).

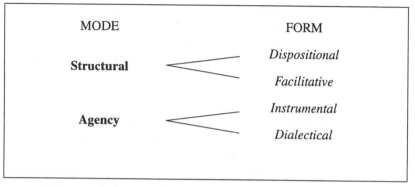

Figure 17.2   A Differentiation of Power

The essential feature of Clegg's portrayal is that the typical expression of *Dialectical* power is to effect digressively constituted points of interest to destabilise social relations, examples of which can be observed as:

- the fracturing and/or reorganising of group membership,
- the transformation of rights and responsibilities,
- the strengthening and/or weakening of allegiances,
- the disciplining or punishment of people subjectively, and/or,
- the making and/or reversal of social arrangements.

The social acceptance of the Agency mode of power stems from a perception that it will be used in the *Instrumental* form. It is this assumption of procedural reason and goodwill that allows the *Dialectical* form. But the question remains whether *Dialectical* power is an intention, or the result of a valuation by unhappy recipients.

Alliance Theory

More than a quarter of a century ago – with the 'rational choice' paradigm as the dominant operational thesis – authors such as Cyert and March were not only perplexed by the impact of the plurality of 'interest groups' operating in complex government administrations, they were also concerned that bargained decision outcomes were deemed socially acceptable. The emergent view indicated that decisions were logical if the plurality of 'interest groups' agreed on outcomes. Much study has followed, with the resultant supposition that 'interest groups' coalesce into communities to effect a decision outcome satisfactory to the majority. From the context in which the 'interest groups' operate, three different (but related) theoretical propositions have emerged:

Policy communities: those with a common interest in fashioning the way a product, service, or process is structured; typically focused on seeking consensual agreement (normally) to *harmonise resource usage*.

Policy networks: those with a common interest in fashioning policy issues and problems; typically focused on the properties or processes used by members of one or more policy community to interact, and/or bargain, across (inter)dependent relationships and aimed at *stabilising the management of a resource* (see Rhodes and Marsh, 1992, pp. 181–205).

Policy regimes: those with a common interest in fashioning the outcome of a product, service, structure or process; typically focused on means to minimise conflict to *facilitate resource development*.

While these separations are important, it is the features in common that form 'alliance theory'. For example, alliances tend to develop as specialists seek common outlooks or orientations. Alliance relationships may include actors outside the organisation in charge of policy development (or articulation). Rhodes and Marsh (1992) describe alliances between governmental representatives (as regulators) and economic interest groups (the regulated) such as business organisations (reactive against regulation) and labour unions (proactive for regulation).

Critically, alliances form as a means of organising how an issue is to be managed, or a matter resolved. Thus, the focus is on fashioning the methods that underpin how decisions will be made. This theme is reinforced by Considine (1994, p. 103) who notes that at the core of each alliance there exists 'informal and semi-formal linkages between individuals and groups in the same policy system'. Furthermore, 'when viewed as a total pattern of involvement and participation . . . (alliances) constitute a key aspect of the social capital of the policy system, helping us distinguish the dynamic from the static' (Considine, 1994, p. 103).

Considine (1994) uses the term 'static' to represent the formal organisational ties or patterns, the larger systemic linkages (such as the functional relationship between organisations or departments, and the macro-political economic ideology) and the normative institutional modes for social behaviour. The term 'dynamic' represents the 'informal and semi-formal linkages between individuals and groups in the same policy system' (1994, p. 103). There is a focus towards commonality about problems and solutions in terms of policy – even though there remains conflict over what can or might be done. In other words, the term 'static' refers to structural issues, while 'dynamic' refers to cultural, or agency, issues.

These points show how a decision maker can be 'socialised' to produce decisions that conform to group expectations. That an organisational actor has difficulty being independent is explained by psychological theories on the norms of social responsibility, reciprocity and equity. In conjunction with a group-held view of appropriate behaviour expectation, these norms are used to ensure a person acts within the desired general boundaries. Thus, a person receives positive or negative sanctions according to how they both act, and relate with others, in the group. Against the positivist assumption of a vertical orientation of power, here power also has a lateral (and cultural) attribute that is a function of the administrative process.

In government administration, the post-structural endeavour has shown that theories of governmental process have incurred considerable revision. By exploring revisions to decision, power and alliance theories, this second part of the chapter showed that contrary to the premise of structural determinism, cultural interactions characterise (and shape) the situational context in which administrative action is undertaken. As natural resource management is a series of ideas communicated in situational contexts, the administrative management process will encounter contextual and cultural norms favoured by those managerial actors having a part to play in the selection of some outcome and/or the implementation of a management plan.

THEORISING 'GOVERNANCE'

Against the positivists' vertical model of government, the term 'governance' embodies a major shift in thinking towards the way western society has fashioned the governing process and how resource allocation is undertaken. The term is applied in democratically pluralist societies where government interacts with private and other public organisations in which the vertical structure of power has largely ceased to be the dominant referential form of authority (Rhodes, 1996).

Mayntz (1993) asserts that modern western government is a partial failure because it can neither command the necessary resources nor gain the mandate to properly effect its will. In other words, government is neither the omnipotent agent nor panoptical regulator as previously theorised (Foucault, 1980). March and Olsen (1995, p. 5) also point to a growing public perception that confidence in the system of government has waned as 'an agent of the public' primarily because of a 'consciousness of the corruption and irresponsibility of state power'. Increasingly, effective governing requires an interaction with major stakeholders in both the process and/or the outcome. At the core is an acceptance that governing involves complexity, and innovative solutions may transcend the governmental jurisdiction – whether legally, spatially and/or ideologically – and so necessitate stakeholder cooperation. Thus, successful governing has focused on the capacity to ensure action occurs without any legal requirement that change will necessarily take place.

For Stoker (1998, p. 17), the 'essence of governance is its focus on governing mechanisms which do not rest on recourse to the authority and sanctions of government'. These are:

1. a set of institutions and actors that are drawn from but also beyond government,
2. the blurring of boundaries and responsibilities for tackling social and economic issues,
3. building on the power dependence involved in the relationships between institutions involved in collective action,
4. acknowledging the autonomy of self-governing networks of actors,
5. recognising the necessity to get things done in ways that do not rest on the power of government to command or use its authority.

The practice of governance is typically less structurally formalised than 'government' and embodies semi-permanent – but, sometimes temporary – arrangements. Whatever the combination of actors, perhaps most importantly, the underlying motive for a governance arrangement is to effect an ideology. This is often premised as general principles or values.

An essential attribute in this portrayal is the subject of power. In Foucault's (1982, p. 21) conception, to govern is 'to structure the possible fields of actions of others'. Thus, market power or ideological commitment is as effective in fashioning an outcome as is the rule of law. Importantly, each power holder has a capacity to obstruct or influence, but none has a singular capacity to control (and thus totally realise an outcome). This depiction of governance as the outcome of coalitions of interests acquiescing or organising to effect mutually beneficial outcomes, employs a 'very loose Gramscian sense of hegemony . . . [with] "blocs" of thought, culture, and modes of production that transcend national boundaries' (Holsti, 1992, p. 33).

The very notion of governance depends on the idea of reform; reform being both the process and outcome of initiatives for change. As Rein and Schön (1993, p. 145) describe, reform or policy discourse refers to 'the interactions of individuals, interest groups, social movements, and institutions through which problematic situations are converted to policy problems, agendas are set, decisions are made, and actions are taken'. Governance is as much a path to get things done without formalised authority as it is the debate over how the problem issue might be framed and negotiated. This process (of semi-participatory democracy) is exercised in values, ideology, and argumentation. Unlike positivist assumptions, the outcome need not be rational. Rather, all that is required is that it be logical to the participants and marketable to the wider community of judgement.

The premise of structural determinism embodied in positivist theory does not explain how resource distributional issues are managed at the level of region, state, or nation. Understanding governance also requires a comprehension of 'alliance theory', as it is the cultural and normative aspects that shape the interactional linkages between individuals and groups within each policy system.

CONCLUSION

The premise of this chapter is that the impact of post-structuralism in the social sciences has induced a theoretical revision – especially in the conceptualisation of how government and public sector administration is undertaken. This has implications for the natural resource manager who draws on theories when undertaking her or his tasks. Perhaps the most revealing outcome is that the idea of structural certainty within theoretical propositions as a basis to make resource and/or management decisions has been abandoned. Instead, theoretical explanations are now situated in both the context of the action and the culture of the actors.

The post-structuralist proposition embodied within the theories canvassed here is that the cultural parameters, normative standards and procedural patterns in any situation will largely be determined by the actors operating within that context/arena. That is not to say that actors in each context/situation/arena will determine guiding parameters which are at odds with the larger cultural and ideological patterns existing in the society. Rather, it indicates that there is no predeterminable certainty as to how the group will fashion its arguments and actions.

For the natural resource manager, the message from the chapter is that administrative actors search for cultural meanings to enact their tasks. In this context, a manager can no longer make assumptions and/or expectations as to how others may resolve a matter to effect an outcome. This means that the manager dependent on third-party solutions cannot rely on logic as a basis to predetermine outcome possibilities. Rather, the probability of an outcome will relate to culture, that is, the collective array of ideologies and expectations informing the actor's decision making. Without doubt, the post-structuralist approach elevates the role of political process in the operational function of resource management.

That public sector natural resource management is increasingly a sharing of responsibilities between other governing agencies and the private sector, makes governance theory clearly pertinent. Where 'getting things done' is increasingly seen as more important than blind adherence to structural rules, the observation that actors hold insufficient power to structure outcomes but sufficient to veto the actions of others is important. This reinforces the observation of 'alliance theory' that in order to gain status and/or standing from outcome deservedness, actors seek agreements with others. For the public sector natural resource manager, patterning outcomes according to collective agreements instead of authoritative power means that the relevance of sanctions changes. Though the threat of hierarchical authority sanctioning remains, any application may require agreement with actors horizontally across the situational context.

The public sector natural resource manager is now operating in an environment that is less structurally certain and is often normatively changing. Moreover, the types of solutions for natural resource management issues rely less on what may be deemed the most logical outcome, and more on the breadth of agreement amongst other actors involved with support and/or implementation.

REFERENCES

Baudrillard, J. (1978), *Writing and Difference* (trans., A. Bass), Chicago: Chicago University Press.

Benton, T. (1981), '"Objective" Interests and the Sociology of Power', *Sociology*, **15** (2), 161–184.

Best, S. and D. Kellner (1991), *Postmodern Theory: Critical Interrogations*, London: Macmillan.

Bettenhausen, K. and J. Murnighan (1985), 'The Emergence of Norms in Competitive Decision-making Groups', *Administrative Science Quarterly*, **30** (3), 350–372.

Burger, T. (1977), 'Talcott Parsons, the Problem of Order in Society, and the Program of an Analytical Sociology', *American Journal of Sociology*, **83**, 320–334.

Butteriss, C. and J. Sinden (1994), 'Rural Waste Management in New South Wales: An Economic Application of the Precautionary Principle', *Australian Journal of Environmental Management*, **1** (3), 156–173.

Calantone, C. (1997), 'Canadian Non-market Depletion Rules: A Simulation Study of Resource Protection Formulae', *Socio-Economic Planning Sciences*, **31** (3), 217–230.

Clegg, S. (1989), *Frameworks of Power*, London: Sage.

Clegg, S. (1990), *Modern Organizations: Organization Studies in the Postmodern World*, London: Sage.

Considine, M. (1994), *Public Policy: A Critical Approach*, Melbourne: Macmillan.

Derrida, J. (1978), *Writing and Difference*, Chicago: Chicago University Press.

Derrida, J. (1981), *Dissemination*, Chicago: Chicago University Press.

Emy, H. (1974), *The Politics of Australian Democracy: An Introduction to Political Science*, Melbourne: Macmillan.

Feldman, D. (1984), 'The Development and Enforcement of Group Norms', *Academy of Management Review*, January: 47–53.

Fiske, J. (1990), *Introduction to Communications Studies* (2nd edition), London: Routledge.

Foucault, M. (1979), *Discipline and Punish: The Birth of the Prison* (trans., A. Sheridan), London: Allen Lane.

Foucault, M. (1980), *Power/Knowledge, Selected Interviews and Other Writings 1972–1977* (translated and edited by C. Gordon), Brighton, UK: Harvester Press.

Foucault, M. (1982), 'The Subject and Power', in H. Dreyfus and P. Rabinow, (eds), *Beyond Structuralism and Hermeneutics*, Chicago: University of Chicago Press, pp. 15–28.

George, C. (1972), *The History of Management Thought,* (2nd edition), Englewood Cliffs, NJ: Prentice-Hall.

Gramsci, A. (1971), *Selections from the Prison Notebooks*, London: Lawrence and Wishart.

Ham, C. and M. Hill (1984), *The Policy Process in the Modern Capitalist State*, London: Harvester Wheatsheaf.

Hobbes, T. (1968), *Leviathan*, Harmondsworth: Penguin.

Hogarth, R. (1980), *Judgement and Choice*, New York: Wiley.

Holsti, K. (1992), 'Governance Without Government: Polyarchy in Nineteenth-Century European International Politics', in J. Rosenau and E. Czempiel (eds), *Governance Without Government: Order and Change in World Politics*, Cambridge: Cambridge University Press, pp. 30–57.

Janis, I. (1982), *Groupthink,* (2nd edition), Boston: Houghton Mifflin.

King, R. (1986), *The State in Modern Society: New Directions in Political Sociology*, London: Macmillan.

Linstone, H. (1984), *Multiple Perspectives for Decision Making*, New York: North Holland.

Lukes, S. (1974), *Power: A Radical View*, London: Macmillan.

March, J. (1994), *A Primer on Decision Making: How Decisions Happen*, New York: The Free Press.

March, J. and J. Olsen (1995), *Democratic Governance*, New York: The Free Press.

Marx, K. (1973), *Grundrisse*, Harmondsworth: Penguin.

Mayntz, R. (1993), 'Governing Failures and the Problem of Governability: Some Comments on a Theoretical Paradigm', in J. Kooiman (ed.), *Modern Governance: New Government–Society Interactions*, London: Sage, pp. 9–20.

Mitchell, T. and L. Beach (1990), '"Do I Love Thee? Let Me Count . . ." Toward an Understanding of Intuitive and Automatic Decision Making', *Organizational Behavior and Human Decision*, **47**, 1–20.

Moon, B. (1998), 'Reforming the Queensland Land-use Planning Legislation: An Agenda Driven by Myth and Rhetoric', *Australian Planner*, **35** (1), 24–31.

Münch, R. (1988), *Understanding Modernity: Toward a New Perspective Going Beyond Durkheim and Weber*, London: Routledge.

Nisbett, R. and T. Wilson (1977), 'The Halo Effect: Evidence for Unconscious Alteration of Judgements', *Journal of Personality and Social Psychology*, **35**, 250–256.

Outhwaite, W. (1999), 'The Myth of Modernist Method', *European Journal of Social Theory*, **2** (1), 5–25.

Parsons, T. (1951), *The Social System*, New York: The Free Press.

Popper, K. (1972), *Objective Knowledge*, Oxford: Oxford University Press.

Rein, M. and D. Schön (1993), 'Reframing Policy Discourse', in F. Fischer and J. Forester (eds), *The Argumentative Turn in Policy Analysis and Planning*, London: UCL Press, pp. 145–166.

Rhodes, R. (1996), 'The New Governance: Governing Without Government', *Political Studies*, **44**, 653–667.

Rhodes, R. and D. Marsh (1992), 'New Directions in the Study of Policy Networks', *European Journal of Policy Research*, **21**, 181–205.

Rorty, R. (1982), *The Consequences of Pragmatism*, Minneapolis: University of Minnesota Press.

Selman, P. (1997), 'The Role of Forestry in Meeting Planning Objectives', *Land Use Policy*, **14** (1), 55–73.

Simon, H. (1976), *Administrative Behaviour: A Study of Decision-making Processes in Administrative Organization*, (3rd edition), New York: The Free Press.

Stewart, R. and I. Ward (1992), *Politics One*, Melbourne: Macmillan.

Stoker, G. (1998), 'Governance as Theory: Five Propositions', *International Social Science Journal*, **50** (1), 17–28.

Swap, W. (1984), 'Destructive Effects of Groups on Individuals', in W. Swap and Associates (eds), *Group Decision Making*, Beverly Hills, CA: Sage, pp. 54–79.

Taggart, W., D. Robey and K. Kroeck (1985), 'Managerial Decision Styles and Cerebral Dominance: an Empirical Study', *Journal of Management Studies*, **22**, 175–192.

Weber, M. (1968), *Economy and Society: An Outline of Interpretive Sociology*, New York: Bedminster.

Weber, M. (1986), 'Domination by Economic Power and Authority', in S. Lukes (ed.), *Power*, Oxford: Basil Blackwell, pp. 28–36.

18. 'Changing People to Change Things': Building Capacity for Self-Help in Natural Resource Management – a Governmentality Perspective

Lynda Herbert-Cheshire

INTRODUCTION

There is agreement amongst most commentators today that something needs to be done to secure the future of rural and regional Australia. Precisely what form those measures take is an issue that has recently come under debate following: the continued environmental degradation of Australia's agricultural lands; the so-called 'failure' of the welfare state to seriously address the problems of poverty, unemployment and social disadvantage in rural regions; and the removal of many of the direct and indirect subsidies from governments that have traditionally propped up primary industries. New discourses which have been emerging since the early 1990s have responded to these failings by advocating an alternative, more holistic, approach to natural resource management which relies on bottom-up models of community self-help, partnerships with government and local empowerment. More generally, these same representations form part of a larger discourse of rural development which, in recognition of the interconnectedness of many of the difficulties faced by rural producers and their local economies, now seeks to implement strategies directed at the cultural, economic, social and environmental sustainability of rural life.

While this idea of community self-help has been inspired by US initiatives of the 1970s and 1980s (Keane, 1990, p. 292) it is increasingly evident that a rhetoric of self-help is being supported by, and gradually being adopted into, governmental discourses of natural resource management and rural development. These discourses have employed the language of community and empowerment and focus heavily on the idea of a partnership between the state and community groups.[1] While responsibility for action is now placed firmly in the hands of rural people themselves, state and federal

government agencies have, in turn, taken on a new 'enabling role' (Goodwin, 1998, p. 9) of providing support, encouragement, advice, training and motivation. In keeping with their new role, it is perhaps not surprising that a significant degree of effort of these agencies is directed at educational programmes of 'capacity building' which set out to enhance the ability of rural people to take on the role that has been set out for them.

To date, Australia's National Landcare Program has been the most significant manifestation of community self-help in the area of natural resource management, with the formation of over 4200 community Landcare groups since its inception (Lockie, 1999, p. 599). While '"empowerment" and "community ownership" have been central motifs of the Landcare Program' (see Martin, 1997, p. 45) some authors have been sceptical of the extent to which power is genuinely devolved to the local level and have regarded the general shift towards self-help as an attempt by governments to creep away from their own responsibilities under the guise of self-determination and empowerment (see for example, Bryson and Mowbray, 1981; Cruickshank, 1994; McLaughlin, 1987; Murdoch, 1997; Sher and Sher, 1994). Clearly, these two perspectives remain in disagreement over the true empowering potential of community self-help, yet, as Martin has pointed out in his critical analysis of Landcare, they are, nevertheless, united by a sovereign–subject metaphor in which power is constructed as a resource that can be shared with, or acted upon, individuals and their communities (1997, p. 47).

Following the work of Martin and others (for example, Higgins, 1998; Lockie, 1998, 1999) this chapter takes an alternative line of enquiry. It draws upon the governmentality work of Foucault (1991) and Rose (1993, 1996a, 1996b) to explore how power under an advanced liberal formula of rule is deployed through a range of governmental technologies of self-help. These include funding, programmes, calculations, techniques, apparatuses, documents and procedures which seek to 'create' individuals and communities capable of rational self-government and yet whose conduct is consistent with specific objectives (Rose and Miller, 1992). What this means for programmes like Landcare and similar community-based resource management or development groups is that any kind of action will not do. Rather, an advanced liberal formula of rule supports specific forms of action that are in line with the general shift towards agricultural intensification (Lockie, 1999), economic rationalism, and enhancing the productiveness and competitiveness of Australia's rural economy in the global market (Lawrence et al., 1999; Lawrence, 2000).

Such techniques in natural resource management are, by now, fairly well documented and a growing body of sociological literature has emerged in recent years which has provided a refreshingly critical, and highly theoretical, approach to these issues (see Higgins, 1998; Lockie, 1998, 1999; Martin, 1997). It is neither necessary nor possible to undertake a review of the literature here: it is sufficient to say that while this research makes its own contribution to this knowledge, it also provides new insights by focusing more sharply upon a specific process within the community self-help approach. The issue for many government agents and extension officers is that while self-help is recognised as a far more sustainable approach to resource management, it cannot be expected that all individuals will have reached the required level of 'capability and preparedness to embark on a co-operative and co-creative development for the benefit of all' (Gannon, 1998, p. 29). To this end, experts and state government agencies like the Queensland Department of Primary Industries (DPI) and the Office of the Public Service, have initiated programmes which seek to build the capacity of individuals to initiate community-based, socially responsible strategies of resource management and development for the benefit of all.

Known as 'capacity building' by those familiar with the new discourse, these programmes are the main focus of this chapter which begins by summarising the key features of the self-help approach and its rhetoric of empowerment. More specifically, it suggests that current attempts to enhance the capacity of rural people to help themselves are directed not so much at providing them with the required support or skills for sustainable land management practices, or even the political skills to question the new deregulated environment in which they find themselves (Martin, 1997), but more at seeking to change their mindset so they may become more psychologically conditioned to embrace this new existence:

> Capacity building is essential for empowering people to open to new attitudes to change and to be motivated in order to reach a level of preparedness to operate to their maximum potential for the development of their community. (Gannon, 1998, p. 29)

In the light of such ambitions, this chapter argues that capacity building programmes like leadership development courses, business advisory centres, motivational conferences and community appraisal workshops operate as 'indirect mechanisms' (Rose and Miller, 1990, p. 2) which frame individual and group ambitions, thereby ensuring they remain compatible with the broader goals of these state agencies. This exercise of power through these mechanisms, it has been argued, is less a matter of the direct imposition of 'state' will and more a case of 'action at a distance' (Rose and Miller, 1990) as governments seek to shape the environment in which people make their choices (Gordon, 1991). In this way people and communities 'freely' choose to conduct themselves according to a culture of self-help, entrepreneurialism and market imperatives. Before doing this, it is worth spending time exploring the self-help approach in a little more detail.

SELF-HELP APPROACHES TO NATURAL RESOURCE MANAGEMENT

The Bottom-Up Approach

There is an increasing expectation on rural people today that they will become actively involved in the planning and management of their own resources. Frequently justified on the basis that rural people are better placed to know their own problems and consequently seek their own solutions, this represents something of a shift in government policy. According to McCallum and Hughey (1999) community-based resource management in the 1990s was the combined result of two factors: the failure of local government agencies to adequately address environmental problems with their own limited resources, and a public sector management philosophy increasingly centred upon efficiency and cost recovery.

Language of Community

While the relationship between locality and community has long been under debate in the field of community studies (see for example, Pahl, 1970; Stacey, 1969) Australia's rural regions continue to be characterised within political discourses by a strong sense of community and a culture of self-help. Strong, cohesive communities are seen as essential to the economic and social, as well as the environmental, regeneration of rural Australia and rural community development is frequently cited by governments and experts as the first step towards a sustainable future. Since the early 1980s (see Bryson and Mowbray, 1981), 'community' has become increasingly politicised as a growing range of welfare provisions has been shifted to the private or voluntary sector, prompting Rose (1996a, 1996b) to write of a new form of governing through community. He suggests that community-building exercises seek to intensify and act upon individuals' allegiance to particular communities so that they are prompted to participate in projects of mobilisation, reform or regulation on their behalf. An alternative form of 'action at a distance', governing through community, similarly operates as an indirect way of acting upon the conduct of free, autonomous citizens by shaping their decision making within the context of their families and communities (Rose, 1996a).

Rise of the Expert

It has already been mentioned in this chapter that, within political discourses, the state now works in partnership with community groups in the delivery of policies and services (Murdoch and Abram, 1998). More specifically, the vital link in this partnership is provided by an emerging body of experts whose role is to 'operationalise' (Cruickshank, 1994, p. 49) the connection between helping and self-help by training individuals in the 'art' of self-government. According to Rose (1993, p. 298), advanced liberalism requires a specific relationship between political authorities and the expert whereby the latter is increasingly located in the sphere of the community. This close link with the community fulfils an important legitimising function for many extension officers or state agents who identify themselves as rural people and who subsequently believe their common background with their clients justifies their authority far more than any skills they may possess in issues of resource management.

Changing Mindset

It is also increasingly recognised by political authorities that sustainability is impossible to achieve simply by underwriting development of declining rural industries within regions. Some of the harshest critics of government intervention, for example, have argued that subsidies remove the incentive for farmers and local communities to become more competitive, thereby locking them into a 'cycle of dependency' (Wise, 1998, p. 89). They suggest that a far more sustainable alternative is to redirect money and energy away from attempts to underwrite uncompetitive farming practices towards strategies which seek to change the attitudes of farmers and to enhance their capacity for self-help. Rather than seeking to address the wider, structural, causes of land degradation, therefore, the self-help philosophy adopts an agenic approach of 'changing people to change things' (Gannon, 1998).

A Rhetoric of Empowerment

One final feature of the self-help approach is the frequency with which it is accompanied by an assumption that, in enabling rural people to help themselves, they somehow become empowered in the process. However, the underlying message of some commentators (see for example, Gannon, 1998) suggests that empowerment does not simply arise through the removal of 'disempowering' structures of government intervention, but, increasingly, occurs through exposing rural people to the vagaries of the international economy. The empowered citizen in advanced capitalism is one who has the 'freedom' to compete in the global market place and who embraces that freedom by adopting dynamic production and marketing strategies that enhance her or his competitive advantage. It is argued by Martin (1997, p. 48), however, that such hegemonic discourses of empowerment marginalise an awareness of how power is actually constituted in the way agricultural production has been organised in late capitalist societies and, consequently, how this can 'discipline' personal and political conduct.

TECHNOLOGIES OF GOVERNMENT – CREATING SELF-GOVERNING INDIVIDUALS

In response to Martin's (1997) comments, the governmentality perspective of Foucault and Rose can be employed to suggest that the trends towards self-help are symbolic in the sense that they represent a new, advanced, liberal form of governing rather than a simple reduction in the role of the state. As a very broad rationality, earlier forms of liberalism placed limits on the extent to which political authorities could legitimately exercise power over civil society (Burchell, 1996), thereby creating a separate sphere of society that was essentially regarded as non-political (Rose, 1993). Although the legitimacy of government continued to be dependent upon the well-being of its citizens (Rose, 1993), it was recognised that the governing of a 'free' society could be achieved without necessarily resorting to disciplinary technologies of police, surveillance or direct social control (Rose and Miller, 1992). Instead, liberalism sought to govern society 'at a distance' by using technologies to create individuals who were capable of regulating their own conduct and who could, accordingly, be governed through their freedom (Rose, 1993).

While continuing to adopt such technologies for governing at a distance, advanced liberalism represents a shift from the more classic liberalism in that governments now recognise a need for some form of intervention – albeit in a very indirect form – to ensure individuals align their conduct in a way that is consistent with Federal government ambitions (Rose, 1993). The well-being of rural Australians remains a concern for federal and state governments, yet it cannot be denied that late capitalist government ambitions extend further than issues of equity and incorporate strategies of economic advancement for the nation as a whole (Garlick, 1997). Unlike the 'welfarist' formula of rule, government intervention under advanced liberalism is not intended to provide a safety net for unviable rural producers (Garlick, 1997, p. 277). Nor does the government wish to directly undertake programmes of environmental management itself. Instead, through the use of new technologies such as funding programmes, community workshops, leadership training courses and farming advisory centres, governments seek to shape the discursive and environmental conditions in which rural producers initiate their own programmes of resource management. In so doing they 'freely' choose to conduct themselves according to the hegemonic principles of competition, efficiency, effectiveness and entrepreneurialism.

By its very nature, therefore, a relationship of governing under advanced liberalism relies on the creation of active subjects (Cruickshank, 1994, p. 47) who are capable of aligning their conduct with the wider political and economic ambitions of state agencies. As Rose (1996a, p. 348) has observed, however, it is likely that some individuals will lack the necessary skills or sensibilities for rational self-management and will consequently require training before they become active and capable of self-government. It is to this end that so-called 'capacity building' is initiated. As the name suggests, the technique of capacity building seeks to alter the behaviour of those people perceived to lack the power, hope, consciousness and initiative to help themselves (Cruickshank, 1994, p. 32). Capacity building features prominently in contemporary discourses of community self-help and, despite the rhetoric of empowerment that frequently accompanies it, should be seen as a mechanism through which state power can be exercised to discipline the personal and political conduct of rural Australians (Martin, 1997, p. 48). It is true that rural producers in Australia are increasingly being encouraged to 'help themselves' but this does not necessarily mean that they are to be left to their own devices. Federal and state governments have a vested interest in seeing farmers become more competitive and consequently initiate and/or support programmes which encourage farmers to learn those new skills. As a result, 'state' power continues to be exercised through such programmes, not only because of the way they encourage rural people to think about resource management in terms of market imperatives but also because they simultaneously marginalise the opportunity for alternative forms of action to take place.

CHANGING PEOPLE TO CHANGE THINGS: INDIVIDUAL AND COMMUNITY CAPACITY BUILDING

It is increasingly obvious that in the context of resource management in particular, and rural development more generally, governmental energies and resources have been targeted primarily at strategies to enhance the capacity of rural people to help themselves. However, rather than seeking to equip them with the political skills for challenging the deregulated environment in which they find themselves, or even the necessary technical qualifications for sustainable land management practices, capacity building exercises are predominantly directed at changing the personality or mindset of rural people. As Keane (1990, p. 292) notes, this represents a shift in government investment away from physical capital towards investment in developing the knowledge, skills and entrepreneurial abilities of local populations, and in changing their attitudes.

For example, the 'victim mentality' of rural people, caused by too many years of government support, and their inability to 'embrace change' (see Gannon, 1998), is often regarded as a major factor in the failure of agricultural enterprises. The refusal to relinquish uncompetitive production practices or to be open to new attitudes to change is frequently cited as the greatest weakness of rural producers and, consequently, becomes the target of many self-help activities (see Cruickshank (1994) for a similar discussion regarding the US war on poverty). While those who are more sympathetic to the circumstances of rural Australians recognise that many are simply so oppressed and disaffected by drought, poor commodity prices, environmental degradation and feelings of hopelessness and despair that they have lost the desire or the energy to help themselves, this negative attitude is still perceived as particularly damaging given the popular images of Australia's rural regions as traditionally comprised of strong, self-reliant and cohesive communities (Wise, 1998, p. 95).

Governments have provided rural producers with a 'stimulus' (Cruickshank, 1994) to help themselves by removing what Gannon (1998, p. 26) calls the 'contra-entrepreneurial support structure(s)' of state intervention. Inadequate on its own, individual and community capacity building supplements this move by equipping individuals and communities with the required subjective capacities (Rose, 1996a) that lead them to willingly embrace the concept of self-help. It is important to note, however, that programmes of capacity building are not simply founded on remedies to address the powerlessness, demoralisation or even apathy of farmers. Nor are they solely directed at creating positive individuals who have the required level of enthusiasm, passion, belief and hope (Gannon, 1998) that might make a difference. More than that, capacity builders seek to alter the attitudes and actions of rural people towards the changes that are taking place in the global economy and to equip them with the necessary skills for successfully responding to those changes.

One such technique of capacity building that deserves a mention here is the Queensland Department of Primary Industries' Building Rural Leaders Program (1999). It has been designed to assist primary producers and agribusiness staff in developing effective leadership, strategic thinking and good business skills. Developed in 1992, the programme comprises six training modules which focus on issues of embracing change and personality types as well as the more market-driven requirements of strategic management, thinking and innovation, business planning, marketing and improved self-reliance (Building Rural Leaders Program Fact Sheet, n.d.). In its paper on Community Capacity Building (CCB), the Office of the Public Service (CCB Cluster, 1999) identified the Building Rural Leaders Program as one of a number of CCB strategies which increased people's level of control over their individual and collective social, economic (and perhaps environmental?) futures.

The rhetoric of enhanced control is consistent with the community self-help philosophy. Yet, as it has already been argued, such techniques clearly intend to do more than simply increase rural people's capacity for action. Additionally, and more importantly, they also seek to 'fundamentally transform' (Cruickshank, 1994, p. 32) that capacity in the process by equipping primary producers with the required skills to respond to globalisation and to embrace flexible adaptability, structural adjustment, competitiveness, efficiency, effectiveness and entrepreneurialism. Indeed, as the Building Rural Leaders Program proudly advertises, the process of 'building rural leaders' involves *transformation not just information* (1999, italics in original). Day (1998, p. 92) is entirely accurate in his observations when he says that what is generally involved in such plans is '.a transformation of values and attitudes freeing the spirit of competition, initiative, self-reliance, risk taking, and so on'. More succinctly, as Wright (1998, p. 105) puts it: 'the spirit of capitalism must enter the soul'.

GOVERNMENT THROUGH EMPOWERMENT: CONSTRAINING ACTION AND LAYING BLAME

For those people like Gannon (1998) who advocate the self-help approach to natural resource management and rural development, its empowering potential for rural people is a fundamental strength. However, if contemporary strategies of community self-help are predominantly built upon programmes of capacity building which, in turn, seek to create efficient, entrepreneurial and competitive individuals who are expected not only to survive but thrive in a deregulated international economy, one is forced to recognise the continued exercise of 'state' power through such strategies. By focusing upon programmes which seek to alter the attitudes and behaviour of rural producers to the changes that are taking place in the global economy, capacity building could be seen, in its present form, to exclude what Buller and Wright (1990, p. 12) suggest is the fundamental characteristic of genuine development: 'an increased social and political role for local communities in the definition and choice of their own development objectives, and access to the material resources and political means to sustain them'.

In contrast, capacity building encourages individuals to work within, and even embrace, hegemonic discourses of natural resource management. In effect, this provides little opportunity for criticism of those discourses or structures, or for the emergence of alternative management practices. Lockie (1999, p. 606) has demonstrated this clearly in his analysis of Landcare funding and discourse which, he suggests, helps deal with some of the negative environmental externalities of agricultural production rather than providing any profound reassessment of current farming systems. Well-meaning state agents who facilitate such activities are, in effect, only really lending support to the already dominant idea that globalisation and deregulation are natural, unstoppable phenomena which must be structurally adjusted to, or successfully managed, if there is to be any hope of survival. Any criticism or resistance by rural people against the dominant discourse is, moreover, dismissed by those who support it as further evidence of their negativity, their inability to change, or their lack of entrepreneurialism. As Day (1998, p. 92) has rightly suggested, the outcome of this ideology is a belief that rural people have suffered because of their reluctance to change or because of their lack of the supposedly necessary entrepreneurial skills. Shifting responsibility onto individuals in this way takes the focus off government actions which have contributed to the degradation of rural environments and overlooks many of the wider forces driving structural adjustment (see Lawrence, 2000). Holding rural people responsible for their own failure, therefore, helps justify a form of social action that is directed less at tackling the underlying causes of environmental damage and more through programmes of capacity building, at changing the response of those who suffer from them most.

CONCLUSION

Contemporary discourses of natural resource management in Australia are increasingly moulding themselves on US and European models of bottom-up, community-based, initiatives which involve a 'new' kind of partnership between varying levels of government and local people. While the responsibility for tackling land degradation is now placed firmly in the hands of rural communities, the task of state agencies is to ensure that individuals have the capacity to bear that responsibility and, moreover, to initiate strategies which are consistent with national objectives. To this end, programmes of individual and community capacity building are becoming more significant within governmental policies of land management.

While this 'sharing' of power (Martin, 1997) and enhanced community autonomy have been regarded as sources of empowerment for local people, it has been suggested in this chapter that a more fruitful line of inquiry follows the governmentality approach of Foucault and Rose. It is important to explore how power is embedded, and how actions occur, within programmes like capacity building. Focusing largely on strategies to equip individuals and communities with the required entrepreneurial skills and attitudes for participation in the global economy, capacity building encourages individuals to work within, and even embrace, the economic and political environment in which they operate. This has the dual effect of providing few opportunities for resistance to, or criticism of, dominant discourses while simultaneously denying the possibility of alternative resource management practices to occur. It is through such measures that state agencies under an advanced liberal formula of rule can guide the conduct of individuals, not so much by direct 'state' intervention, but more by 'shaping' the environment in which rural people make their decisions about appropriate courses of action. Those who choose to operate outside the current paradigm, or who express criticism of it, are marginalised and regarded as 'unable to change' or 'negative' and are ultimately held responsible for the continued decline of their farms, their communities and their natural resources. How sustainable these 'band-aid' treatments are, or to what extent they can reverse the continued decline of Australia's agricultural lands, without any simultaneous attempts by governments to address the long-term structural causes of the environmental crisis is presently dubious.

NOTES

1. A good example of this is provided by the Rural Partnership Program. Managed by the Commonwealth Department of Primary Industries and Energy in consultation with state and territory departments of agriculture and natural resource management, the central tenet of the Program is 'Communities and governments working together for strategic rural development'.

REFERENCES

Bryson, L. and M. Mowbray (1981), 'Community: The Spray–on Solution', Australian Journal of Social Issues, 16 (4), 255–267.

Buller, H. and S. Wright (1990), 'Introduction: Concepts and Policies of Rural Development', in H. Buller and S. Wright (eds), Rural Development: Problems and Practices, Aldershot: Avebury, pp. 1–24.

Burchell, G. (1996), 'Liberal Government and Techniques of the Self', in A. Barry, T. Osborne and N. Rose (eds), Foucault and Political Reason: Liberalism, Neo–

Liberalism and Rationalities of Government, Chicago: University of Chicago Press, pp. 19–36.

Community Capacity Building Cluster (CCB) – Government Service Delivery Project (1999), Community Capacity Building in Queensland: The Queensland Government Service Delivery Project, Office of the Public Service, 21 April 1999.

Cruikshank, B. (1994), 'The Will to Empower: Technologies of Citizenship and the War on Poverty', Socialist Review, 23 (4), 29–55.

Day, G. (1998) 'Working with the Grain? Towards Sustainable Rural and Community Development', Journal of Rural Studies, 14 (1), 89–105.

Foucault, M. (1991), 'Governmentality', in G. Burchell, C. Gordon and P. Miller (eds), The Foucault Effect: Studies in Governmentality, Hemel Hempstead: Harvester Wheatsheaf, pp. 87–104.

Gannon, A. (1998), 'Mastering Change: A New Paradigm in Building Positive Futures for Rural Communities', Proceedings from the Positive Rural Futures 1998 Conference, Biloela, 28–30 May 1998, Brisbane: Office of Rural Communities, pp. 20–41.

Garlick, S. (1997), 'Regional Economic Development: New Partnership Challenges for Local Government', in B. Dollery and N. Marshall (eds), Australian Local Government: Reform and Renewal, Melbourne: Macmillan, pp. 276–293.

Goodwin, M. (1998), 'The Governance of Rural Areas: Some Emerging Research Issues and Agendas', Journal of Rural Studies, 14 (1), 5–12.

Gordon, C. (1991), 'Governmental Rationality: An Introduction', in G. Burchell, C. Gordon and P. Miller (eds), The Foucault Effect: Studies in Governmentality, Hemel Hempstead: Harvester Wheatsheaf, pp. 1–51.

Higgins, V. (1998), '"Self Reliance", Governance and Environmental Management: A Case Study of the Rural Adjustment Scheme', paper presented to the Sixth Agri-Food Network Meeting, Rockhampton: 27–29 August 1998.

Keane, M. (1990), 'Economic Development Capacity Amongst Small Rural Communities', Journal of Rural Studies, 6 (3), 291–301.

Lawrence, G. (2000), 'Global Perspectives on Rural Communities: Trends and Patterns', paper presented at the International Landcare Conference, Melbourne Convention Centre: Melbourne, 2–5 March.

Lawrence, G., I. Gray and D. Stehlik (1999) 'Changing Spaces: the Effects of Macro-social Forces on Regional Australia', in C. Kasimis and A. Papadopoulos (eds), Local Responses to Global Integration: Toward a New Era of Rural Restructuring, Aldershot: Ashgate, pp. 63–87.

Lockie, S. (1998), 'Landcare and the State: "Action at a Distance" in a Globalised World Economy', in D. Burch, G. Lawrence, R. Rickson and J. Goss (eds), Australasian Food and Farming in a Globalised Economy: Recent Developments and Future Prospects, Melbourne: Department of Geography and Environmental Science, Monash University, pp. 15–28.

Lockie, S. (1999), 'The State, Rural Environments and Globalisation: "Action at a Distance" Via the Australian Landcare Program', Environment and Planning A, 31, 597–611.

Martin, P. (1997), 'The Constitution of Power in Landcare: A Post–Structuralist Perspective with Modernist Undertones', in S. Lockie and F. Vanclay (eds), Critical Landcare, Centre for Rural Social Research Key Papers No. 5, Wagga Wagga, NSW: Charles Sturt University, pp. 45–56.

McCallum, W. and K. Hughey (1999), 'Towards an Evaluative Model of Community-based Environmental Management in New Zealand?', paper presented at the International Symposium on Society and Resource Management, Brisbane: 7–10 July 1999.

McLaughlin, B. (1987), 'Rural Policy in the 1990s – Self Help or Self Deception', Journal of Rural Studies, 3 (40), 361–364.

Murdoch, J. (1997), 'The Shifting Territory of Government: Some Insights from the Rural White Paper', Area, 29 (2), 109–118.

Murdoch, J. and S. Abram (1998), 'Defining the Limits of Community Governance', Journal of Rural Studies, 14 (1), 41–50.

Pahl, R. (1970), Patterns of Urban Life, London: Longman.

Queensland Department of Primary Industries (1999), Building Rural Leaders Program Fact Sheet.

Rose, N. (1993), 'Government, Authority and Expertise in Advanced Liberalism', Economy and Society, 22 (3), 283–299.

Rose, N. (1996a), 'The Death of the Social? Re–figuring the Territory of Government', Economy and Society, 25 (3), 327–356.

Rose, N. (1996b), 'Governing "Advanced" Liberal Democracies', in A. Barry, T. Osborne and N. Rose (eds), Foucault and Political Reason: Liberalism, Neo–liberalism and Rationalities of Government, Chicago: University of Chicago Press: pp. 37–64.

Rose, N. and P. Miller (1990), 'Governing Economic Life', Economy and Society, 19 (1), 1–31.

Rose, N. and P. Miller (1992), 'Political Power Beyond the State: Problematics of Government', British Journal of Sociology, 42 (2), 173–205.

Sher, J. and K. Sher (1994), 'Beyond Conventional Wisdom: Rural Development as if Australia's Rural People Really Mattered', Journal of Research in Rural Education, 10 (1), 2–43.

Stacey, M. (1969), 'The Myth of Community Studies', British Journal of Sociology, 20 (2), 134–147.

Wise, J. (1998), 'Community Education: The Sleeping Giant of Social and Economic Development. Exploring the Dynamic Interface between Community Learning and Community Development', Proceedings from the Positive Rural Futures 1998 Conference, Biloela, 28–30 May 1998, Brisbane: Office of Rural Communities, pp. 83–96.

Wright, R. (1998), 'Reinventing Good Government? Entrepreneurial Governance and Political Virtue in the Nineties', Arena, 11, 97–118.

Index